Shooting for Hope

Shooting for Hope
Providing Preventive Patterns of Care

SUSAN J. PRESLEY

CASCADE *Books* • Eugene, Oregon

SHOOTING FOR HOPE
Providing Preventive Patterns of Care

Copyright © 2025 Susan J. Presley. All rights reserved. Except for brief quotations in critical publications or reviews, no part of this book may be reproduced in any manner without prior written permission from the publisher. Write: Permissions, Wipf and Stock Publishers, 199 W. 8th Ave., Suite 3, Eugene, OR 97401.

Cascade Books
An Imprint of Wipf and Stock Publishers
199 W. 8th Ave., Suite 3
Eugene, OR 97401

www.wipfandstock.com

PAPERBACK ISBN: 979-8-3852-1939-1
HARDCOVER ISBN: 979-8-3852-1940-7
EBOOK ISBN: 979-8-3852-1941-4

Cataloguing-in-Publication data:

Names: Presley, Susan J., author.

Title: Shooting for hope : providing preventive patterns of care / Susan J. Presley.

Description: Eugene, OR : Cascade Books, 2025 | Includes bibliographical references and index.

Identifiers: ISBN 979-8-3852-1939-1 (paperback) | ISBN 979-8-3852-1940-7 (hardcover) | ISBN 979-8-3852-1941-4 (ebook)

Subjects: LCSH: Religion and politics—United States. | Gun control—United States | Firearms and crime—United States. | Violent crime—United States—Prevention.

Classification: BL2525 .P74 2025 (paperback) | BL2525 .P74 (ebook)

VERSION NUMBER 031825

Unless otherwise indicated, Scripture quotations are taken from the Holy Bible, New International Version®, NIV®. Copyright © 2011 by Biblica, Inc.® Used by permission of Zondervan. All rights reserved worldwide.

Scripture quotations marked KJV are from The Authorized (King James) Version. Rights in the Authorized Version in the United Kingdom are vested in the Crown. Reproduced by permission of the Crown's patentee, Cambridge University Press.

Scripture quotations marked NRSV are from the New Revised Standard Version Bible, copyright © 1989 National Council of the Churches of Christ in the United States of America. Used by permission. All rights reserved worldwide.

For the Survivors:
We're searching for a better way.

Contents

List of Illustrations and Tables | ix
Acknowledgments | xi
Abbreviations | xiii
Introduction | xv

Chapter 1: Big Picture, Big Hope | 1
Chapter 2: The History: How We Got Here | 15
Chapter 3: What We Think We Know | 20
Chapter 4: What Happened at Mother Emanuel AME | 35
Chapter 5: What Happened at Burnette Chapel Church of Christ | 44
Chapter 6: What Happened at First Baptist Church | 54
Chapter 7: Who Is Dylann Storm Roof? | 61
Chapter 8: Who Is Emanuel Kidega Samson? | 77
Chapter 9: Who Is Devin Patrick Kelley? | 88
Chapter 10: What Are We Doing as Churches? | 101
Chapter 11: The Racial Component | 112
Chapter 12: Moving Forward: Recognition | 126
Chapter 13: Taking Action Before Trouble Happens | 137
Chapter 14: Taking Action After We Spot Trouble | 159
Chapter 15: It Works: Stories of Hope | 170

Appendix A: Dylann Roof Manifesto | 179
Appendix B: Emanuel Samson Note | 185
Appendix C: Letter from Dylann Roof to Christian Picciolini, December 2017 | 186

Appendix D: Letter from Emanuel Kidega Samson to Susan Presley, 2021 | 187

Appendix E: Dylann Roof Jailhouse Drawings | 188

Appendix F: Letters from Dylann Roof to His Mother and Father | 192

Appendix G: Six-Week Curriculum: *Unity in Conflict* | 194

Appendix H: Pro Se Motion to Remove and Replace Appointed Counsel | 208

Bibliography | 213
Index | 221

Illustrations and Tables

Increase in Mass Shootings | Chapter 1
Warning Signs | Chapter 12
Emanuel Samson Note | Appendix B
Letter from Dylann Roof to Christian Picciolini | Appendix C
Letter from Emanuel Kidega Samson to Susan Presley | Appendix D
Dylann Roof Jailhouse Drawing of Ghosts and Cross | Appendix E
Dylann Roof Jailhouse Drawing of Cross with 14/88 | Appendix E
Dylann Roof Jailhouse Drawing of Jesus | Appendix E
Dylann Roof Jailhouse Drawing of Cross | Appendix E
Dylann Roof Letter to Mother | Appendix F
Dylann Roof Letter to Father | Appendix F
Pro Se Motion to Remove and Replace Appointed Counsel | Appendix H

Acknowledgments

SINCE THIS BOOK HAS its roots in my doctoral dissertation, the number of people that should be thanked could be longer than the book itself. During my work at Louisville Seminary, I was blessed to have advisors Shannon Craigo-Snell and Angela Cowser who advocated for my work when others thought it too daunting a task. Shannon is also a contributor to this book. Dianne Reistroffer was a strong advocate through the entire journey.

Two churches have also been pillars of support. During my studies I pastored First Presbyterian Church in Mendota, Illinois, and while writing this book, I am now pastoring First Presbyterian Church in Mexico, Missouri. Both wonderful communities of faith have bolstered me, cheered me on, and celebrated my victories. Anyone would be fortunate to be undergirded by either of these church families.

While writing and researching, friends and colleagues consistently offered ideas, thoughts, critiques, food, and drink to aid the writing process. Special thanks go to close friends Max Hazell and Sarah Dierker. Sarah's infernal positivity and Max's vast stores of knowledge combined with constant humor make this a wonderful friendship. Likewise, Sandra Weber and Micah McNeal, colleagues in ministry, have been sounding boards, givers of wisdom, and are the inventors of the title of this book. Rob Dalton was a dedicated editor and proofreader.

The book and the research behind it (which continues) would not be possible without the support of friend and research assistant Sarah Dierker. Why she has lent enormous support to such a difficult subject is a mystery, but together we have traversed much difficult terrain, enjoyed many victories, and been moved and changed by countless stories. She will also surely be appalled that I just wrote a paragraph with only three sentences, which irritates her to no end.

Thanks are also due to all those who agreed to be interviewed for this project.

Finally, but most importantly, are the two closest to my heart: my mother, Paula Presley, and son, Jimmy Ray. Both believe in me and imagine greater things for me than I can fathom myself. My mother's academic success as editor of the *Sixteenth Century Journal* has been inspirational, but her ability to jump societal hurdles on her way to success has made her my role model. Jimmy's love of life, his belief that people are essentially good, his wild and untamed joy and imagination, and his confidence that his mother can conquer the world remind me that life *is* good, people *are* good, and God *is* good. I am blessed indeed.

Now, let's go make the world a better place.

Abbreviations

AME	African Methodist Episcopal
CE	Common era
CHC	Chaplain Corps
DoD OIG	Department of Defense Office of Inspector General
DSR	Dylann Storm Roof
ELCA	Evangelical Lutheran Church in America
EMDR	Eye movement desensitization and reprocessing
FLETC	Federal Law Enforcement Training Center
FBI	Federal Bureau of Investigation
ICOC	International Churches of Christ
NAACP	National Association for the Advancement of Colored People
NEMA	Nebraska Emergency Management Agency
NIV	New International Version
NPR	National Public Radio
PTSD	Post-Traumatic Stress Disorder
RBG	Red, black, green
RPGs	Role-playing games
RV	Recreational vehicle
SCLC	Southern Christian Leadership Conference
SUV	Sport utility vehicle
TRC	Truth and Reconciliation Committee

Abbreviations

U.S.	United States
U.S. DOJ	United States Department of Justice
UCC	United Church of Christ
USAF	United States Air Force
USN	United States Navy

Introduction

EVERY DAY, ANOTHER CHURCH signs up for a safety seminar.

Every week, another church installs more security cameras.

Every month, another church makes lockdown policies for its buildings.

We understand why. We get it. Fear is an emotion that's easy to sympathize with when mass shootings appear in news media as frequently as they do. A shooting in a place of worship seems even more heinous than most others, somehow, and it is obvious why parishioners, ministers, lay leaders, and committees in houses of worship are frightened. This is a problem that surpasses denominational and even religious bounds. Traditional or progressive, liberal or conservative, Christian, Jewish, Sikh, Buddhist, Muslim, or otherwise, communities of faith are looking for a solution. We desperately want a way to feel safe in the place that is meant to be our sanctuary.

Feeling scared is common. What's rare is for a church to examine itself. It's unusual for a church to wonder if they've somehow unintentionally been complicit in the problem. It's uncommon for a church to actively work on recognizing warning signs in potentially violent persons, both in and out of their congregation. It's profoundly unusual for a church to include a preventative curriculum in its Sunday schools, Bible studies, confirmation classes, and Sunday sermons. Most of all, it is surprising to find a church that puts fear aside in order to look forward with hope to the possibility of stopping violence before it happens. Fear is paralyzing. It halts our belief that God can work, and it throws the emergency brake on our belief that action will help. Fear freezes us in place and makes hope impossible.

Hope, however, leads to education and action. With the goal of always working in the direction of hope, this book looks at where we are, how we got here, and how we can move toward a better tomorrow. The chapters that follow examine the stories of three mass shooters and explore the

Introduction

details of the shootings that those three carried out in churches. The three individuals and the crimes they perpetrated are as follows:

- On June 17, 2015, Dylann Storm Roof killed nine and injured one at Emanuel American Methodist Episcopal Church (colloquially known as Mother Emanuel) in Charleston, North Carolina. You may remember what happened that day. Pastor and South Carolina Senator Rev. Dr. Clementa C. Pinckney was one of those killed, and his funeral eulogy was delivered by President Barack Obama.

- A lesser-known church shooting happened on September 24, 2017. Angered by Roof's actions, Emanuel Kidega Samson decided to respond in kind. He killed one and injured seven at Burnette Chapel Church of Christ in Antioch, Tennessee. Samson's goal was to kill at least one more white person than Black persons killed by Roof.

- The third shooting reviewed here happened on November 5, 2017. Devin Patrick Kelley killed twenty-seven churchgoers and injured twenty-two at First Baptist Church of Sutherland Springs, Texas, then took his own life.

Through a study of similarities and differences between these three shooters and the horrendous acts they carried out, a positive way forward is proposed: prevention. The backgrounds of all three men are examined in these pages, including where, how, and by whom they were raised; their mental health histories; their criminal histories; and histories of drug use. Most relevant to this work, their religious backgrounds are examined, including what they were taught both in and out of church.

This book also focuses on moving beyond gun laws, guards, armed parishioners, and security systems. What you won't find here is a discussion of the Second Amendment, arguments for or against access to weapons, or a review of proposed gun control laws. You won't find a description of the latest security technology targeted to churches. None of those practices is inherently harmful, but they are fear-driven and reactive measures rather than proactive. By the time those measures are needed, a person has already decided to harm people.

This book does not advocate for or against stricter gun control or discuss gun control from the angle of keeping weapons out of the hands of shooters. Apart from a discussion on security measures and whether parishioners should be armed, the issue of who should and shouldn't own a gun is left for Second Amendment and gun control experts. Much

Introduction

in-depth, accomplished work has been done on all sides of this topic. Many volumes by specialists both in and out of the field of gun ownership have been written on every side of the issue imaginable. From proponents of gun ownership to those who would support a unilateral ban on firearms and all points of view in between, the matter in question has been covered well.

The original question that started the doctoral study upon which this book is based was: "If no gun had been available, would this person still have hurt people?" The subtitle of this book addresses the universal need for churches to first ask themselves how they have missed opportunities to educate their faith communities about ways to prevent violence. Second, it speaks to the possibility that churches can approach the future in a way that offers opportunities to act preemptively before a person maliciously picks up a weapon.

After a mass shooting in 2022, Rev. Harry "Max" Hazell II, CHC, USN, a Navy chaplain, former pastor, and former middle school history teacher, summed up the situation on his Facebook post of May 25, 2022, this way:

> The anti-gun citizen and the gun-owning citizen react with just as much shock and grief at this kind of tragedy . . . and both are just as passionate about the solution. Unsurprisingly, it's the same solution they desired before the tragedy, when they weren't reeling from the effects of it.
>
> That's a good thing, by the way. Lawmaking should be dispassionate, for the most straightforward of reasons: heightened emotions make us think solutions to complex problems are simple.
>
> They never are.
>
> In the lust for simplicity, people attacked Muslims after 9/11, or vandalized Chinatowns because of Coronavirus, or decided all white/black people were "the enemy." They passed sweeping legislation for the Patriot Act, or wiretapped certain communities, or declared war on nations, hoping, praying that if this final simple thing were done, the problems would all vanish.
>
> But it doesn't work like that, as frustrating as it feels.
>
> There are no simple solutions. Life is complex, and the path through it requires complex thinking. Slogans won't heal the country, but earnestly seeking complex solutions together might.
>
> All of this is a plea for more talking with each other; WITH, not AT. "Bold solutions" tend to be the simplest ones, and they always, always, always have follow-on effects that diminish the rights of others.

Introduction

This book echoes Hazell's thoughts and vehemently advocates for churches to mitigate violence through building relationships. This is indeed a heartfelt appeal to talk with each other rather than to only attempt to hide from violence. Churches are uniquely poised to teach nonviolence, to recognize warning signs in individuals, and to do the hard work of leading the community in change before violence escalates and destroys lives. This involves intentionally setting fear aside and opting for a posture of hope. Hope makes us look forward to a future without violence. Without hope, we'll stay where we are. We, as the church, can lead communities into a future that is bright with possibilities rather than dim with despair.

The chapters that follow are based on a decade-long study of mass shootings in the United States from 1940 through 2022. Data from over five thousand mass shootings that occurred during those years have been and continue to be researched. The result is one of the largest, most comprehensive databases of mass shootings in the United States. The information collected not only reveals important stories but helps give information on multiple data points. Information revealed includes the frequency of mass shootings, the time of day shootings happen, and the location of mass shootings. The age, gender, and race of shooters, motives, intended victims, and the relationship of the shooters to their victims is studied. Information on the frequency of drive-by mass shootings, whether the shooter left a manifesto-type document, and other data points have been diligently collected.

Not included in that database are a very small number of incidents that can be categorized as self-defense. In those cases, the shooter was not a perpetrator and did not set out to harm anyone. All other mass shootings, however, are included. All research, information, data, and conclusions contained in this book are specific to the United States. Other countries and cultures certainly have issues regarding violence, but the United States has a particular history that requires specific study and action.

In an effort to better understand the role of theological socialization in relationship to violence in general, a broad review of past and current literature on the issue and surrounding the topic was conducted. Works that are quoted are contained in the bibliography, but multiple other contributors helped with the formation of ideas and conclusions as the project progressed. Experts gave important data, and survivors shared compelling experiences.

Introduction

The work completed here was strengthened from many interviews. Two of Dylann Roof's pastors contributed (Rev. Dr. Tony Metze, from Roof's childhood; and Roof's current pastoral advisor, Father John Parker). There was an interview with Rev. Sharon Washington Risher (whose family and a friend perished at Emanuel AME) and an interview with Peter and Linda Warren, leaders of Youth with a Mission, a facility where a twenty-four-year-old former member of that program shot and killed five and wounded five. Lisa Krantz, a photojournalist who won a Pulitzer Prize for her work after the Sutherland Springs shootings, was kind enough to visit with me at length. An interview with Sherri Pomeroy, wife of the pastor of Sutherland Springs Baptist Church, can be found in chapter 14. An anonymous source connected to the Uvalde school shooting offered input. Other interviews were conducted with law enforcement officials, educators, coaches, and students (most of whose names were changed at parental request) for opinions, ideas, and consideration.

This work also benefited from communication via letters and answered questionnaires with attorneys and court officials involved in both Roof's and Samson's cases. Court records that quoted persons under oath who were directly involved in shootings were given the most credence, as was communication with one of the judges who presided over Roof's cases, but hundreds of news reports and articles were read and/or viewed. This point was specifically driven home by one of Roof's ministers, Rev. Dr. Tony Metze, who believes his words in many of his interviews in the past have been taken out of context. From a legal research standpoint, law reviews and law journals were incorporated into the readings. Related to Roof's and Samson's court appearances, tens of thousands of pages of court records were obtained online through multiple courts in Tennessee, Virginia, and South Carolina.

Though personal histories, mental health backgrounds, and criminal histories are explored, it is important to note that the major focus of this book is the religious socialization of Roof, Samson, and Kelley and the church's ability to help prevent violence. All three of the shooters discussed herein were raised in churches, and all three have religious backgrounds. Two had pastors and youth leaders who studied with them, worked with them, and tried to mentor them. The third shooter had attended church some and briefly participated in church activities, and had an extended family who faithfully attended church. This book reveals that faith and religious experience, socialization, and lack of religious training regarding potential violence and how to deal with it helped to shape the perpetrators' beliefs and actions.

Since findings on these topics vary, I will surely be wrong on some points. By the time you read this book, more details on the shootings or the shooters may have come to light. However, the final result remains the same. With interviews, questionnaires, court records, and published material, this book examines how the faith and church experiences of all three shooters impacted their motivations and their decisions to murder churchgoers during a church service. The hope is that the information here offers a possible course for future action that churches can take to help mitigate the problem.

Pastor Joey Spann of Burnette Chapel spent three months after the shooting recovering from his wounds. His words upon his return to the pulpit sought to unite all worshipers in the church universal: "When he attacked Burnette Chapel, he attacked every body of worshippers, wherever they may be. That's why I think so many people are touched by what took place at Burnette Chapel. When we were attacked, you were attacked."[1] With that awareness in mind, we search for a better way.

---

1. Tryggestad, "We Do Not Go," paras. 5–6.

Chapter 1

Big Picture, Big Hope

I APOLOGIZE. REALLY, I'M sorry, but here's a spoiler alert: much of this book is dark. It's dark because this is a dark topic, yet it is incredibly, vitally important, and I promise that it moves towards hope. The material covered here is difficult for us to think about. You may believe you're resilient and have read many difficult things in your life, but there are few people who can walk away from the descriptions given here and remain unaffected. The stories may be hard to read and may be even more difficult to act upon, but we are not called to flee from the dark. As individual people of faith and as the larger, collective church, we are called to be the light in the dark. Jesus said, "You are the light of the world. A town built on a hill cannot be hidden. Neither do people light a lamp and put it under a bowl. Instead, they put it on its stand, and it gives light to everyone in the house. In the same way, let your light shine before others, that they may see your good deeds and glorify your Father in heaven" (Matt 5:14–16). That instruction implies that we go into the darkness, that we stand in the dark, and that we reflect the light of Christ in the world. We can't make the dark lighter by hiding from it.

Though the topic of mass shootings is difficult, painful, and often emotionally taxing, we must face the issue to make progress in our work for the kingdom of God. Denial of the urgency of the problem poses a serious risk to all of us. As you make your way through the chapters that follow, keep the light in mind. Look for the hope in these pages: the living hope that is possible through Jesus. And when necessary, take a break, take a walk, gather yourself, and come back to read more.

A BROAD FOCUS—
MASS SHOOTINGS IN THE UNITED STATES

It would be optimal if this book was not timely. The problem is that discussions about mass shootings have been terribly relevant for years in the United States. The rate of mass shootings is escalating, and easy access to news about them leads to an increase in fear at an equal or greater rate.

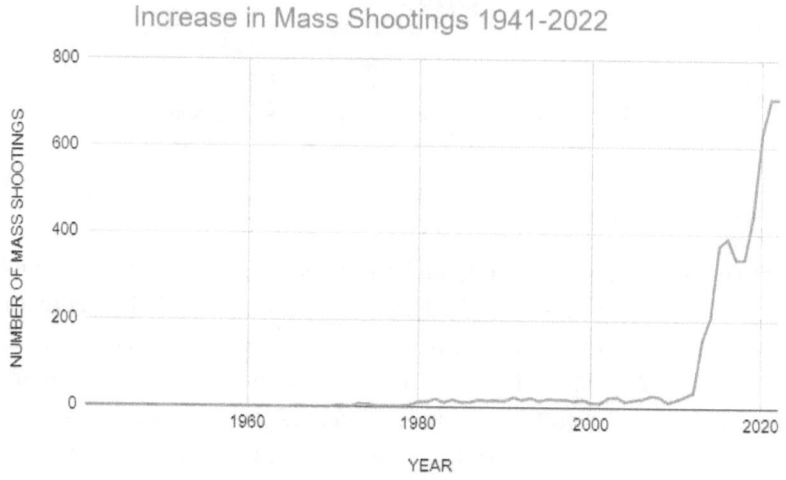

From 1940 through 2012, the number of mass shootings per year remained in single or double digits each year; in each of those years, there were fewer than 100 mass shootings. There was a dramatic rise in violence in 2013 with 155 mass shootings in that year alone, and the total began to increase exponentially from there. In 2022, the number of these horrific events in the United States—for 2022 alone—had jumped to 713. The reason for this dramatic increase is open to speculation. Life stressors such as poverty, family discord, or job stress could be factors. Generalized anger could be the culprit. Interestingly (or maybe coincidentally), 2013 is also a time when use of social media dramatically increased. This increased communication and the spread of ideas, but whether a causation exists that led to the drastic increase in mass shootings is open to study.

One commonality seems to stand out: mass shooters tend to be really angry. The Secret Service found that in more than half of the mass shootings since 2016, the assailant had a grievance, either personal or work related they were trying to settle.¹ The presence of a grievance seems to be the largest common denominator for perpetrators. The urgency, then, is that we figure out how to reach people before they ever turn that grievance into action, and before they consider picking up a gun. Our job is to help them find a better way.

Mass shootings seem to be in the news and on social media constantly, especially when the shootings happen near large metropolitan areas. Rural residents are often afraid to visit nearby big cities because every evening, their news coverage includes the number of shootings that happened in the large nearby city that day. I remember being with my mother at her senior apartment complex in rural northern Illinois, and every day a group would turn on the evening news to find out how many people had been shot in Chicago the day before. "Don't go to the city," I remember being told. "You'll get shot!" I went to Chicago frequently, since my son lived there for fifteen years. I have yet to be shot in the Windy City. And yet, while it seems like mass shootings are constantly in the news, statistically only a fraction of them are covered by news outlets.

Personally, I noted the uptick in mass shootings in about 2014. My interest was piqued, and I began pondering what the cause could be. With a then-recent (2010) bachelor's degree in journalism, I wondered if there was actually a statistical rise in incidents or if that was simply an issue of the media suddenly giving them more airtime. A little study showed that, no, there had definitely been an escalation of mass shootings in the United States. The dramatic rise was both alarming and terrifying. My next two questions are what drove me to study the issue for the ensuing decade: If no gun had been available, would the perpetrator still have hurt people? Why do we want to hurt and kill each other so much?

However, because news outlets have limited time and space in which they can convey information, stories about mass shootings tend to highlight specific cases that are of broad interest, while the bigger picture can be neglected. The part with the long-range statistics doesn't make the nightly news. Fear-based news stories are incredibly compelling. The problem is that the big picture, which comes from trends, data, and statistics, tends to get lost or outright ignored in favor of shock-based storytelling. The American church has bought into the fear, and the fear of this kind of violence is so strong, it's nearly tangible.

---

1. Cho, "Many Mass Attackers," para. 1.

When a mass shooting happens in a place of worship, immediate and intense news coverage usually follows, perhaps because houses of worship historically have been thought of as safe havens. That's what the word "sanctuary" is all about, after all. This is true not only in the United States, but the idea of a church as a refuge dates back many centuries to a wide variety of places and cultures. For example, in the 1200s, a person could hide, or seek sanctuary, in a church for up to forty days, and sometimes longer. People undergoing persecution have historically fled to churches as a safe space. In the 1960s, some American churches housed draft resisters, as those churches sought to support conscientious objectors. In modern church parlance, some congregations have opted to adopt the term "sanctuary churches." This signals that they actively work to house and protect undocumented persons from arrest or deportation. Church as a safe place is ingrained into our minds. Church is supposed to be the place where harm can't find us.

When a church shooting garners news coverage, fear ensues among the otherwise faithful. Good, well-intentioned people wonder how their congregations can protect themselves or any worshiper that enters their buildings.

Because of fear, churches tend to go in one of two directions:

- They either want to advocate for stricter gun control, or
- They want to build tighter security systems.

The idea is that if we take away the weapon and/or access to our parishioners, violence won't happen. There are two problems with this thinking: First, removing access to guns doesn't remove a desire for violence. Second, it doesn't turn a violent person into a peace-loving one if you take away their access to a gun. In the approximately five thousand mass shootings studied leading up to the writing of this book, it has never been shown that if a door had been locked, the shooter would have put his gun away and opted not to harm anyone.

NARROWING THE FOCUS—FREQUENCY OF VIOLENCE IN PLACES OF WORSHIP

In the United States, the church has a problem that is as old as the country itself. The solution to every problem in American society, from unemployment to domestic discord, seems to be violence. This issue has grown and festered and turned into a shooting problem. Gun violence has resulted in countless deaths and untold ruined lives.

The definition of *mass shooting* in this work is four or more people injured or killed in a single event and general location, including the shooter. Stanford University's definition of mass shooting is partially used for this survey. "The definition of mass shooting used for the Stanford database is three or more shooting victims (not necessarily fatalities), not including the shooter." Stanford's then goes on to exclude any violence considered to be "identifiably gang, drug, or organized crime-related."[2] When gang, drug, or organized crime-related shootings are omitted, that does three things: First, it makes the data inaccurate. Second, it says that the lives lost in those situations somehow matter less than lives lost due to other mitigating factors. Third, to not include the shooter as a victim dehumanizes him or her. Further, if a bystander is injured or killed in a gang, drug, or organized crime-related shooting, it would be difficult to know how to categorize that victim. For these reasons, this study includes all victims of mass shootings. As Christians, we believe that all people are made in the image of God, so all lives are included.

The *Historical Dictionary of Human Rights* defines a *massacre* as the murder of people, usually civilians. The text notes that murderers and legal defense teams usually contest the term "massacre" and consider it inflammatory.[3] The shootings discussed in this work, however, certainly qualify as massacres. Whatever nomenclature we use, the problem of mass shootings, massacres, or murders is both a religious and a secular one. Somehow, though, people of faith seem to feel a particular propensity for protecting themselves. This is an issue of people among all faiths that is increasing in frequency, and Christian churches are not alone in the problem of attacks at houses of worship. Religious institutions of all types have been affected by attacks on mosques, synagogues, temples, and faith-based community centers. Even a Church of Satan was a target.

Between 1940 and 2001 (a sixty-year span), only eight mass shootings occurred in worship spaces within the United States. Six were at Christian churches, one was at a Buddhist temple, and one was at a Jewish community center. Again, that's eight shootings in sixty years. These events were:

---

2. Stanford University, "Mass Shootings in America," svv "Definition of Mass Shooting."

3. Fomerand, "Massacre."

- 1974 at Our Lady of the Rosary Church in Union City, California (one killed, three injured)
- 1977 at St. Aloysius Catholic Church, Spokane, Washington (one killed, four injured)
- 1980 at First Baptist Church in Daingerfield, Texas (five killed, eleven injured)
- 1991 at Wat Promkunaram Buddhist Temple in Waddell, Arizona (nine killed, none injured)
- 1999 at Wedgwood Baptist Church in Fort Worth, Texas (eight killed, seven injured)
- 1999 at St. John Fellowship Baptist Church in Gonzalez, Louisiana (four killed, four injured)
- 1999 at North Valley Jewish Community Center in Los Angeles, California (one killed, five injured)

From 2002 to 2022 (a twenty-year span) there were twenty-five mass shootings. Twenty were at Christian churches, four were at Jewish synagogues and other establishments, and one was at a Sikh temple. Those twenty-five shootings in twenty years are as follows:

- 2005 at Living Church of God, Brookfield, Wisconsin (eight killed, four injured)
- 2006 at The Ministry of Jesus Christ in Baton Rouge, Louisiana (five killed, one injured)
- 2006 at Jewish Federation in Seattle, Washington (one killed, five injured)
- 2007 at First Congregational Church in Neosho, Missouri (three killed, five injured)
- 2007 at Youth with AaMission in Arvada, Colorado, and New Life Church in Colorado Springs, Colorado (five killed, five injured)
- 2008 at Unitarian Church in Knoxville, Tennessee (two killed, seven injured)
- 2012 at Sikh Temple of Wisconsin in Oak Creek, Wisconsin (seven killed, four wounded)

- 2013 at Uptown Baptist Church in Chicago, Illinois (one killed, four injured)
- 2014 at Word Tabernacle Church in Rocky Mount, North Carolina (none killed, four injured)
- 2014 at Jewish Community Center in Overland Park, Kansas (three killed, none injured)
- 2014 at Ebenezer Church in Atlanta, Georgia (none killed, four injured)
- 2015 at Emmanuel Church of God in Brooklyn, New York (two killed, four injured)
- 2015 at Emanuel American Methodist Episcopal Church in Charleston, South Carolina (nine killed, three injured)
- 2017 at the Immaculate Conception Pastoral Center in Sacramento, California (none killed, four injured)
- 2017 at Cathedral of the Cross in Birmingham, Alabama (none killed, six injured)
- 2017 at Zion Lutheran Church in Des Moines, Iowa (one killed, three injured)
- 2017 at Burnette Chapel Church of Christ in Antioch, Tennessee (one killed, seven injured)
- 2017 at First Baptist Church in Sutherland Springs, Texas (twenty-six killed, twenty injured)
- 2018 at Bethlehem Star Missionary Baptist Church in Chicago, Illinois (six injured)
- 2018 at Tree of Life synagogue in Pittsburgh, Pennsylvania (eleven killed, seven injured)
- 2019 at Chabad of Poway synagogue in Poway, California (one killed, three injured)
- 2021 at New Shiloh Missionary Baptist Church in New Orleans, Louisiana (two killed, two injured)
- 2022 at The Church in Sacramento, California (five killed, none injured)

- 2022 at Geneva Presbyterian Church in Laguna Woods, California (five killed, one injured)
- 2022 at Destiny of Faith Church in Pittsburgh, Pennsylvania (none killed, five injured)

Those incidents were heinous enough, but a simple tally of the killed and injured worshipers only scratches the surface. Roof, Samson, and Kelley are not the only shooters who have had the desire to harm churchgoers; they are just three of those who were successful in their quest to kill (Kelley in particular). Some potential killers hoped to unleash massive violence on churches but were thwarted. Three recent examples follow, all of which were unsuccessful. These are but a small representation; countless other attempts exist.

The first example happened on the afternoon of October 24, 2018, a Wednesday. First Baptist Church of Jeffersontown, Kentucky, was having their regular Wednesday evening Bible study when Gregory Bush tried to gain entrance with the purpose of shooting parishioners. The church had taken the precautions that many of us think of as the most effective means of prevention: they had locked their doors. Bush attempted to go into the church building, video surveillance shows, by pulling and banging on multiple doors of the premises. Though he was thwarted by the multiple locked entryways, Bush did not suddenly decide that he wasn't feeling violent after all. He did not put his gun away and go home.

Instead, he went to a nearby Kroger grocery store. A grocery store can't be locked during business hours, after all. Ten minutes after leaving the church, he fired shots both inside the grocery store and outside in the parking lot. Two people were killed: The first, Maurice E. Stallard, was inside. Stallard was shopping with his grandson, and Bush followed Stallard and the grandson the length of an aisle before shooting the man multiple times. Bush left the child unharmed. Then in the parking lot, Bush approached Vickie Lee Jones and shot her several times, killing her. A man with a handgun asked Bush what was going on, and Bush, without responding, began walking toward him with the gun drawn. The third victim fired at Bush, and Bush returned fire. After about a minute, Bush stopped shooting and walked away. He then met another man with a firearm and said, "Don't shoot me. I won't shoot you. Whites don't shoot whites."[4] Bush fled but was caught and arrested. He was charged with multiple hate crimes, including

---

4. Bailey and Ross, "Whites Don't Shoot Whites," para. 8.

killing a victim on the basis of race or color and attempting to shoot or kill a victim on the basis of race or color.[5] He is serving a life sentence in prison without the possibility of parole.

First Baptist Church of Jeffersontown, Bush's originally intended target, is a Black church. Bush has stated on multiple occasions that his actions that day were racially motivated, including the attack on Kroger. All victims there were Black. Billy Williams, a church administrator, said in an interview that he was glad their security was in place and that they were praying for the victims from the nearby grocery store.[6] Though their prayers are surely appreciated and undoubtedly no malice was intended by the church towards the shoppers, Bush's violence was not stopped that day. A person who wants to commit violence will find a way to do so. The locked church doors did not stop the attack; they just moved the violence down the street. Locking the doors merely delayed and relocated the inevitable.

The second example of an unsuccessful church attack is a non-firearm situation. The potential for violence in and against churches is not limited to gun use; many weapons can be put into play when a person is seeking to do harm. In November 2019, a sixteen-year-old high school girl plotted to kill members of Bethel African Methodist Episcopal Church in Gainesville, Georgia. The girl was meticulous. She collected knives and detailed her plans to kill in writing. As the would-be assailant is a minor, her court records, including her name and other identity, are not public. From the limited records available, we know that she owned T-shirts that said "Free Dylann Roof" and that she told her school counselors this would be a racially motivated event. She had a deep desire to cut African American persons with knives and other sharp-edged weapons. Like Dylann Roof, the girl searched online for an African American church and eventually chose Bethel because it was relatively small. She went to the church once, but services had been canceled that evening.

The reason she was stopped was that fellow students spoke up. The girl had shown her notebooks detailing her plans to others, who alerted school officials, who in turn alerted law enforcement authorities. This tragic situation underscores several things: racially motivated attacks are real. Also, while gun violence is a problem, the desire to commit violence is the underlying problem.[7]

5. Chokshi, "Kroger Shooting Suspect," para. 3.
6. Emery, "Minutes Before," para. 12.
7. Hawkins, "White Teen Girl," paras. 1–6.

Third, in September 2023, Rui Jiang was thwarted from committing an attack on Park Valley Church in Haymarket, Virginia. According to a federal grand jury indictment, on a Saturday evening, a concerned citizen alerted police to threatening social media posts by Jiang, including apologies to those he was about to kill. On Sunday morning, the police found the potential shooter at the church's front entrance where he planned to murder as many people as he could. Jiang was armed with a gun, copious amounts of ammunition, and a knife. A mere matter of minutes made the difference, as this was very nearly another church massacre. When police searched his residence, they found that Jiang had written five copies of a single letter, all of which read, in part, "To the families of those men about to be slain—I am sorry for what I have done and about to do. May your tears not be cried in vain, but to celebrate how your loved ones had lived."[8] As of this writing, Jiang is in prison while his case makes its way through the court system.

The motives for these examples and others, whether executed, attempted, or only planned, are vastly different. Roof, Samson, Bush, and the unnamed minor girl all had racially based motives. Kelley had issues with family members and Christianity in general. Anti-Semitism remains rampant in our country and was responsible for multiple shootings at Jewish facilities. Jiang's motives were related to anger at men in relationships while he struggled to find a partner. The reasons people attack groups of people are varied, but the common denominator, as stated earlier, is that there is usually a grievance. Chapter 12 elaborates on this and covers how to recognize when a grievance is about to turn to violence. What remains constant, though, is that in each mass shooting, cues were missed and opportunities to intervene failed to be acted upon before the person chose to pick up a weapon and kill people.

Another person whose situation deserves consideration is Lee Boyd Malvo, whose story sheds further light on the radicalization of young people. In 1999, Malvo was baptized in the Seventh Day Adventist Church. In 2002, Malvo was one of the persons dubbed "the DC snipers." Read those dates again: there's only a three-year difference between them. The DC snipers were a duo who had cut a hole in the trunk of a Chevrolet Caprice so that shots could be taken from this concealed location. This was a clever tactic that made it incredibly difficult for witnesses and law enforcement to determine the source of the shooting. The two snipers who carried out their

---

8. United States Department of Justice, "Virginia Man Charged," para. 2.

attacks managed to avoid capture and arrest for three weeks. The pair killed three and critically injured two in the nation's capital. Seven others were killed and seven injured in shootings leading up to the DC attacks. The city and surrounding area were in a panic.

Malvo was a boy (age fourteen) when he met John Allen Muhammad (age thirty-eight). The younger male had struggled socially but was warmly welcomed by the considerably older Muhammad. At one point, Malvo's mother was deported from the United States and Malvo was left to live with Muhammad. Over years of knowing one another and through a friendship with the Malvo family, the older man managed to groom the boy to be a sniper and a murderer. Malvo was sixteen and seventeen years old during the time of the attacks the pair carried out. Like Roof, Malvo was young when radicalized and grew up with a church background. Like Samson, Malvo is an immigrant.[9] Like many mass shooters, Malvo was an outcast looking to belong.

THE PROBLEM: MASS SHOOTINGS IN PLACES OF WORSHIP

The three mass murderers studied in depth herein, Roof, Samson, and Kelley, explicitly shot people who had gathered in churches. Roof's reason was racially motivated, Samson's was retaliation, and Kelley's was a family dispute that escalated. In all three cases, churches were where they could find large groups of people in a vulnerable position. These three cases are highlighted because of the commonality of the location and church backgrounds of the shooters, but also because of the differences in denominations and motivation. The three incidents are detailed in further chapters, but a very brief picture of each event follows.

- First, on June 17, 2015, Dylann Roof entered a Bible study, sat through the entire class, then killed nine people and injured one at Emanuel African Methodist Episcopal (AME) Church in Charleston, South Carolina.[10] One of his goals was to start a race war with his actions. Roof is on death row in an Indiana prison.

- Second, on September 24, 2017, Emanuel Samson killed one person and injured seven at Burnette Chapel Church of Christ in Antioch,

---

9. Kovaleski and Sheridan, "Boy of Bright Promise."
10. Frazier et al., *We Are Charleston*, 1–4.

Tennessee. Samson stated that his acts were in response to Dylann Roof's actions in North Carolina. Burnette Chapel is a multiracial church, and Samson had regularly attended a few years prior to this incident. Wrestled down by a deacon, Samson was held until arrested by police. He is serving life without parole at a prison in Tennessee.

- Third, on November 5, 2017, Devin Kelley killed twenty-six people and wounded twenty-two at First Baptist Church of Sutherland Springs, Texas. The church was familiar to Kelley, as his ex-wife's family attended there. Kelley, though he had once attended a different Southern Baptist church and had volunteered during a church's vacation Bible school, had become adamantly and vehemently anti-religious. A bystander shot and wounded Kelley, who eventually took his own life.

One of the most notable commonalities between these three events is that the faith and church experiences of Roof, Samson, and Kelley impacted their decision to murder churchgoers during a church service. All three have church and religious backgrounds, but none of the three had a church background that helped them decide against violence.

Differences also exist between the three situations. Two of the shooters, Samson and Kelley, had attended the churches they attacked. Samson chose a church where he had regularly attended a few years prior. He was known there by the pastor and many parishioners. The other shooter who knew the church he chose to attack was Devin Kelley, who shot dozens of churchgoers at his ex-wife's family's church. He had attended events there in the past. Dylann Roof, however, took a different path. Rather than causing harm to the Lutheran church of his childhood, he chose a historic Black church to make a racist statement. Roof had known none of the people at Mother Emanuel personally.

One other vital comparison between the three shooters shows that while all had serious behavioral and mental health issues, two denied having any such problems. Roof in particular went to great lengths to hide his issues. One shooter, however, is remarkable in that he doggedly sought help. Devin Kelley repeatedly recognized problems in himself and reached out for professional help many times over many years. This is discussed in detail in chapter 10. Kelley is a prime, tragic example of how not only warning signs must be addressed, but cries for help must be heard as well.

RELIGIOUS SOCIALIZATION OF ROOF, SAMSON, AND KELLEY

One way to look at what led Roof, Samson, and Kelley to attack people in a church is through an examination of their religious socialization. *Socialization* is the process or processes used by persons, groups, or institutions to help individuals function within their given society. This contributes to the targeted person's development of their personality. The *Handbook of Cross-Cultural Psychology* explains that this process occurs in multiple ways, including imitation, identification, play, role taking, language acquisition, contact with books, media, and all other means of learning.[11] Different types of socialization affect all people. Economically, socially, and institutionally, Roof, Samson, and Kelley had fairly similar histories. In part, the conceptual framework of the cycle of socialization is used to learn more about these three situations. The theory briefly describes socialization as follows:

- Persons are born into a world that contains biases, stereotypes, prejudices, traditions, and history.
- First-degree influencers, including family, teachers, and loved and trusted persons, socialize individuals. Social norms, roles, rules, and values further shape us.
- Institutional and cultural socialization follows, which include institutions as culture—a church can be an influencer on both a conscious and unconscious level.[12]

The chapters that follow explore and describe three cases of religious socialization. Questions are asked about whether denominations and individual local churches are abdicating their responsibility to offer a different cultural message about violence than what exists in the rest of society and culture. Through this lens, we can focus more on prevention and emphasize being proactive rather than reactive.

---

11. Berry et al, "Socialization."
12. Harro, "Cycle of Socialization," 2.

REACHING FOR HOPE

The very idea of a church shooting is terrifying. Fear is rising among the faithful, but the increasing frequency of violence in churches is not inevitable. It's real, it's evident, and it's changeable. We'll take a hard look at the factors, both inside and outside of the church, that might have contributed to shaping these three people's beliefs and actions; we'll consider why we're so afraid; and we'll examine what's worked well historically and what hasn't. Churches have the resources and can learn and develop strategies to recognize potential violence before it occurs. God called us the church to save the world, after all. God wouldn't have given us that mandate if we weren't supposed to work towards the welfare of our churches and our communities. It's not an easy path, and it's a path that takes time, but it's a path we must walk.

Chapter 2

The History: How We Got Here

WITH THE CREATION OF the 24/7 news cycle, it's understandable for us to believe that violence is a new issue in our country. When we were growing up, we likely didn't see this much violence in the nightly news or online. The belief that this is a recent problem, though, would be a misconception. Though murder by way of mass shootings has increased dramatically in recent years, the concept is far from new. Mass shootings have been happening in the United States since the early 1900s, but as Americans, we tend to forget our violent past. This seems to be especially true when churches are historically involved in either perpetrating the violence or neglecting to prevent it. The history of Christianity-related violence far predates 1900, though. The Christian faith isn't unique and isn't alone in this, of course—the river of violence runs deeply through most, if not all, religions. The faith that was built around Jesus, who promoted peace, did not invent the glorification of violence by way of religion. However, Christianity has not been immune to the effects of violence within its ranks. The experience of religion-related violence is long and complex, and until America gains an understanding of our own past as well as the development of our complacency toward violence, we cannot change our present or future.

HISTORICAL REVIEW

Violence takes many forms. Many volumes have been written and thousands of hours of study have been devoted to each of these, and the surface of each is barely scratched here. This is not an exhaustive list, but rather a gloss of the situation to serve as a refresher of our history. We can surely remember additional examples, but these will serve as a starting point. Let's back up historically.

Martyrdom

The idea of the blood of the martyrs predates both Islam and Christianity. In some situations, classifying a death as martyrdom is seen as giving respect to those who have had violence perpetrated on them. However, often the focus shifts from the person to the act. In those cases, the person becomes secondary, and the violence itself becomes glorified and held in great awe. One famous early story of martyrdom is that of the siege of Masada. This event was recorded by Josephus and dates between 73 and 74 CE. Depending on which historian is to be believed, for between seven weeks and two years, Jewish Sicarii rebels fortified themselves against the Romans in the Judean Desert in southern Israel. A siege initiated by the Romans ensued, which led to the mass suicide of the Sicarii rebels hiding there. In memory of the siege, the saying "Masada will never fall again" is an ancient promise. The story has an enormous place in Jewish history and culture, with the rebels seen as heroes.

The second example of religious martyrdom crosses religious boundary lines. Women who sacrifice themselves for either men or children have historically been seen as martyrs in religious circles. In particular, much study has been done on the martyrdom of Mary, mother of Jesus. Kathleen Gallagher Elkins dives deeply into this enlightening topic in *Mary, Mother of Martyrs: How Motherhood Became Self-Sacrifice in Early Christianity*.[1] The extremes of death have softened over time, but even in modern American culture, women who overextend themselves physically, mentally, and emotionally for men or children are still seen as valiant and sacrificial, not only by men, but often by other women.

Religious Wars

A century or so later, the Crusades began. The Crusades were a series of wars and conflicts from the eleventh through thirteenth centuries that

---

1. Elkins, *Mary*, 1–3.

began with European Christians fighting Near Eastern Muslims for control of holy sites that both religions claimed belonged to them. Modern historians estimate that there were about 1.7 million deaths during the nearly two hundred years of ruthless fighting, while other scholars posit between 3 and 9 million lives were lost. Those who died on both sides of the conflict have been elevated to martyr status. Violence in the name of religion is a very, very old concept indeed.

Recently, I learned of a pastor colleague who was leading a class in his church, and the topic of the Crusades came up. After his description of the historic massacres included in those wars, an attendee who had never heard of the Crusades was appalled and asked, "But where were the Christians?" The pastor had to explain that the Christians were right there, killing Muslims. The Christian leader at that time, the pope, the head of their church, had told them to go fight, so they did.

Other historic examples of the church committing violence in the name of religion are plentiful, and religious wars also cross nearly all boundaries of religion and belief systems. Even Buddhists, traditionally seen as peace loving, participated in the Sri Lankan Civil War (1983–2009). Like any religion or tradition, Buddhism includes people with a wide variety of beliefs within it. Typically a pacifistic, peace-loving system of belief, some Buddhists have participated in war. Even Jainism, which promotes noninjury to even the smallest living creature, makes exceptions for war in cases of self-defense or injustice. The Jain tradition uses a military and soldiers to fight in these broadly defined situations.

There are so many more wars that have been fought in the name of religion than can be mentioned: the Thirty Years' War, the Anglo-Spanish War, the Eighty Years' War, the Taiping Heavenly Kingdom rebellion, the Conquest of Ceuta, and the Mughal-Maratha Wars resulted in millions of deaths. Surely some have been omitted here, but the point stands.

Religious Justification in the United States

In the United States, the early days of our country were rife with violence wrapped in religious justification. To this day, the entire concepts of manifest destiny and divine providence continue to affect society. As soon as nonnatives landed in North America, the new arrivals believed that expansion was their birthright. It was all somehow thought to be part of God's plan for them, to be fruitful and multiply and fill the continent with people like themselves, despite that an entire culture already lived here. The newcomers thought they were God's chosen people (a concept inherent in this line of thought), and they, as the embodiment of godliness and civilization, must spread their culture and their religion as far as the land would take them. The new arrivals did not come in peace. They aimed to keep going and going until they ran out of habitable land and assumed that would be where God wanted them to stop.

This is not mere speculation hundreds of years after the fact; it's first-hand testimony. Christians who came to America during the early days of the country wrote copiously about themselves as personal instruments of God's will. They wrote these missives as they continued heading west and slaughtering native peoples. The "settlers" believed they were carrying out mission work as they went out to tame the West. It's important to know that when we're talking about manifest destiny, the "West" at that time was only as far west as Missouri, not all the way to the western California coast. The early settlers were pushing the boundaries of the colonies because, after all, they believed it was their right. They felt obliged to fulfill the will of God.

The reasoning for the belief that this murderous rampage was an appropriate course of action lies in Old Testament Scripture. A profusion of imagery exists in the book of Deuteronomy about the struggle that Israel had against the Canaanites. According to the fifth book of the Old Testament, under the leadership of Joshua, the Israelites conquered the land of Canaan and civilized it. The encroaching North American settlers internalized these Scriptures and viewed themselves as God's chosen people, much like the Israelites. Because of this, when they encountered indigenous people who were fighting against them and what they felt was the living out of God's will to conquer, the settlers viewed the native people as modern-day Canaanites. The intruders convinced themselves that, in the name of the deity, it was their job to conquer the native people and "civilize" the land. In Deuteronomy, the Israelites discovered that the Canaanites performed sacrifices, both animal and human; consequently, the Canaanites were viewed as savages. Similarly, those coming to North America saw unfamiliar practices among native tribes that they didn't understand and drew an unfounded parallel.

In warfare, we create an enemy, and we create a justification for the enemy. The concept of a paper tiger addresses this practice. We make ourselves believe that the enemy are more powerful than they actually are so we can justify using overwhelming force against them. In modern times, a paper tiger is seen as a sort of joke in modern warfare, because we talk about the enemy making themselves a paper tiger. But historically, a paper tiger is this idea of us building them up in our collective psyche so we can use force and methods that are out of proportion to the situation. Then, when we win the battle or the war, we convince ourselves that we have been clearly chosen to be God's people. It's an inhuman practice, but it's a great method for building up esprit de corps: a sense of team spirit that says, "Together we can accomplish anything against this tribe that is so evil. God is on our side! We're very good at this, so let's go attack another tribe and take over another land!"

Jumping ahead to the American Civil War, the violence perpetrated on so many while Scripture was used as an excuse is beyond the grasp of modern-day sensibilities. The national motto of the Confederacy was the Latin *Deo vindice*, or in English, "God as our protector/defender." The idea was that God preferred the Confederacy over the Union and would protect them. In the meantime, preachers in both the North and the South launched holy wars against each other from their pulpits. Sermons about why God preferred either side were in abundance.

Moving forward to 2017, arguments over religion that escalate to violence were still happening. After years of debate about separation of church and state, a monument of the Ten Commandments was erected on the grounds of the state capitol in Little Rock. The next day, Michael Tate Reed, age thirty-two, drove his car into the six-thousand-pound piece of concrete and destroyed it while shouting, "Oh my goodness, freedom!" The incident was captured on video. It wasn't Reed's first time destroying publicly placed displays of the commandments. He was arrested in 2014 in Oklahoma City for a similar act. Though many staunchly disagree with the commandments being posted on government property, most spoke out against the violent destruction of property.[2]

Hopefully, this brief dive into our violent past has laid some groundwork about where we've come from. Both our country and our faith have deep histories of violence, and those histories are intertwined. At the same time, our Christian faith calls us to strive for peace. What we've done so far has not worked, and mass shootings are at an all-time high. It's time to imagine a new starting point.

---

2. Lee, "Destruction," para. 1.

Chapter 3

What We Think We Know

WHEN TALKING WITH FRIENDS, relatives, or colleagues about the problem of mass shootings, it's likely you have encountered people who believe they know precisely what's happening in the country, how often and in what way the incidents happen, and what the overall problem is. They probably think they know the solution too. It's rare to encounter someone with absolutely no opinion on the national crisis of mass shootings. Maybe you're one of those people who believes they know the answers. After all, we all mean well, we all want mass shootings to stop, and isn't that what we're all searching for: an answer that will end the madness?

The problem is that data doesn't come to us in level, measured ways. Rather, we get news stories as they occur, and we hear about only a fraction of mass shootings that happen in our country. Through no fault of those hearing the stories, common misunderstandings about mass shootings abound. Those misconceptions lead us to conclusions that don't fit. This chapter seeks to inform about what data shows, and to dispel commonly held beliefs.

Assumptions are a result of our own experiences or stories we've been told, and they can build and solidify themselves in our consciousness even more if fear is involved. When we repeatedly hear about shootings at houses of worship, assumptions kick into high gear. Misinformation and lack of questioning can create ideas that embed themselves in our minds over time and can be quite difficult to dislodge. If people and organizations are open to understanding data and evidence, assumptions can be tested. In some cases, those assumptions are confirmed, but in others, they're found to be incorrect and should be challenged.

SURPRISE FINDINGS

Statistics are fascinating. Just when we think we know something, data and evidence can move the needle for us. Information about approximately five thousand mass shootings dating between 1940 and 2022 was used in the study that led to this book. The details learned are interesting at best and disturbing at worst. Much of it surprised me and may take you by surprise too. Perhaps a good look at it can change our understanding of how we can work for safety and nonviolence.

Mass Shootings by State

Do you think you live in either a safe or a dangerous state? Over the years studied, the occurrence of mass shootings categorized by state were recorded. The five states that endured the most tragedies of this type were:

- California: 480
- Illinois: 451
- Texas: 344
- Florida: 291
- New York: 232

Population-wise, this ranking makes a lot of sense . . . almost. The more populous a state is, the more mass shootings they've had, which is perfectly logical, with one notable exception: Illinois. That state ranks second in mass shootings, but sixth in population in the country.

If we look at the number of mass shootings compared to the state's population on a per capita level, the results are even more alarming for Illinois. The number of mass shootings per number of people in those states is as follows. (For reference, the lower the number of people, the more likely a person is to be a victim of a shooting in that state.)

- Illinois: 1 mass shooting per 27,826 people
- Florida: 1 mass shooting per 77,700 people

- California: 1 mass shooting per 81,177 people
- New York: 1 mass shooting per 84,358 people
- Texas: 1 mass shooting per 88,672

This comparison changes the narrative quite a bit, with a person being nearly three times more likely to be involved in a mass shooting in Illinois than in the next most dangerous state, Florida. Who knew the Midwest was in this kind of turmoil? The data shows California to be far less scary than it seemed to be at first. As for Illinois, shootings in the Chicagoland area disproportionately raise the number of mass shootings in that state. During the eighty-two-year span studied, 326 mass shootings have happened in Chicago. Alarmingly, nearly all of those (318) happened in a single decade, between 2013 and 2022. By comparison, during that same eighty-two-year period, the second most mass shootings were in Philadelphia, with fewer than half as many as Chicago: 134. In those same years, 18 mass shootings happened in New York City, 69 in Los Angeles, and 64 in Miami. Clearly, there is much work to be done by our neighbors in northern Illinois.

Law Enforcement Fatalities

Another statistic that might come as a surprise is that law enforcement officers are often injured or killed in mass shootings. In 120 of the cases studied for this project, at least one law enforcement officer was hurt or killed. Sometimes the officers are shot as they respond to another shooting. Once, on March 30, 1981, law enforcement officers were hurt in a mass shooting as they were protecting someone. That situation involved the attempted assassination of President Ronald Reagan. But other times, the law enforcement officers themselves were the target of a shooter's ire. In February of 1971, three law enforcement officers attempted to serve a warrant in Dallas, Texas. They called two other officers and asked them to bring some consent forms to the residence, but while they waited, the officers were taken hostage. When the two officers came to bring the paperwork, they, too, were taken hostage. All five of the officers were driven down a dirt road near a river. Three were killed, one was injured, and one escaped to call for help. The two shooters were each sentenced to quadruple life sentences, but one was deemed rehabilitated and was paroled after sixteen years. Law officers, though usually armed, are at high risk.

CORRECT ASSUMPTIONS

There are a few areas where what we presume to be true about mass shooters is correct. For example, we tend to assume that most mass shooters are male, which is true 98 percent of the time. When women are mass shooters, their victims are usually family, or the woman has accompanied a man as an assistant in a shooting. The average age of a shooter is another area where our assumptions tend to be correct. Young men, that is, men under thirty years of age are most likely to be mass shooters. When incidents from 1940 through 2022 are calculated, the median age of a mass shooter is twenty-seven. Those who committed their acts in houses of worship have a median age of twenty-six. These two factors, sex and age, may be the end of our correct widely held assumptions.

INCORRECT ASSUMPTIONS

White Men as Majority Perpetrators

Those of us who stayed abreast of current events in the 1990s and 2000s likely remember the term "going postal." In those two decades, twenty-six shootings occurred either in post offices or outside of them, but by employees of the United States Post Office; eight of these were mass shootings. Nearly all the perpetrators were white, and all but one were male. The idea that mass shooters were largely white men garnered great public intrigue and gathered steam until it embedded itself into the national social conscience.

During those two decades, however, postal-related shootings were only the tip of the iceberg. There were more than four hundred mass shootings across the country in those years. Of the shooters whose races are known, more were nonwhite than white. The idea that most mass shooters are white men never had a basis in reality; it was only media coverage and popular culture that caused us to believe it was true. The myth persists, but on the contrary, the total racial makeup of mass shooters (from 1940 to 2022) is approximately 62 percent Black persons, 21 percent white, 13 percent Hispanic, 2 percent Asian, 1 percent Middle Eastern, and 1 percent other races or mixed race.

Frequency of Apprehensions and Arrests

Another assumption Americans tend to make is that most mass shooters are immediately detained, arrested, and tried in the criminal justice and court systems. This is an assumption that is no longer accurate. It was true until about 2013, when mass shootings began their rapid increase. During the last decade, each year brings more mass shootings that remain unsolved. Law enforcement and judicial systems can't keep up. Also, very often—about one third of the time—the shooter is deceased. They were either caught in some cross fire, killed by law enforcement, or more likely, they took their own lives.

Fear of Strangers

One widespread misconception is that we tend to believe in "stranger danger." It's a lesson that we, as a society, teach children so that they're not abducted by kidnappers or traffickers. Stranger danger is the belief that someone unknown to us is more likely to kill or otherwise harm us than someone we know. Again, the data doesn't support that idea. Even for children, according to the Child Crime Prevention and Safety Center, most abductions are committed by a family member. Only 25 percent of abducted children are taken by strangers.

As for mass shootings, the same concept applies. Statistically, more shootings involve people known to the shooter than only strangers. In either type of shooting, a stranger or known person can be caught in the cross fire, but since mass shootings are usually the result of a grievance, the victims are usually known to the shooters.

When we narrow our focus to shootings in places of worship, most church shootings, including two of the three church-related shootings studied herein, involve victims who were known to the shooter. Communities of faith worry endlessly about security and about letting strangers in the doors after a worship service begins, but a person is more likely to be killed by someone known to them than by an unknown entity.

Types of Locations of Mass Shootings

One interesting data point has to do with the types of locations in which mass shootings tend to occur. For the roughly five thousand mass shootings studied, fifty categories of locations were identified. Places were categorized in groups such as air/bus/train/terminal, bar/nightclub/pub, grocery/market, lake/waterway/beach, and so forth. What was discovered is that more mass shootings happen in residences than anywhere else. Some situations involve break-ins, some are caused by family members who live in or have access to the home, and some are acquaintances endangering acquaintances. More than any other place, though, a person is more likely to be shot in their own home by a large margin. The second most frequent location for mass shootings is just generally outdoors. This does not include instances that occurred in specific places like a park, an outdoor basketball court, a parking lot, or a similar place. The street or standing in front of one's own home or in front of a place of business is the second leading location for mass shootings. The third-ranking type of place for mass shootings is bars/nightclubs. The incidence of violence that happens in these establishments is alarming. Alcohol can impair judgment, though, and poor judgment combined with a grievance can lead to erratic behavior.

Further, it may come as a surprise that a high number of mass shootings are the result of drive-by shootings. Of the shootings studied, 480 were the result of shots fired from a vehicle. Because of the melee that ensues when people shoot from cars, these incidents and those who perpetrate them are incredibly hard for law enforcement to find, investigate, and prosecute.

Frequency of Indoor vs. Outdoor Incidents

Another misconception has to do with whether most mass shootings happen inside of buildings. Overall, most mass shootings don't happen indoors. More than twice as many occur outdoors, and a person is much more likely to be killed in a parking lot than they are inside a building. Yes, indoor shootings do happen, but far more occur in parking lots than in churches or any other structures. Two of the three shootings highlighted in this book began outdoors.

Efficacy of Locking the Doors

For churches, possibly the most widespread misunderstanding is that tighter security in our churches will keep us from being victims of a shooting. The safety measures that are popular tend to fall into two categories:

arming parishioners and locking doors. Both practices have limited benefit but are also deeply flawed, and neither measure addresses the problem of why a person wants to kill others.

The Christian church as a whole has an interesting history when it comes to locking the doors of our church buildings. In the sixteenth century, Reformer John Calvin broke from the Catholic Church. While he was in Geneva, Calvin strongly promoted the notion that the church doors of a church should be locked at all times except for during worship service times. As a Reformer, Calvin was trying everything he could to distance the Protestant Church from Catholicism, and the instinct for Reformers at that time was to run as far from the Catholic Church as possible. Calvin was concerned that if the buildings were left unlocked, people might come in, assume that any religious object in the building was a relic or icon, and lapse into what he considered "superstitious" religious activity, praying or worshiping in more traditionally Catholic ways. That was an interesting reason to lock the doors indeed.

Calvin had a second reason for keeping people out during the week as well. The theologian and pastor wanted to emphasize that the life of the church was not relegated to Sunday service times or the walls of the church building. Church life, Calvin believed, was to be lived out in the world, in the community, and in the home. All of earth is God's, and any place can be a sanctuary if you're prayerful while you're in it.

Calvin's concern about relics and icons is no longer an issue when it comes to church security. However, vandalism, theft, and personal safety are all reasons doors are often locked during non-service times. Catholic parishes have historically kept their sanctuaries unlocked between Masses so the faithful can come in to pray at any time, but that practice is changing. Many parishes now require a person to ring a bell to be allowed in during non-Mass times. This is practiced to protect both people and property.

As recently as 2010, I was a member of a church in a town of 17,000 that unlocked the doors at sunrise and locked them again at sundown. Anyone could come in to pray, prepare a classroom, practice a musical instrument, or whatever else they wanted to do during the week, whether the pastor and administrator were in the building or not. So many keys to that church had been distributed that there was a running joke: when a new person moved to town, they were given a city map, cookies from the town's welcoming group, and a key to the Presbyterian church. In the years since then, however, even that church has changed its policies and now locks the doors during non-service times. Only a few people in church leadership have keys, and the church office keeps track of who has those keys. Many, if not most, church buildings have the same or similar policies.

I am not untouched by the threat of violence inside the church. In 2017, I served in a church that encouraged me to lock the doors during the week during office hours, but I refused. Both the office administrative assistant and I didn't feel unsafe in our town of 7,700, and we wanted people to be able to come into the building if a staff member was there. I grew up in Detroit, Michigan, the administrative assistant was from New York City, and we figured people were more afraid of us than we were of them.

Then one day, when I was in the building alone, Mike (not his real name) stopped by the church. Mike was a church member who struggled with multiple illnesses, both physical and mental. To control pain that was caused by an accident that had happened decades earlier, he used both prescription and illegal medications. His life was lived in constant pain, and it took a toll. In the weeks leading up to this event, Mike had endured hallucinations and alternately thought I was an angel or a demon. On this particular day that he stopped in my office, he thought I was demonic. As Mike stood in my office doorway screaming, I noticed he was tapping a long Bowie knife that was strapped to his hip. It wasn't a gun, but I'm fairly certain that a knife with a long blade can do some serious damage. As I instinctively began to reach for the phone on my desk, he yelled, "What are you going to do? Call the Gestapo?" I calmly said, "I'm thinking maybe, yeah." Mike said, "Fine! I'll leave!" He left, paced in the parking lot for a long time, and eventually went on his way.

Nearly every time I've related that incident, I've been told it is evidence for why church doors should always be locked. But let's think that through: First, Mike fit the statistical norms in that he was neither a stranger to me or to the church. Mike was a church member and was one of the volunteer custodians. He had a key to the church, as he regularly cleaned different areas. Second, if the door had been locked and Mike had knocked or rung a bell, I'd have had no reason not to let him in. I wouldn't have noticed the knife (it was in a sheath the same color as his pants), he was well known to me, and I enjoyed talking with him when he was feeling well. He asked interesting, deep, theological questions. I would have let him in immediately.

The end to Mike's story is tragic. He lost the battle with mental illness and took his life later that same year. Earlier in his life, he had been a smart, creative, clever schoolteacher, coach, mentor, and musician. Adults who had had him as a teacher spoke at his funeral about the powerful and wonderful impact he had had on their lives. I learned a lot from Mike. Perhaps the most lasting lesson is that he once asked me if, when we pray for sick people at church, we can pray for those with mental illnesses too. "Not every time," he said, "But maybe once in a while?"

Locking the doors of a church can be a gut reaction to situations like that day with Mike. It may feel like a logical step on a security level. After all, in our modern day, most people lock their doors when they leave their house or when they go to bed at night. Some people keep the doors locked at all times, even if they're home and awake. Many or most of us lock our car doors. The idea of a locked door is comforting, so it's understandable that locking doors during a church service has become popular.

The difficulty comes when we begin thinking about locking our buildings not only during non-service hours but while the worship services are happening. During a time when church attendance is widely on the decrease, locking people out of worship services seems counterproductive to spreading the good news of the gospel. Yet, the idea of locking worshipers into the church once a service starts and keeping everyone else out has engendered much discussion and is gaining popularity. Communities of faith who are otherwise friendly and welcoming have begun locking their doors ten or fifteen minutes after worship services start in order to protect themselves from mass shooters. What makes us think that mass shooters run late? Dylann Roof was on time to the Bible study at Mother Emanuel. Though it might feel safer to lock people out after the service starts, experience and data show us that it only gives us a false sense of security, and the concept of locking potential shooters out simply doesn't work. Let's look at statistics, gleaned from real events, relating to church shootings and locked doors.

Since 1940, thirty-two mass shootings have happened in places of worship. Of those thirty-two, twelve happened during an actual worship service. The other twenty were before or after worship, between services, or at other events being held inside the church. Attacks have also occurred during services that are not regularly scheduled weekly services, such as when attendees are leaving funerals or memorial services. This includes the Emanuel AME shooting in North Carolina. Dylann Roof went to a Sunday evening Bible study, not a regular Sunday morning worship service.

An example of a church shooter that began shooting before he even entered the building is Emanuel Samson, who began his crime at Burnette

Chapel by shooting a woman who had gone out to her car for a cough drop. Others were shot on the threshold of that church as they were exiting the building after the service had concluded.

Somehow, our collective conscience seems to think that locking doors after a church service starts will prevent a shooting, but that is historically and statistically inaccurate. Of the recorded worship place shootings, in only two is it possible that locked doors would have stopped the gunman.

- In two church shootings, door barricades were in place, and the shooter broke them down.
- In two church shootings, door guards were in place, and the shooter talked his way around the precaution.
- In thirteen church shootings, people were shot outside the building.
- Twice, the people who were shot were not in the sanctuary. They were in the lobby or narthex.
- Once, the shooter shot from outside through the windows.
- Four times, the shooter attacked during a non-service time such as an after-service luncheon or a Bible study or between services.
- In five church shootings, the shooter either was known to the congregation or simply looked harmless and would have been let in regardless of what security was in place.

The reality is that modes of prevention such as locked door policies make multiple assumptions about who potential shooters are and how they will carry out their attacks. They assume a shooter will be a stranger, that they will shoot only indoors, and that they will be late for whatever event they're coming to. In the three cases studied in this book, two of the shooters (Samson and Kelley) were known at the churches where they carried out their crimes. Neither would have been denied entry if security measures had been in place. The one fatality caused by Emanuel Samson occurred in the parking lot. As for Devin Kelley, he began shooting in the parking lot too. Regarding Dylann Roof, security systems would not have stopped his spree either. He arrived to the Mother Emanuel AME Church on time and sat through an entire Bible study before killing nine and injuring three.

When we lock the doors, who are we saying shouldn't be let in if they do happen to be late? Who would be denied entry? Are we suspicious of all we encounter? Short of a person actively waving a weapon, it seems that all would-be worshipers, known and unknown, would and should be welcomed into the worship space. Most churches claim that all are welcome in their buildings and at their worship services. If that is true, why would we lock the doors? Locking people out of our worship spaces sends the opposite message. It limits who can participate in worship and fellowship. Also, tightening security measures in ways that involve screening people who come through the doors unduly burdens volunteer ushers and greeters with the task of deciding who should be allowed to enter church buildings and who should not.

A scenario does exist where a church shooter was thwarted by a locked church door, and it is heart wrenching. As mentioned earlier, that system worked at First Baptist Church of Jeffersontown, Kentucky. That is, it worked to the extent that the shooter was locked out of the church, but it did not cause him to put his gun down and change his course of action. Instead, he went immediately to a grocery store and killed multiple people. The ripple effect of those doors was certainly not intended, but the result remained disastrous. Locking people out of church does not calm violence; it moves the violence to another location. It is assumed that the good people of First Baptist of Jeffersontown, and anyone reading this book, does not wish for anyone to be shot, whether in their own place of worship or at another location.

Christians are called to live like Jesus, who spent his life being a servant to others and not causing harm. He took it to the extent that he literally died in our place. As a church, Jesus is our model. The locked doors, at best, might save our lives, but in saving our lives they might cause harm to others. They block us from sharing the joy of a worship service with anyone who doesn't make it into the building in time or anyone whom church security guards deem unfit to come in. Locked doors may rob us of the opportunity to live ultimately like Jesus did.

Efficacy of Arming Parishioners

One idea that is gaining popularity is that churches should put together armed security teams or that legally qualified parishioners should be encouraged to carry concealed weapons into worship spaces. Though there have been a few instances where that helped, arming parishioners can lead to irreversible problems. Susan Rockett, past president of the National Association of Women Law Enforcement Executives and retired police chief of Mexico, Missouri, explained the danger of arming churchgoers. In a 2024 interview, Rockett said her department once received a call from a pastor whose church had been having problems with a person in particular. That person had sparked quite a bit of fear within the congregation, and the church board had decided to arm everyone in the church.

The police chief explains her reply. "I said, 'Well, if you have a situation like that and guns are drawn and we're called, do not have that gun in your hand when we get there. We will shoot the person with the gun.' The perpetrator needs to be out, like on the ground. In this day and age, if someone calls and says, 'We've got an active shooter in the building,' we have a protocol that we're going to follow. Everybody's going to be super charged up. Just . . . please don't put yourselves in harm's way. That's what I'm going to tell you now, but what I really want to tell you is . . don't do that. Don't do that." Rockett went on to say that arming church members is just not necessary, and she does not know if that's truly what the church intended.[1]

This sentiment played out in real time in the Burnette Chapel shooting and could have resulted in a much larger tragedy. In that situation, Robert Caleb Engle, a parishioner, armed himself with a weapon he retrieved from his vehicle and held Samson until the police arrived. However, Sergeant Geoffrey Odom of the Metropolitan Nashville Police Department was the first to arrive on the scene and, according to court records, "Sergeant Odom walked into the church sanctuary and saw Caleb pointing a pistol at Defendant who was lying on the floor. He initially thought that Caleb was the shooter, until he was informed that Defendant, who was lying motionless and covered in blood, was the actual assailant." The assumption is completely reasonable.

Rockett adamantly encourages churchgoers to not take carrying a weapon into church lightly. "If there's a shooting in a church . . . Let me just tell you, nobody comes away from a shooting unscathed," she said. She told of a colleague who was shot in the chest but survived because of a bulletproof vest. The officer returned fire, hitting the shooter in the leg. Nobody died, but now, decades later, that officer still has PTSD. She's still afraid of the dark. Nobody comes away unscathed.[2]

---

1. Susan Rockett, interview by author, May 5, 2024.
2. Susan Rockett, interview by author, May 5, 2024.

The Effect of Video and Role-Playing Games

Another misconception some people hold is that video games and role-playing games lead to shootings. In my preparation for this book, while I was interviewing teenagers, one of the adults in the room said we couldn't ignore the effect of video games as a cause of violence. For decades, Americans, ranging from religious leaders to politicians, have tried to blame violent behavior, especially when exhibited by younger persons, on video games that contain violent elements. Before video games were created, Dungeons and Dragons was (and sometimes still is) feared to lead to all manner of societal ills. Modern video games, especially first-person shooter games, have raised the ire of those who wish to blame violence on entertainment. If we consider reason and evidence, though, we can find out the reality of the consequences of video games on violence in society.

In 2023, Stanford Brainstorm Lab meticulously reviewed eighty-two medical research articles, the whole of which included all the reputed literature and studies that purported to show links between video games and violent behavior. A link could not be established. A review of FBI data of the thirty years that violent video games have been available did not show that the games cause an increase in actual violence. The same Stanford study noticed an interesting decrease in violence following the release of extremely popular violent video games. One theory is that for potentially violent people, the games serve as an outlet, thus helping to prevent acting on those urges.[3]

Massey University in New Zealand gathered twenty-eight studies, similar to the way Stanford researched the issue. The studies collected information on over twenty-one thousand people, and the Massey researchers released a report published in the *Royal Society Open Science* journal. Their findings included a miniscule correlation between gaming and aggression, but not enough to even be classified as a "small effect." The report decisively concluded that there is no support for the notion that violent video games affect aggression in young people.[4]

Another study takes the same question in a different direction. The American Journal of Play completed a study in 2020 and determined that all types of video games can help improve social and cognitive skills, help with mood management, and may even decrease violence in the real world.

---

3. Dupee et al., "Stanford Researchers."
4. Przybylski and Weinstein, "Violent Video Game Engagement."

When balanced with other life responsibilities, the research showed that video games can be a worthwhile activity for most youth.[5] Despite the religious and societal fearmongering placed upon the music and video game industries, the fear of it turning young people towards violence is not merited. Video games are not causing violence.

Video games aren't the only hobby shouldering blame. RPGs, or role-playing games, are sometimes looked at as problematic too. Dungeons and Dragons is one of many role-playing games. In these, players take on the role of beings and act out storylines. These can be played around a table, similar to a board game, or the storylines can be played out live, often by people who dress in character. The games have rules and game masters who direct the play. However they are played, Dungeons and Dragons and other role-playing games can be a healthy recreational outlet for people who might otherwise be marginalized. A person might be socially awkward or might have difficulty finding a romantic partner or any other social struggle. But in a role-playing game, that person is connected to other people, and for a few hours they get to actually have control over their own situations and make meaningful decisions for their characters. People playing these games quickly learn that their actions have consequences, without having to learn it within the harsh realities of real life. For example, if a player decides to role-play that they're going to kill everyone in the town, there are swift consequences to those actions.

Through the incredible rise of Dungeons and Dragons and other role-playing games since the 1980s, we can reason that the benefits of the games and what people get from them are needed and desired in society. Critical Role is a group of role-playing gamers who have played live games both online and in person. In October of 2023, Critical Role played a live event at Wembley Arena in London. This is the stadium where such legendary acts as Beyoncé, Queen, and Madonna have played. Over twelve thousand people attended the event.[6] Attendees paid to sit in a stadium and watch people play a role-playing game. That speaks loudly to the need for this sort of activity.

These things that some Christian groups have demonized in society such as video games, Dungeons and Dragons, and other role-playing games (and entertainment in general) may actually be part of the solution. These activities may be part of the way in which we can reach out to people.

---

5. Markey, "Video Game Play," 87.
6. Mann, "From Twitch to Wembley," para. 8.

Participants who are deeply invested in these and similar activities have an outlet that could be an alternative to violence. The relationships are grounding. Wherever a person finds community, that group of people can be a stabilizing factor in their life. Instead of vilifying certain types of music or games that we may not quite understand or personally find appealing, we should be working to make sure those things are being used to build relationships and build community. This can be true of sports, music, or any such activity. They are all ways for us, as humans, who are always crying out for community.

Consider Dylann Roof, who had no community. He was isolated in his home, rejected by peers and in-person social groups. Because of that, when he had a question about Trayvon Martin and wanted to learn, he fell into a negative community instead of a positive one. Had a productive, positive community been available, where he could have felt welcome and accepted, things could have gone very differently for him and the people of Emanuel AME. We vilify things like leisure activities because it's easier to blame things for our problems and society's ills than to look at ourselves and see how we can improve. As a result, we push away people who harmlessly enjoy those activities. We may mean well when we do this, but we can begin the journey on the road back to one another. We can certainly be part of the solution.

SUMMARY

If we allow ourselves permission to move beyond emotion and the messages that media, politicians, and religious leaders are sending us, we will be swayed by evidence and data, and our strategies will change. We will resist the temptation to align ourselves with unproven assumptions. We will recognize that the odds of us enhancing our safety through measures like security guards and locked doors are nearly nonexistent. We will stop trying to find ways to place blame for mass shootings on outside factors and take a look at what we can do in the way of prevention. If we believe statistics and peer-reviewed studies, no longer will we make it our priority to hide from a shooter. Instead, our plan of action will focus on preemptive work such as education, prevention, and recognizing potential violence before it occurs. This will allow us, as communities of faith, to create space in which we can learn and grow and potentially save lives and help facilitate healing.

Chapter 4

What Happened at Mother Emanuel AME

INTRODUCTION

ON JUNE 18, 2015, Americans woke up to the news that evil had unfolded the night before at Emanuel AME Church in Charleston, South Carolina. Of all church mass shootings in the United States, this one may be the most well known. At the time, it received intense press coverage. Follow-up news stories continued in the weeks, months, and even years that followed.

Mother Emanuel, as the church is known, was established in 1816. It is the oldest Black church in the Southern United States, standing as a proud historical landmark in both secular and religious realms. The AME denomination to which it belongs was originally founded as a group of Christians seeking to end racism and slavery. From its onset, the church's cofounder, Denmark Vesey, championed these causes. For his efforts, he was subsequently arrested in 1822 for plotting a slave revolt.[1] The denomination has a history of promoting education, determination, and racial uplift. During a labor strike for hospital workers in 1969, the church hosted civil rights leaders, including Coretta Scott King, Martin Luther King Jr., and Booker T. Washington. The ensuing march began on the steps of Mother Emanuel.[2] Moving forward to modern times, Clementa Pinckney was not only the pastor at Mother Emanuel but a state senator with a history of working for

---

1. Khimm, "Clementa Pinckney's Political Ministry," para. 8.
2. South Carolina Department of Education, *2025 Calendar*, June 22.

racial justice. In 2001, Pinckney said, "Our church was founded on social policy. We have always been vocal about social equality since the 1700s. I come from that tradition."[3] Justice is in the DNA of this church.

In the Deep South—that is, southern states that are typically highly religious, including Texas, Louisiana, Alabama, Mississippi, Florida, Georgia, North and South Carolina—a long-standing tradition of some Christian churches is to meet on Wednesday nights for various activities.[4] Youth groups gather, choirs rehearse, the devout meet for prayer meetings, meals are shared, and faithful parishioners come together to study the Bible. On that particular and awful Wednesday night in 2015, Dylann Roof came to Mother Emanuel church and joined such a Bible study. This group was led by Myra Thompson.

The class almost didn't happen that evening. It had been a busy day at the church, with a licensing ceremony, a business meeting, and other well-attended activities. Rev. Pinckney had worked that morning in his position as state senator, campaigning for then-presidential candidate Hilary Clinton. It had been an exhausting day for so many. "Should we have Bible study tonight?" The faithful debated. In the end, they decided to stay the course and have their gathering. The meeting started almost two hours late, about 8:16 p.m., with a lower than usual attendance. Those factors surely decreased the number of Dylann Roof's victims. The nine lives lost that day were Rev. Dr. Clementa Pinckney, Cynthia Marie Graham Hurd, Susie Jackson, Ethel Lee Lance, Depayne Middleton-Doctor, Tywanza Sanders, Daniel L. Simmons, Sharonda Coleman-Singleton, and Myra Thompson. Thompson led the Bible study.

SHOOTER PREPARATION

Events in Dylann Roof's life leading up to the shooting at Mother Emanuel are vitally important to the story. One day in 2012, after hearing repeated mentions of the name Trayvon Martin in the news and daily interactions, Roof, who was seventeen at the time, turned to the search engine Google. He looked up Trayvon Martin's name and the phrase "black on white crime" to learn about the situation. What appeared first and most prominently in the search results were links to white supremacist groups, which Roof clicked on and explored. He joined some of the discussion groups

3. Frazier et al., *We Are Charleston*, xiv.
4. Frazier et al., *We Are Charleston*, 1.

he found. It was there that Roof was welcomed into community, accepted even with his quirks, and made to feel like a valued part of a tight-knit group. Roof quickly adopted the racist and violent ideology of these organizations. After years of being shunned by his peers, Roof was welcomed and appeared to be respected as an equal. Soon, it was clear to him that Black people should be eliminated. For further exploration into how this happened, chapter 8 describes Roof's journey into white nationalism and white supremacist groups.

After that Google search, Roof then meticulously scoured the internet, researched and studied ways to solve what he considered to be the problem: the existence of Black people. Initially, he considered targeting a "Black festival" but changed his mind because of the pressure of having his actions limited to a specific day, as well as the complications of potential security at a festival. In the end, he determined that one particular church, Emanuel African Methodist Episcopal Church in Charleston, South Carolina, would be a perfect target. Other churches were considered, and a list of African American churches was found in his car after his arrest.[5] Ultimately, though, Emanuel AME was chosen because it is a historic Black church with a deep, rich legacy in the denomination, in culture, and in anti-racism work, and is important to the history and culture of its geographical region. Dylann Roof had ascertained that Mother Emanuel was a church of faithful parishioners who were largely African American, and his goal was to make a statement of racial hatred that would be heard far and wide. Roof chose this innocent target intentionally.

In 2015, prior to the shootings at Mother Emanuel, Roof wrote and published a manifesto at www.lastrhodesian.net (no longer an operational website) entitled "rtf88." The document outlined his white supremacist views (appendix A). Roof dedicated four and a half pages to his hatred of Black persons, eight sentences to Jews, seven sentences to Hispanics, and eight sentences lambasting patriotism. Four sentences, however, were used to explain that he took no issue with people of East Asian descent. In court, however, he explained that while Asian people have higher IQs than white people, he still believed white people were superior. Roof then issued a call to action, explaining that nobody was doing anything but "talking on the internet," that "someone has to have the bravery to take it to the real world,"

---

5. United States v. Dylann Storm Roof, "Brief of Appellant," 51.

and "I guess that has to be me."⁶ Dylann Roof has never made his motives a secret.

Videotaped law enforcement and court records tell this story well. In an interview with police the day after the shooting, Roof explained why he chose Mother Emanuel church, and he self-identified as a white nationalist. The following exchange is from court records of the interview, with "CJ" and "MS" being the interviewing detectives and "DR" being Dylann Roof. Spelling and grammatical issues are left untouched, as this is the official court record.

> CJ: So is that why you chose that church?
>
> DR: Well, yes.
>
> MS: Because you were looking for African Americans.
>
> DR: Right, right. I wasn't going to go to another church because there could of been white people there.
>
> MS: So you didn't want to kill any white people? Or shoot any white people?
>
> DR: (Laughs) Oh, no.
>
> MS: You just wanted to shoot the black people.
>
> DR: Right, yeah.
>
> CJ: What was the reason why you chose Charleston as your location, why that particular area there?
>
> DR: Well, the reason I chose Charleston is because it's just, I like Charleston.
>
> CJ: Uh huh.
>
> DR: It's really nice down there. It's a historic city. At one time, I think it had the highest ratio of black people to white people in the whole country, when we had slavery. And then the other reason is just because that AME church was historic, too. It was a historic AME church. I mean, I guess that's pretty much the reason.
>
> MS: How did you find out about that AME church in Charleston? Did you research it on the internet?
>
> DR: Yeah, I just looked up black churches.⁷

Later in the same interview:

6. Roof, "Manifesto," para. 36.
7. United States Attorney's Office, "Full Dylann Roof Confession," 16:06–16:38.

DR: Right, well, you know, obviously I realize that these people, they're at church, they're not criminals or anything but that's not the point. What is, that criminal black people kill innocent white people every day.

CJ: So what was your point then? What point were you trying to make? You said right there these people are in church, they're innocent.

DR: Right.

CJ: So what was the point of targeting them?

DR: Because, I just knew that would be a place there would be, a small amount of black people in one area.[8]

Fueled by that racism, Roof made approximately a half-dozen trips to Charleston between December of 2014 and June of 2015. These trips were made to canvass the area, do surveillance, and prepare for the shooting. Mother Emanuel was one of the places he visited on those trips as he planned his attack. It was during that visit that he learned of the Wednesday night Bible study.

On the evening of June 17, 2015, security video shows that Roof drove to the church, sat in his car for about thirty minutes, then entered the church's fellowship hall. This is the room where the Bible study had gathered, and Roof asked if he could join. Rev. Pinckney stood to greet him and offered him a Bible and study guide, which Roof took.

Roof had entered the church building through a regular church door. If security had been present at that door, there would have been no obvious reason to stop him. His weapons were concealed, and he appeared to simply be a person interested in a Bible study and the people in attendance. Churches are in the business of welcoming people, after all. If the church had had a practice of locking the doors after a meeting began, Roof would still have been in the room that night. He was on time for the Bible study.

What those eleven people in that room did not know was that Roof had entered Mother Emanuel with a concealed Glock pistol and eight magazines, each loaded with eleven hollow-point bullets. Roof asked specifically to sit next to Rev. Pinckney. He sat through the entire forty-five-minute meeting, during which the group studied and discussed Mark 4, particularly the parable of the sower.

---

8. United States Attorney's Office, "Full Dylann Roof Confession," 29:31–30:09.

THE SHOOTING

At the end of the meeting, the entire group stood and invited Roof to join them in a closing prayer. As they closed their eyes to pray, Roof drew his pistol. He killed nine people and injured three with shocking intentionality. He walked through, circling the room as people hid under tables, and reloading multiple times. Roof shot Rev. Pinckney first. Immediately, Rev. Daniel L. Simmons tried to stop the shooting and check on his pastor and was shot and killed. Roof then shot the others in the room. According to the coroner, each victim was shot at a minimum of between five and ten times. Pinckney's wife and daughter heard the commotion and called 911 from the church office.[9]

On the first day of courtroom testimony, Felicia Sanders, one of the three survivors of the shooting, said that during the massacre, Roof stated, "I have to do this because y'all are raping our women and taking over the world." Sanders continued, "That's when he put about five bullets in my son. Seventy-seven shots in that room, from someone we thought was looking for the Lord."[10] In a later courtroom appearance, survivor Polly Sheppard gave a chilling account of the events in a courtroom testimony. The following exchange is from the transcript of those court proceedings in the US Court of Appeals in 2020. Spelling and grammatical issues are left untouched, as this is the official court record.

> Q. Were you able to hear the gunshots as they were fired?
>
> A. I could hear them, yeah.
>
> Q. Were you able to see the casings as they kicked out of the gun?
>
> A. I did.
>
> Q. As the defendant shot, could you see his boots as he walked closer to you?
>
> A. I did.
>
> Q. When he got to the end of the row of tables, where you were laying, tell us what happened.
>
> A. He told me to shut up.
>
> Q. Why did he—What were you doing?

---

9. Frazier et al., *We Are Charleston*, 4.
10. United States v. Dylann Storm Roof, "Motion to Appropriate," 18.

A. I was praying out loud. He told me to shut up. And he asked me, Did I shoot you yet? And I said no. And he said, I'm not going to. I'm going to leave you here to tell the story.

Q. And when you say Tywanza rose up, what do you mean by that? Was he able to stand up or just prop himself up?

A. He rose up on his elbow and propped up and he started talking to him.

Q. And what did Tywanza, in an effort to distract the defendant, what did he tell him?

A. He said—he asked him, Man, why are you doing this? We mean you no harm. Why are you doing this? So he said, I have to. I just have to. You're raping our women and taking over the nation.

There was a pause in the proceedings here. When they resumed, this exchange occurred:

Q. And what did the defendant do at that point?

A. He shot Tywanza.[11]

Moments before the shooting, Tywanza Sanders had sent a Snapchat of the Bible study. Roof is seen in that social media post. At the time, the social media platform Snapchat allowed ten-second videos, which is what this one is. This short clip is widely available online and shows class participants with Sanders's caption, "Bible study knowledge planter."[12]

HOW AND WHY IT STOPPED

Roof tried to keep shooting the Bible study participants but had run out of ammunition. Security camera footage shows that at 9:06 p.m., less than an hour after he entered Mother Emanuel, he left through the same door that he'd entered. Roof then got into his car and left the scene, leaving the dead and dying behind, and drove toward Nashville. He told both Polly Shepherd and law enforcement agents his plan was to take his own life once police surrounded him. Apparently serious about this idea, Roof had saved one magazine of ammunition for this purpose.[13]

---

11. United States v. Dylann Storm Roof, "Brief of Appellant," 51.
12. News 24, "Snapchat from Charleston Victim," para. 1.
13. United States v. Dylann Storm Roof, "Brief of Appellant," 47.

Emergency responders descended upon the church quickly. Their presence was needed and helpful, but Roof was at large, and tensions in both the church and the community remained high. No one knew if he might come back to the scene and shoot more people, or if he'd headed to another location to continue the violence. Images from the church security cameras quickly circulated across the country, and a phone bank was set up for people to call in tips if they saw him. Even Roof's own father, Franklin Bennett Roof, saw the broadcasted photos of his son from security footage. The senior Roof called in his son's identification. Multiple others recognized him as well and called in with identifying information. After a tense night, the following morning police received a tip that his car had been spotted, and they pulled the killer over at 10:40 a.m. in Shelby, North Carolina. When asked what happened, he said, "I killed them. Well I guess, I mean I don't really know." He also said, "I am guilty. We all know I'm guilty."[14] Law enforcement arrested Roof without incident.

The video of the interview with Dylann Roof, conducted by law enforcement, the morning after the shootings is harrowing. Viewing the interview and hearing Roof's voice might humanize him to some viewers and listeners who had previously thought of him only as a type of monster. When the investigators asked him to tell them what happened the night before, he haltingly said, "I went into that church in Charleston . . . and, uh . . . I . . . I did it." Investigators asked, "You did what?" Roof waffled. The officer said, "I know it's tough sometimes to say it." Roof answered, "It's not that I don't want to say it because I don't want to make myself seem guilty. I just don't really like saying it."[15] In the interview, he is asked how many people he killed, and he guesses five but is "really not sure."[16] Roof's voice is that of a young man who sounds confused and unsure of himself, rather than the tough, gruff, bloviating person that might be expected.

CONVICTION AND SENTENCE

On December 15, 2016, Roof was convicted on thirty-three federal counts. Nine convictions were for racially motivated hate crimes resulting in death, three were for racially motivated hate crimes in an attempt to kill, nine convictions were for obstructing religious exercise resulting in death, three

---

14. United States Attorney's Office, "Full Dylann Roof Confession," 7:13–7:15.
15. United States Attorney's Office, "Full Dylann Roof Confession," 6:22–6:57.
16. United States Attorney's Office, "Full Dylann Roof Confession," 8:45–9:08.

convictions were for obstruction of religious exercise in an attempt to kill using a weapon, and nine convictions were for the use of a firearm to commit murder. On January 23, 2017, he was sentenced to fifteen concurrent life sentences and eighteen concurrent death sentences. Roof is currently on death row at a maximum-security prison in Terre Haute, Indiana. He has filed multiple motions for a new trial or judgment of acquittal and has filed multiple appeals. All have been unsuccessful. In October 2022, his death penalty appeal went to the United States Supreme Court, and the sentence was upheld.

INTERVIEWS AND COMMUNICATIONS

I wrote to Roof in prison, to hear his account of the story, but received no reply. Other interviews regarding Roof himself are in chapter 7. These include conversations with two of his pastors.

SUMMARY

The horrific events that happened on that June day are remembered by many. Reverend Clementa Pinckney's eulogy was delivered by President Barack Obama, and the entire service was broadcast live on national television, which further cemented the event into our collective national psyche. Many studies have been and continue to be completed, analyzing every second of Roof's six-minute rampage and the moments beyond.

The horror of that day almost defies description. The other side of the coin must be shown. If we're going to speak of the terrible, let us also remember the good and work for better. Let us look forward with hope to a time when these types of events are rare, if not unheard of. Let us work toward recognizing the troubled and potentially violent people like Dylann Roof before they take another innocent life. As we move further into this study, ways to recognize warning signs and what to do about them will be discussed. Most importantly, further chapters will cover how to help people before they begin to show signs of potential violence.

Chapter 5

What Happened at Burnette Chapel Church of Christ

INTRODUCTION

TWENTY-FIVE-YEAR-OLD EMANUEL KIDEGA SAMSON was not secretive or mysterious about why he entered a church he used to attend, Burnette Chapel Church of Christ, on September 24, 2017. Two years and three months earlier, Dylann Roof had killed nine people and injured one at Emanuel African Methodist Episcopal Church in Charleston, South Carolina, as a self-proclaimed racial statement. Samson stated that his actions were in response to Roof's actions. The day Samson shot people at Burnette Chapel, he left a note on his car's dashboard explaining that his goal was to kill one more white person than the number of Black people Dylann Roof had killed (appendix B). In an attempt to accomplish his goal, Samson went to the multiracial Burnette Chapel in Antioch, Tennessee, where he had once been an active parishioner.[1] He killed one (Melanie Smith Crow) and injured seven others (Linda Bush, Catherine Dickerson, Marlene Jenkins, William Jenkins, Pastor Joey Spann, and Peggy Spann). Robert Caleb Engle was injured when he was pistol-whipped as he stopped the carnage.

Burnette Chapel Church of Christ has historically been a diverse congregation in multiple ways. Current pictures on the church's web page show a broad racial mix of people, as well as a wide range of ages and people

---

1. Grinberg and Stirling, "Picture," paras. 9–11.

with varying accessibility needs.[2] Their worship services began being live streamed in March 2020, and a variety of ethnicities, races, and physical abilities are represented in the congregation and worship leadership. African, Hispanic, white American, and worshipers of unknown origins are seen and heard in the voices that participate in their services.[3] This church is the very definition of a diverse body of believers. Though persons of multiple races were in attendance that day and Samson had opportunity to shoot nonwhite people, all of his victims were white.

Emanuel Samson did not act in a sudden burst of passion. Much like Roof, his actions were well thought out, planned, and documented. He chose a church with which he was familiar and wore a mask, presumably not to be recognized. He attacked a church where people said he had been friendly, even to one of the people he shot. He left multiple notes and messages explaining what he was about to do.

DAY BEFORE

Maya Hill and Emanuel Samson had been dating for about four months at the time of the shooting, and Samson is the father of one of her children. The night before he attacked Burnette Chapel, the couple argued about his plans to move in with his father. This was a change in their previous plan, which involved the possibility of buying a house together. Hill said that usually after an argument, Samson liked to be left alone. That night, though, she said he held her all night long after the argument, which was very rare behavior for him. The morning of the shooting, Samson was agitated, and the couple exchanged texts that were described by Hill as hostile. After Samson left her home, Hill found a note he had left her explaining that he was going to shoot himself that day. She immediately began to drive around looking for him but was not successful.[4]

Samson previously had had an unarmed security license, but it had expired. Two days before the shooting, he attended a class to update that license. However, the guns used that day were not Samson's. He had sold his own guns the prior summer but was holding his cousin's guns for him as a favor at the time of the shooting. The cousin was in and out of trouble and was afraid for his life and safety, and had trusted Samson with the guns. The

---

2. See http://www.burnettechapel.org/.
3. E.g., Burnette Chapel, "Sunday, August 16th, 2020."
4. State of Tennessee v. Emanuel Kidega Samson, "Appeal," 13.

cousin says he did not know about Samson's homicidal or suicidal thoughts. Samson regularly kept these guns in his car to keep them out of reach of his girlfriend's children.[5]

Samson told the court that in the days leading up to the shooting at Burnette Chapel, he was extremely depressed and felt "kind of numb." He described rapid mood changes during those days and said when his mood dropped, he would sometimes place a gun to his head, which is consistent with his father's testimony that Samson sometimes verbalized suicidal ideation.[6]

SHOOTER PREPARATION

On September 27, 2017, a beautiful Sunday morning, Samson left Maya Hill's home about 8:30 a.m. He was scheduled to work both of his part-time jobs that day, but not until 11:00 a.m. At 10:01 a.m., he sent an email to his employer stating that he appreciated the opportunity to work there but would not be returning. Samson dressed in a T-shirt and leather jacket that portrayed human targets. Both had phrases "Just Another Day" and "FLETC," which is an acronym for the Federal Law Enforcement Training Center in Glynco, Georgia.

Samson drove around for a while, then headed to Burnette Chapel. He parked his blue Nissan Xterra near the church entrance, left two guns and ammunition on the front passenger floorboard of the car, left the vehicle running, and donned sunglasses and a mask. Before he entered the church, he left a handwritten note on his dashboard, which appeared to be torn from a journal, also found in the car. Specifically, the note read, "Dylan [sic] Roof is less than nothing. The blood that 10 of your kind is that of the color upon the RBG flag. 1 up bitch," and a smiley face.[7] A copy of this note is available in the appendix (appendix B).

RBG is a reference to red/black/green, the colors of the Pan-African flag, sometimes called RBG, the black liberation flag, and the Marcus Garvey flag. The flag is tricolored with equal horizontal stripes of red, black, and green, and the flag was designed by the Universal Negro Improvement Association in 1920. The scrawled term "1 up" references Samson's desire to "one up" Roof by killing one more person than Roof had killed. As stated

---

5. State of Tennessee v. Emanuel Kidega Samson, "Appeal," 21.
6. State of Tennessee v. Emanuel Kidega Samson, "Appeal," 8.
7. Tamburin, "Lawyers Read," paras. 23–24.

in court records, the note was essentially Samson's declaration of his motive and intent to carry out a mass shooting in a church, similar to or more violent than the one perpetrated by Dylann Roof on June 17, 2015.[8]

Samson's attack began in the church parking lot. If guards had been posted at the church doors, or if the doors had been locked during the service, the violence would not have been stopped. Three of the people shot that day were leaving the building, and Samson entered the building as people were leaving at the end of the service—a time when the doors would have been opened in any case. He was known to the people there. Any posted guard would have welcomed him in.

THE SHOOTING

Samson carried two handguns, extra ammunition, and a double-edged knife with an approximately five-inch blade and sheath with him as he walked from his car toward the church, just as the worship service was ending. While still in the parking lot, Samson shot Melanie Crow Smith, twenty-eight, once in the face and three times in the back as she walked to her car for a cough drop. Smith, a mother from Smyrna, was carrying a Bible and sermon notes.

People both inside and outside the building heard the shots but assumed the first two shots were firecrackers.[9] After the third and fourth shots, multiple courtroom witnesses explained, they realized that there was a problem. Pastor Joey Spann and his wife, Peggy, had proceeded to the back of the church auditorium after worship service, as was his usual practice, to greet and shake hands with members as they left. Pastor Spann had spoken to Melanie as she left the building. He stepped into the vestibule to speak with others when he heard the gunshots. He then walked outside, looked around, and saw Samson walking quickly up the sidewalk—a "strong" walk, as Spann said in court—wearing a neoprene mask and holding a gun. With the goal of protecting those still in the building, Pastor Spann walked back through the vestibule door and yelled for everyone to run.

Pastor Spann realized what was happening, attempted to get people to run, and made multiple other efforts to stop the shooting and to save lives. The next shots came when Samson walked toward the church and shot William and Marlene Jenkins, an elderly couple who were leaving to

---

8. State of Tennessee v. Emanuel Kidega Samson, "Appeal," 18.
9. State of Tennessee v. Emanuel Kidega Samson, "Appeal," 12.

walk to their car. Mr. Jenkins, eighty-four, was using a walker that day and said he was only a step or two outside of the door when Samson shot him three times in the legs. Jenkins fell against the door frame as he tried to turn and go back inside the church. William Jenkins's wife Marlene, eighty-three, described the scene. "Joey backed up into the church and he hollered, 'Everybody get back!' Well, when he shot my husband, I didn't get back, I went toward him, my husband, because he was laying on the ground." Pastor Spann went into the church to continue to warn people, but Marlene stayed with William Jenkins. In courtroom testimony she said, "After that, I was looking down at . . . my husband, where he was laying, and he hadn't moved. I thought he had killed him. He was laying down and he hadn't moved, and I thought, 'Well, he has killed him, he might as well kill me too.' That's just how I felt about it." Samson then shot Marlene Jenkins in the arm as she held it up to protect herself. "Then I saw him [William Jenkins] move," Marlene said. "He was trying to get to me."

Another parishioner who attended that day, Catherine Dickerson, was outside of the church but ran back inside, where Samson then shot her in the leg. She fell down, crawled to the foyer, and lay down under the water fountain with her purse over her face. She hoped that if Samson saw her again, he would assume she was dead. She heard more shots as Samson made his way through the sanctuary.

Peggy Spann was standing outside of the church when she saw Samson with a gun and warned her husband, Pastor Joey Spann. Samson shot Peggy Spann as she tried to reenter the church. Wilma Crow, aunt of Melanie Crow, had been heading to the parking lot with Melanie but stopped to talk. She heard the shots that killed Melanie and she saw Peggy Spann fall. She ran to the kitchen and encountered Joey and Peggy Spann's nephew, David Morales. Together they ran to a house next door, hid behind a shed, and called 911. They returned to the church after the police arrived, and Wilma was led to where her niece's body was lying in the parking lot.

Linda Bush, who had been talking to Pastor Spann, was shot in the back of the leg as she attempted to run away and fell face first, "half in the door and half out." She pretended to be dead, and Samson stepped over her. Samson kept shooting, and Pastor Spann threw a wooden prayer box at him, but the box "just bounced off of him," Spann said. Samson then shot Pastor Spann once in the chest and once in the finger. Other shots were fired did not hit anyone. "I was moving forward, and I fell," Joey Spann said. "My finger was dangling off." Peggy Spann testified in court that as she fell to the floor with her leg injury, she saw the hole in her husband's suit jacket. She asked him if he was okay, and the pastor answered, "He's killed me. I'm sorry, I'm dying." They told each other they loved each other. Peggy Spann said that "everything was fading off" after that.

Mary Pitts and Linda Stafford ran inside the women's restroom when they heard the gunshots, and Ms. Pitts locked the door. Samson began firing shots into the walls and door of the restroom. Ms. Pitts got down in a stall and put her head in her lap and held her Bible to the side of her head hoping it would protect her if one of the bullets penetrated the stall. Ms. Stafford stood in the last stall and called 911. Later, Mary Pitts assisted Marlene Jenkins with towels and water until emergency responders arrived.

Armilla Bishop attempted to run to the front of the church when she heard gunshots but was knocked down. She crawled under the front pew and heard "the gunshots getting closer and closer." Ms. Bishop saw Samson's shoes as he walked down the aisle and up to the baptistry door and stopped. She described the scene this way: "As he was standing at the front of the church, he had a gun out firing towards the back of the church. Then, all of a sudden, a clip was ejected, a magazine was ejected, and it landed on the floor by the pews, another one was put in. And then, as I'm lying there, I thought, he kind of brought the gun down just a little bit, so I thought maybe he had seen me. But then he brought it back up and started firing at the back of the church again."

The stories from those who ran for cover and were not shot, recorded in courtroom testimony, are harrowing. Tammy Luker described Samson as the "bogeyman walking down the aisle coming to get you, and you have nowhere to go."[10] Minerva Rosa, who had blood on her as a result of administering aid, said of some of the injured victims, "Our church is senior people. They didn't make it out." Danny Carter, church treasurer, had walked forward to collect the offering when he heard gunshots. Carter had initially assumed Samson intended to steal the offering, but Samson was not interested in the donations. Carter immediately went to the youth classroom to tell his wife and the children to stay in the classroom. He then saw a man with hearing differences and ran to protect him. Samson looked at them and fired his gun into the floor but did not shoot them.

---

10. State of Tennessee v. Emanuel Kidega Samson, "Appeal," 15.

HOW AND WHY IT STOPPED

A church deacon, twenty-two-year-old Robert Caleb Engle, had attended the service that day with family members. Engle testified in court that he was hiding between the first and second pews near the front of the sanctuary. As Samson walked up the aisle and passed him, Engle began to follow Samson.

> As soon as I was an arm's length away, I remember reaching down and trying to grab his firearm and ended up grabbing his leather jacket and ripping it around the cuff. He had then turned around and pistol-whipped me. I can recall between three to five times on the top of my head. After he had pistol-whipped me, this was towards the vestibule now, I had dropped down to my knees and scurried into the right side of the pews and hid in between there. From there, he had, his back was towards the vestibule, and he had walked all the way back towards the pulpit. And I was peeking up from between the two pews, and that is whenever I'd seen him coming back towards the vestibule again. And I had stood up in front of him and he extended his arm. And the only thing I can remember is I just shoved my left arm out in front of him. And then I heard a gunshot. And we had stood there for what seemed like an eternity. I looked down at myself and I looked up at him, and then he fell down to the floor.[11]

Samson first pointed the gun at Engle and pulled the trigger, but the gun's clip was empty. Samson began to hit Engle in the head with the gun and at some point reloaded. Samson then fired the weapon and accidentally shot himself in the chest. Engle then shouted, "The shooter is down, is everyone OK?" People began emerging from hiding, and James Engle (Caleb's father) walked up and kicked the gun away from Samson's hand and asked Barbara Davis, who had emerged from behind a pew, to stand on the gun until police arrived. Engle's courtroom testimony continued:

> From there, and I remember as I was walking up through the front of the church I had passed a vehicle that was running and I thought that was either Mr. and Mrs. Jenkins' vehicle running and didn't really pay much attention to it. From there, I had gone back in, planted my foot in the small of his back, and I had pointed my firearm at him. I remember I said, "I have a .45 caliber with hollow points loaded, pointed right at you. You move, I shoot."

---

11. State of Tennessee v. Emanuel Kidega Samson, "Appeal," 15–16.

Then shortly after that, the first responding officer, I believe Officer Odom, showed up and he had instructed me to lay my gun aside and I did.[12]

As law enforcement arrived, they asked who the shooter was, and everyone pointed at Samson. Engle had blood dripping from his head and face from where he had been hit with the gun by Samson. James Engle described his horror at seeing his son's bloody face and his assumption that Caleb had been shot. "No," Caleb said, "I just got hit over the head." The senior Engle explained that there's a running family joke that Caleb is hard-headed, but he wondered how else Caleb would still be able to get up, go to his car, and retrieve his own weapon.

CONVICTION AND SENTENCE

In courtroom testimony, Samson claimed he did not remember any details of the shooting apart from accidentally shooting himself. Judge Cheryl Blackburn noted that not remembering an event is not a defense. An insanity defense was also not supported. A forensic psychiatrist affirmed that Samson has a diagnosis of bipolar II disorder, but that under Tennessee law, the shooter did not meet the criteria for an insanity defense.

In court, the psychiatrist explained:

> "There is insufficient evidence to conclude that his mental disease prevented him from appreciating the nature, or wrongfulness, of his alleged actions"; that there is "insufficient evidence to conclude that [Defendant's] severe mental disease rendered him incapable of knowing or premeditated actions"; that Defendant's "capacity to exercise judgment and reflection, prior to acting, does seem to have been compromised by his severe mental illness; and, while his judgment was most likely impaired, it is not possible to definitely opine that he lacked total capacity for premeditation"; and "despite his severe mental diseases he appreciated the wrongfulness and nature of his alleged actions."[13]

In 2018, Emanuel Samson was convicted of the following crimes: three counts of civil rights intimidation, one count of first-degree premeditated murder, seven counts of attempted first-degree murder, seven counts of employing a firearm during the commission of a dangerous felony,

12. State of Tennessee v. Emanuel Kidega Samson, "Appeal," 16.
13. State of Tennessee v. Emanuel Kidega Samson, "Appeal," 9.

twenty-four counts of aggravated assault, and one count of reckless endangerment. He was sentenced to life in prison for the murder of Melanie Crow Smith, as well as 281 years for the other charges, to run concurrently with the life sentence. He is currently an inmate at Riverbend Maximum Security Institution in Nashville, Tennessee. Samson has filed multiple subsequent appeals. All have been denied by the court.[14]

INTERVIEWS AND COMMUNICATIONS

I wrote three letters to Emanuel Samson, who is in a federal prison, to see if he would be willing to talk about what he did. Samson spoke very little in court, and I was interested in hearing his thoughts now that a few years have passed since the incident. He responded to the first letter from me, asking for more details about what I was interested in, but then ceased communication (appendix D).

Pastor Joey Spann and Burnette Chapel did not respond to interview requests. However, an informative article was published in the *Christian Chronicle*, "We Do Not Go to Church Anymore."[15] This commentary helped give a sense of Pastor Joey Spann and the leadership he provides at Burnette Chapel Church of Christ. This article led to the exploration of Burnette Chapel's weekly broadcast services over the last two years. Also, an in-person interview conducted by WKRN in 2018 helped show Pastor Spann's calm persona and bright outlook toward the future of Burnette Chapel and Christianity in general.[16]

When the shooting began, an eight-year-old boy, Micah Carter, hurried with other children into a classroom and barricaded the door. He helped calm the younger children so their cries wouldn't be heard by the assailant.[17] Knowing these children may never feel safe in church again weighs on the heart of Pastor Spann. The church building, which has been renovated since the shooting, now has security cameras in place, Spann says, yet there is a persistent feeling of insecurity. When deciding whether the church should be remodeled with chairs or pews, the members requested pews so if another shooting happened, they could hide under them.

---

14. State of Tennessee v. Emanuel Kidega Samson, "Appeal," 52.
15. Tryggestad, "We Do Not Go."
16. WKRN, "Newsmaker: Joey Spann," para. 3.
17. Schmitt, "Boy Scouts to Honor," paras. 3–4.

SUMMARY

Antioch is twelve miles from Nashville, Tennessee. Outside of that metropolitan area, the shooting at Burnette Chapel remains largely unheard of. One person died, as opposed to nine at Mother Emanuel in Charleston, South Carolina, and twenty-seven at First Baptist of Sutherland Springs, Texas. The parishioners and leadership of Burnette Chapel and the city of Antioch, Tennessee, remember the event well, though. The city and church are intertwined: besides pastoring, Joey Spann teaches a Bible class and coaches basketball at the local middle school and high school. Both the church and the community are moving forward with faith and hope.

For his part, Robert Caleb Engle is uninterested in being labeled a hero. He is interested, however, in prayers for all who were hurt that day. "I ask everyone to pray for the victims, family members of the victims, our church community. Please pray for healing. Also, please pray for the shooter, the shooter's family and friends. They are hurting as well," Engle said in a statement released after the shooting.[18]

Peggy Spann passed away in October 2021 after a battle with COVID-19.[19] Joey Spann continues to pastor Burnette Chapel Church of Christ.

---

18. Chaney, "22-Year-Old," para. 6.
19. WKRN, "Wife," para. 1.

Chapter 6

What Happened at First Baptist Church

INTRODUCTION

Those who attended worship at First Baptist Church of Sutherland Springs, Texas on November 5, 2017, had no idea how their worlds were about to change. That day, Devin Patrick Kelley, age twenty-six, attacked them. He killed twenty-seven people (including himself) and wounded twenty-two, both inside and outside of the church building. First Baptist was not chosen at random—this faith community is his wife's and in-laws' church home.

Since Kelley took his own life after leaving the church, there are no court transcripts to reference in which Kelley was the defendant. In lieu of those records, three types of sources were consulted for this research:

1. Court transcripts from a 2021 federal case brought by Kelley's family and the families of victims against the US government
2. Interviews with reporters and persons associated with the incident
3. A timeline garnered from a wide variety of law enforcement statements and news outlets created to better understand the events as they unfolded

Kelley had an extensive history of domestic violence, workplace violence, and other antisocial behavior (see chapter 9). This chapter discusses the events as they occurred that day.

What Happened at First Baptist Church

SHOOTER PREPARATION

From 2014 through 2017, Devin Kelley had been in the practice of purchasing one gun per year—even though he had a conviction in 2014 that should have disqualified him from purchasing firearms. The gun used in the First Baptist Church shooting had been purchased in April 2016 at a sporting goods store. In 2021, a federal court in San Antonio, Texas, ruled that the United States Air Force (USAF) was 60 percent responsible for the First Baptist massacre. More on Kelley's background with the USAF, their liability in the situation, and Kelley's ability to purchase weapons when he was legally disqualified from doing so can be found in chapter 9.

Devin Kelley was not a stranger to First Baptist in Sutherland Springs. The town has about six hundred residents, and Kelley was known to be married to a parishioner, Danielle (Shields) Kelley. His wife loved the church and called it her second home, though Kelley didn't allow her to go to services often because he didn't want her to be in contact with her mother, Michelle Shields, who attended there. Michelle had recognized Kelley's abusive behavior toward Danielle and had encouraged her to leave him, which angered Kelley.

Though he wasn't a member or regular attendee, Kelley visited First Baptist Church's Fall Festival on the Thursday prior to the shooting, October 31, 2017. His family and in-laws were not with him; he traveled alone. The event is a Halloween alternative hosted annually by the church and includes outdoor activities, which is where Kelley was seen. He acted strangely enough that day to raise alarm among festival attendees, who got a "weird vibe" from him. Kelley wore all black that day, just as he did on the day of the shooting. Those who were concerned about him wondered if he was carrying weapons at the festival. He was examined by a former law enforcement officer. If that officer or anyone else had seen evidence of such, he would have been searched by festival security, but no firearms or other weapons were spotted. In retrospect, it is believed Kelley was in the planning stage on that day.[1]

In the days immediately leading up to the massacre, Kelley had posted a Mark Twain quote on Facebook, saying, "I do not fear death. I had been dead for billions and billions of years before I was born and had not suffered the slightest inconvenience from it." Kelley also made social media posts with photos of himself with a gun. The day before the shooting, Kelley

---

1. Lisa Krantz, interview by author, May 24, 2024.

left his job as a security guard at Summit Vacation and RV Resort on River Road early, stating that he had a headache. He had worked there for six weeks.

On the morning of the massacre, Kelley's widow, Danielle, says he told her to make him a light breakfast, which was unusual, as he was normally a man who enjoyed big breakfasts. After eating it, however, he threw it up. He then said, "We only have an hour left," and Danielle thought he was referring to going to work. They watched television. Next, he made sure their two-year-old boy and five-month-old girl were in their cribs. Kelley then hog-tied Danielle with rope, duct tape, and handcuffs in their bedroom while she screamed and protested. Their son had made his way out of his crib, according to Danielle, and was distressed as he watched his father tie up his mother. Kelley told his son he'd be right back, kissed him, and left to shoot up the church. Kelley was seen driving through town dressed in all-black "tactical-type gear" and was wearing a ballistic-style, bulletproof vest and a black mask with a white skull on it.[2] He had at least three guns with him. On the drive, he called his parents and asked them to go to his home because Danielle needed help. They did and released her. He told his dad, "I don't think it's going to work out."

Similar to Emanuel Samson's attack at Burnette Chapel Church of Christ, this shooting began in the church parking lot. As with that incident, if guards had been posted at the doors of the church, or if the doors had been locked during the service, violence would not have been averted. Kelley shot through windows, and his high-powered weapon easily shot through the doors and walls of the small, older church building. Also, since Kelley was related to a family of the church, he would have been admitted into the service by any security that might have been posted had he asked to come in.

THE SHOOTING

Kelley arrived at the church in his gray Ford Expedition SUV at about 11:00 a.m. Roughly twenty minutes later, he parked across the street at a gas station, got out of his vehicle, and walked toward the church.[3] He crouched and began shooting while still in the parking lot, killing two people. First Baptist has constructed a new building since the shooting, but at the time,

---

2. Koubaridis, "From the First," para. 3.
3. Koubaridis, "From the First," para. 7.

it was a nearly one-hundred-year-old wooden building. Kelley fired 450 rounds. He shot through windows, doors, and the side of the building. As he entered the church, the congregation was singing the old hymn "Are You Washed in the Blood?" Kelley moved around freely at first and continued shooting while yelling, "Everybody die!"[4] Some survivors say he seemed to be pointing at a corner of the sanctuary where Danielle's mother, Michelle Shields, usually sat. Danielle's grandmother, Lula White, was shot and killed, but Michelle was not in attendance that day. Also not in attendance were Pastor Pomeroy and most of his family. His fourteen-year-old daughter Annabelle was present, though, and was shot and killed.

In another similarity to the Burnette Chapel shooting, David Colbath, a survivor who was shot eight times, said that churchgoers originally thought the sounds were fireworks. They quickly figured out the reality, though, as bullets began coming through the wooden door. As he crawled on his elbows through the pews, Colbath prayed, "I love you Jesus. I love you Morgan. I love you Olivia. I love you Jesus. I love you Morgan. I love you Olivia." Morgan and Olivia are his son and daughter. He does not know how many times he repeated it. "He was literally putting people out. He was killing people individually instead of spraying bullets," Colbath said. "He was shooting individuals, and he came over to my side of the church and he shot me in the back right under my neck, and I'm sure he thought he'd killed me." Colbath was shot eight times. He still carries one of the bullets that lodged near his heart.[5]

With the number of people who were killed and wounded, it might be assumed that First Baptist of Sutherland Springs is a medium-sized or even a large church. It was not in 2017. The room in which this tragedy took place was small and had a single aisle separating two rows of seating. Kelley advanced up that aisle, shooting indiscriminately into the pews. Though a few made their way out of the sanctuary, there were few exits and fewer opportunities for escape.

The youngest victim was yet to be born; the oldest was seventy-two. Killed were Sara Johnson, Dennis Johnson, Lula White, Annabelle Pomeroy, Haley Krueger, Bryan Holcombe, Karla Holcombe, Danny Holcombe, Noah Holcombe, Crystal Holcombe, Baby Holcombe, Emily Hill, Megan Hill, Greg Hill, Tara McNulty, Richard Rodriguez, Theresa Rodriguez, Robert Corrigan, Shani Corrigan, Joann Ward, Brooke Ward, Emily Garza,

---

4. Koubaridis, "From the First," para. 9.
5. Petrie, "Survivor," paras. 4–8.

Robert "Scott" Marshall, Karen Marshall, Peggy Lynn Warden, and Keith Allen Branden. As is evidenced by the surnames, several families endured multiple losses. The Holcombe family in particular suffered nine deaths.

After the shooting, Kelley called his parents and his wife, Danielle, who listened together on a speakerphone. Not realizing the shooting had already happened, his family pleaded with him to stop. According to his widow, Kelley said that he had killed many people and kept saying how sorry he was. Danielle testified in court, "He blamed me and said it was my fault, and he shot himself. And that's when I hung up the phone."[6]

HOW AND WHY IT STOPPED

From down the street, Stephen Willeford's daughter heard the gunshots and alerted her father. Willeford, age fifty-five, said, "I kept hearing the shots, one after another, very rapid shots—just 'pop pop pop pop' and I knew every one of those shots represented someone, that it was aimed at someone, that they weren't just random shots." He went, barefoot but armed, to investigate. From inside their home, neighbors watched Kelley leave the church. They said the shooter was methodical and was moving robotically. Quickly, Kelley was confronted by Willeford, a former NRA firearms instructor. From behind a pickup truck, Willeford shot Kelley twice, and the neighbors say Kelley seemed to snap out of something that seemed like a robotic trance. The church shooter dropped his weapon and fled in his vehicle. Willeford fired once more at Kelley. Despite the body armor, Willeford struck Kelley twice, once in the torso through a gap in the protective gear and once in the leg.

Johnnie Langendorff, twenty-seven, happened to drive by in a pickup truck on his way to pick up his girlfriend. Willeford flagged Langendorff down, got into his truck, and together they engaged in a high-speed chase, pursuing Kelley. Willeford explained, "He jumped in my truck and said, 'He just shot up the church, we need to go get him.' And I said, 'Let's go.'" During the pursuit Willeford and Langendorff called the police; Kelley called his parents and wife. Kelley eventually hit a road sign, and his truck overturned. Before police arrived on the scene, Kelley shot himself in the head and died. He was found there, six miles from the church.

6. Conrad, "Wife," para. 2.

INTERVIEWS

Lisa Krantz

By any measure, the events of November 5, 2017, in Sutherland Springs, Texas, were mind boggling and terrible. Not all reports focused on the tragedy, though. Lisa Krantz is a photojournalist and part of a Pulitzer Prize–winning team who authored a series called *A Tragedy Without End*. As her work on that project reflects, her interest was in focusing on the congregation: how they held each other together, loved and supported one another, and how much they leaned on their faith. "That's the unique thing about it happening in a church," Krantz said. "They already have a church family and have that love and support. I wanted to show how victim families and survivors were healing (or not), and what their grief was like." Krantz saw and heard many terrible things in her work on the Burnette Chapel tragedy. But good has triumphed over evil there, and she is sharing that story.[7]

SUMMARY

Hope indeed abounds at First Baptist in Sutherland Springs. One week after the shooting, the congregation held an event that showed the completely revamped sanctuary with all signs of violence wiped away. White wooden chairs, each adorned with one rose and a name, sat where each victim had fallen. In the spot where bloodshed had happened, this church family opened a spot for peace and reflection. That original building is now a memorial, and through generous donations, a new facility has been erected. The rebuilt church building is bright and airy with a high, beamed ceiling and large windows that are higher than the original ones. Chairs have replaced pews.

One week after the shooting, the church also held a community-wide worship service in a tent, as the more than one-thousand-person crowd was too much for the building. Even with a tent, the crowd flowed past the structure's boundaries. Pastor Frank Pomeroy said, "Everyone who gave their life that day, some of which were my best friends, and my daughter . . . I guarantee you beyond any shadow of a doubt they are dancing with Jesus today, and they would tell you today and they would tell you from where they are to keep on fighting. Keep on fighting." He concluded his comments

---

7. Lisa Krantz, interview by author, May 24, 2024.

with an assurance that referenced 1 Cor 13: "Love never fails. It will not." Pastor Frank Pomeroy retired in 2022, and as of this writing, the congregation's pastor search committee is in the final stages of discerning God's will in filling that position. An interview with Pastor Pomeroy's wife, Sherri Pomeroy, can be found in chapter 14.

Hope and faith remain at First Baptist Church. We must strengthen our efforts to prevent another event like this one from shattering even one more life. As Krantz stated so well, we as the church already have built-in church families in which we can do this hard work. We are able to act preemptively, and we simply must.

Chapter 7

Who Is Dylann Storm Roof?

INTRODUCTION

As we begin our exploration into the three mass shooters highlighted in this book, I want to discourage the tendency to label a person as good or bad. None of us, including Dylann Roof, Emanuel Samson, and Devin Kelley, are all good or all bad. We've all done some good things, and we've all done some things that are decidedly not good. Our actions don't define us in total; each of us is still made in the image of God—even Roof, Samson, and Kelley. The backgrounds of the three people examined in these chapters have many differences but share a commonality: they had all participated in the life of a Christian church at some point. As you read about these three churchgoers-turned-murderers, imagine how your own faith community has reacted or would react if a person with similar traits and warning signs was connected to your congregation.

First, we'll look at Dylann Roof, the twenty-one-year-old perpetrator of the June 18, 2015, mass shooting at Emanuel African Methodist Episcopal Church in Charleston, South Carolina. Roof killed nine and injured one.

BACKGROUND

Childhood

Dylann Storm Roof was born on April 3, 1994, in Columbia, South Carolina. Court affidavits show Dylann's parents to be divorced and his father to be physically and verbally abusive. His father remarried but divorced again after a decade of allegations of abuse and infidelity. Dylann was raised in multiple cities in the southern United States. He was transient in schools, attending at least seven different ones in nine years. There is no record of him attending school after ninth grade. Court records reveal that Roof was a "ninth-grade dropout diagnosed with schizophrenia spectrum disorder, autism, anxiety, and depression."[1]

In an interview with a psychologist, Roof's father, Franklin Bennett Roof, said that his son did not grow up racist and is not racist. However, the senior Roof also made racist statements during the brief interview. Court records state:

> Specifically, the father said that as a young child Dylann asked why another child's "thingy" [penis] was so small. Mr. Roof laughed in the retelling and said that the boy "had Asian in him" so that Dylann was probably correct in his size assessment. Mr. Roof was also observed during videotaped visits with Dylann at the jail to joke about sex change operations, to say "that's so gay" in a derogatory fashion, and to remark that Bill Clinton would be the "First Bitch" if his wife were elected president. In viewing videos of their visits at the jail, Dylann was observed to appear uncomfortable and to sometimes tell his father that jokes with sexual content were not funny.[2]

Similarly, Roof's uncle, Joe Roof, spoke with a court-appointed psychologist. Joe said that racism was not part of Roof's upbringing and that he didn't understand where Roof's racist ideas had come from. He believed they emerged fairly recently.

Roof was googling "How to get a Glock" as early as 2008, about age fourteen.[3] Also in 2008, Roof's internet search history includes searches related to racial content, including searches for Aryan Brotherhood.[4] Roof

---

1. United States v. Dylann Storm Roof, "Brief of Appellant," 59.
2. United States v. Dylann Storm Roof, "Brief of Appellant," 52.
3. United States v. Dylann Storm Roof, "Brief of Appellant," 67–68.
4. United States v. Dylann Storm Roof, "Brief of Appellant," 88.

was actively involved in church during this time. A psychiatric evaluation presented in court in 2020 established a timeline of Roof's radicalization and shows the overlap between that period and the time he attended church regularly.

Young Adulthood

According to his stepmother, Roof was "a loner and quiet and very smart—too smart. He was locked in his room looking up bad stuff on the computer. Something on the computer drew him in—this is Internet evil."[5]

Roof turned twenty-one in the spring of 2015. He had already been given a car, and once he turned twenty-one, he was able to buy a gun with birthday money from his parents. Putting those dates together, it appears that Roof's interest in racism and white supremacist ideas began in about 2008. However, the process of racial radicalization by others that led Roof to kill nine people in June of 2015 took place in a little more than a year and a half, beginning in the summer of 2013. His school and medical records do not indicate Roof having racial or violence issues.[6]

In the months before the killings, Roof had asked his uncle, Joe Roof, several times if Joe thought the Holocaust was real. Joe also noted that Roof sounded like he was quoting another source when making statements about Muslims or other minority groups, rather than explaining his own ideas.[7] When Roof tried to speak with his mother or other family members about his developing ideas about race, his fears that Blacks were injuring whites and that the Jewish media were covering it up, his ideas offended others, and he learned to keep them to himself.[8] Rather than hearing his newly discovered ideas that were quickly turning into life-changing beliefs, Roof was shunned by those with whom he shared his thoughts. The people who did listen to his thoughts were those he met in online discussion forums. Through a display of violent images, inaccurate information, purported statistics, and white supremacist ideology, these individuals taught him hate-filled ideas, mostly race based.

Thus ostracized by family, colleagues, and peers whom he knew in person, Roof had nobody to dispel those ideas in a concrete, meaningful

5. Frazier et al., *We Are Charleston*, 22.
6. United States v. Dylann Storm Roof, "Brief of Appellant," 26.
7. United States v. Dylann Storm Roof, "Brief of Appellant," 86.
8. United States v. Dylann Storm Roof, "Brief of Appellant," 69–70.

way. In his FBI interview, he would assure the agents that the internet was his only source of racial knowledge. Most notable for those of us in churches, no racial education or socialization, either positive or negative, came from his church experience. Roof said he had not talked to friends or family, either inside or outside of the church, because, in his words, they would not approve.[9]

MENTAL HEALTH

From a psychological standpoint, Roof's autism spectrum disorder traits have been evident since childhood. Court records reveal that psychological experts determined that Roof had "over-valued" racist views. That is, Roof's views on race were primary and foremost in his life, above every other aspect of his own world or the world around him. Race mattered more than anything to Roof. The experts who testified in court said his beliefs were not delusional and that he possesses no other traits of psychosis. Psychological testing after the murders showed Roof to have a very high intellectual function. Roof tested in the 96th percentile on intelligence tests when compared to national averages for peers in his age range.[10] According to court transcripts, by his adolescent years, Roof displayed emerging schizophrenia spectrum disorder. The combination of his autism spectrum disorder and emerging schizophrenia spectrum disorder, in one expert's opinion, led to his racist beliefs that began at age nineteen.[11]

Roof's time in court after the Mother Emanuel shooting revealed a diagnosis of autism. Also, those court records showed that he would rather be executed than for people to label him as autistic. On November 7, 2016, the following exchange took place between Roof (DEFENDANT) and the judge (THE COURT) regarding this issue. Spelling and grammatical issues are untouched, as this is the official court record.

> THE COURT: You don't want others to think that you did these things because there was something wrong with you?
>
> THE DEFENDANT: Exactly.
>
> THE COURT: And you are willing to have the case tried before a jury with essentially no defense so people won't think that?

9. United States v. Dylann Storm Roof, "Brief of Appellant," 26.
10. United States v. Dylann Storm Roof, "Brief of Appellant," 77.
11. United States v. Dylann Storm Roof, "Brief of Appellant," 15.

THE DEFENDANT: Yes.

THE COURT: And you are prepared to face the death penalty to avoid anyone thinking that?

THE DEFENDANT: Yes.

THE COURT: Mr. Roof, you might understand that I am troubled—I'm trying to figure out why being labeled something would be worse than death. Could you explain that to me, being labeled autistic is worse than death?

THE DEFENDANT: Because once you've got that label, there is no point in living anyway. You see what I'm saying?[12]

Roof also suffered from multiple delusions. According to attorneys in the case, "[Roof] does not believe he's going to be executed, no matter what sentence is imposed . . . because he firmly believes that there will be a white nationalist takeover of the United States within roughly six, seven, eight years, and when that happens, he will be pardoned. And he also believes it probable, although not certain, that he will be given a high position, such as the governorship of South Carolina." His delusional beliefs also involved his ideas about his own body. He thought that contrary to what he had been told by physicians, all his testosterone had collected on one side of his body and made his body asymmetrical. He also thought his forehead was disfigured (it was not and is not) and has attempted to keep it hidden with a bowl-style haircut with bangs that extend almost down to his eyebrows. He also believed his hair was falling out and that he would soon be bald (it has not, and he is not).[13]

DRUG USE

Roof has no history of illegal drug use apart from once being found to be in possession of Suboxone. This drug produces effects such as euphoria or respiratory depression at low to moderate doses. It is unclear whether Roof was using the drug or simply in possession of it.

---

12. United States v. Dylann Storm Roof, "Transcript," 22.
13. United States v. Dylann Storm Roof, "Brief of Appellant," 66.

CRIMINAL HISTORY

Once he connected with his new online community, Roof's descent into antisocial behavior escalated rapidly, and subsequently, interactions with the police began to happen monthly. In February of 2015, as a twenty-year-old, suspicious behavior on his part had led shopping mall employees to alert police. Law enforcement found the above-mentioned controlled substance, Suboxone, on his person. Roof was banned from the mall for a year.

In March of 2015, Roof was found loitering in a park. A search of his vehicle revealed semiautomatic weapon parts. No charges were filed, as no laws had yet been broken. In April of 2015, only two months after having been banned from the mall for a year, Roof returned. He was recognized and was convicted of trespassing. This earned him an extended three-year ban from the mall.

In May of 2015, Roof was found guilty of a charge of entry on another's pasture or other lands after notice, based on an event that had occurred in February of that year. Roof pled guilty and was fined $270.38 by the Columbia [South Carolina] Municipal Court. Roof had no further criminal history and no history of violent activities prior to the mass shooting.[14]

Roof purchased the handgun with which he killed the churchgoers. If a criminal background check had been properly done, according to the law in South Carolina in 2021, it is possible that the drug possession charge would have blocked him from purchasing the weapon. There is continued debate and conflicting records about whether the Suboxone possession was a misdemeanor or felony.

RELIGIOUS HISTORY

Dylann Roof was raised in and was a member of the Evangelical Lutheran Church in America (ELCA) denomination. Rev. Dr. Tony Metze was then and continues to be the pastor of St. Paul's Lutheran Church in Columbia, South Carolina. He has pastored there since 2007. Dylann Roof's family attended St. Paul's when Roof was a child and adolescent. In a January 6, 2021, telephone interview with Rev. Dr. Metze, the pastor stated, "Dylann attended camp for one week in a confirmation ministry where we went

---

14. BeenVerified, "Dylann Storm Roof."

over the Gospel of Luke for a whole week."[15] Roof did not complete the confirmation class. At this time, Roof was about fourteen years old.

In court documents, Metze described Roof as "socially immature and naïve," as well as "robotic." Other descriptors given by the pastor were "not normal, withdrawn and reclusive" and possibly struggling with his sexuality. Roof had difficulty building relationships both inside and outside of church, according to Metze.[16] Nowhere in court documents does Metze mention discussing racism with Roof nor the church hosting classes or events regarding racism.

Bonnilynn Henry was a Sunday school teacher who knew Roof from ages eleven to sixteen. Henry said that Roof did not want to attend confirmation camp. Ms. Henry hypothesized that he did not want to be with people that he did not know. Henry met with Roof's father and urged that he attend because it was required for confirmation and because she believed Roof needed the interaction. She found him to be quiet and withdrawn and thought it would be good for him to go and meet some people and build some friendships. Roof did not want to play games like other young people did. He was adultlike and reserved. Ms. Henry stated that Roof participated in the activities in class, but he was withdrawn and did not interact with the other children. She also said he did not bring friends with him to church like most of the other kids did.[17] What Roof did learn about Christian belief is summarized in a journal he kept in prison.

> Christianity, I cannot agree with the form of Christianity most modern preachers preach. It seems to me that this form of Christianity says, "Leave it to God. There is nothing you can do about it." Okay. Well, maybe we can do something but don't because it's not your place. And I can't agree with this. I see some people who seem to use Christianity as an excuse for not doing anything. They tell themselves they are being pious, but they are really being cowardly. Their pity is their excuse. But Christianity doesn't have to be this weak, feeble, cowardly religion. There is plenty of evidence to indicate that Christianity can be a warrior's religion.[18]

---

15. Tony Metze, interview by author, Jan. 6, 2021.
16. United States v. Dylann Storm Roof, "Brief of Appellant," exhibit 1, 21–40.
17. United States v. Dylann Storm Roof, "Brief of Appellant," 92.
18. United States v. Dylann Storm Roof, "Brief of Appellant," 48.

INTERVIEWS

Tony Metze

Considering his local church's views on racism and race-based crime, Rev. Tony Metze said:

> I think that the best way to sum it up is that when Dylann did what he did, there was just tremendous shock in the congregation that I serve. Now, what the church was forty years ago, I can't speak to. But I know the church that I serve now felt deeply hurt because of course there's this expectation, or not expectation. That's the wrong word. Sort of the image that we would be a church that grew this kid who was mentally ill, but that's been ignored, because he fought that anyway.[19]

Metze did acknowledge that the church he pastors is largely composed of white persons. Metze shared that the one time a Black reporter attended a worship service, the reporter stood out and said she felt singled out.

Sharon Washington Risher

On June 5, 2020, Rev. Sharon Washington Risher was interviewed. Three of her family members and a friend were killed by Roof. She was asked her thoughts about Roof's theological socialization regarding race. Her brief remarks on the issue are as follows:

> Not too long ago there was a Lutheran person I ran into and they wanted to apologize to the whole damn denomination for Dylann Roof, and I'm looking at that woman like, whoa, that's a heavy thing to take upon yourself. I understand where she was coming from and I accepted that. But no matter where you come from, people grow into who they are. You can sit by somebody in church every day and not know what goes on in the psyche of their brains. So, it's hard.[20]

---

19. Tony Metze, interview by author, Jan. 6, 2021.
20. Sharon Washington Risher, interview by author, June 5, 2020.

Who Is Dylann Storm Roof?

COURT RECORDS

John Parker

Father John Parker is the current dean of St. Tikhon's Orthodox Theological Seminary in South Canaan, Pennsylvania, and is the previous pastor of Holy Ascension Orthodox Church in Mount Pleasant, South Carolina. Among his other duties, Father John Parker is Dylann Roof's spiritual advisor and has been since the time of the shootings. He provides spiritual care to Roof on death row. In court records of a competency hearing, Father Parker stated he did not find Roof to be coldhearted or angry, and the priest struggled to reconcile Roof with the crime he committed.[21] Father Parker's comments in a court competency hearing for Roof lend much insight and include the following. Spelling and grammatical issues are untouched, as this is the official court record.

Q. How did you come to know Dylann Roof?

A. In the weeks that led up to the shootings, our lectionary readings, what we read in the church services, are prescribed each year. Many of those readings in the weeks leading up to the shootings were related to if you love those who love you, what credit is that to you. These are Jesus' words: If someone strikes you on one cheek, turn to the other. Do good to those who persecute you, etcetera. We had heard those readings in the two weeks prior.

When the news came, I asked myself who—I was certain that the families of the victims would be surrounded very quickly and in overflowing abundance, and I wondered to myself, who will visit Dylann? So I believe it was maybe the Monday or Tuesday of the next week I went to the jail to visit him. I had been there any number of times to visit parishioners and others. I didn't realize that it would be any different. I was told I couldn't visit without an attorney's approval. So I contacted Ashley Pennington, and after a long conversation, he allowed me to go visit Dylann, which I believe was the Wednesday. It would be maybe exactly one week after the shootings.

I said to Dylann, as I have said to him on a number of occasions, "First, I'm not a mental health expert. However, I have"—this is my answer to him—"I have served 400 hours in a psychiatric hospital. I have been pastor of a church for fifteen years, and I have some parishioners who suffer some pretty severe mental illnesses,

---

21. United States v. Dylann Storm Roof, "Brief of Appellant," 98–99.

including untreatable ones. And so my answer to that is I can't say I haven't seen that in you." And, you know

THE COURT: And what was his response to that?

THE WITNESS: His response is, "Can't you just say no?" And I told him, "It's too complex to say no." And Your Honor, in my opinion, having spent many, many hours with Dylann, the kinds of questions that he has raised to me, um, with respect to—even my court appearance, for example, it was a few days before Christmas—please forgive me, I don't remember the times exactly—when the question formally came up would I come here to be a witness sometime later this week after tomorrow, one of—well, perhaps his main concern was which cross would I wear and what color shoes would I wear. And maybe that says enough. I mean, if I may say as a pastor, I can't imagine how strange it would be to hear this, so I need to acknowledge that up front, I have a hard time labeling that an ideology in him. I have told that to him. I mean, I said it point blank to him. For example, I said to him, "Dylann, you are no white nationalist." And I've said that to him many times. We've had many conversations about that. So with respect to your question, Your Honor, in my time with him in these many hours, though the externals of it all point to ideology, I personally have not seen that.

Please understand—allow me just one further sentence. The point that I was trying to make with that is what I would have pictured in my mind about a person who was capable of doing—not only capable, but having done such a thing, would not be the person—would not be a person like Dylann as I have experienced my visitations with him over this time period. Cold-hearted, angry, I don't know what other words to say about that. Please understand what Dylann did was heinous. I have expressed that to him many, many times, and I'm not trying to defend that at all. I'm simply saying that my pastoral relationship to him has involved—I can't understand how A connects to B. He did it, but—

THE COURT: You can't understand how it happened.

THE WITNESS: The only way I can explain it is mental illness.

THE COURT: But what mental illness and all that is beyond your expertise.

THE WITNESS: It is certainly beyond my expertise, yes.[22]

---

22. United States v. Dylann Storm Roof, "Brief of Appellant," 177–80.

MOTIVATIONS

Upon his arrest and in discussion with law enforcement the day after the shooting, Roof was verbose in explaining his motives, which were entirely racial. He told agents, "You know, black people are killing white people every day on the streets, and they rape, they rape white women, a hundred white women a day." At that point, Roof said he was hoping to start a "movement," but he believed a race war was inevitable.[23]

Roof, who, as of this writing, continues to have court appearances on appeals, has spent ample time in court explaining his beliefs regarding the supremacy of the white race. One example occurred on September 18, 2017, when Roof filed a handwritten "Pro Se Motion to Remove and Replace Appointed Counsel" on the grounds that one of his attorneys was Indian and one was Jewish. Roof's handwritten motion to the court (a copy of which is in appendix H) reads as follows:

> This is a motion to dismiss and replace my current appointed counsel due to a conflict of interest.
>
> The court is aware of my decision to represent myself at my trial, a decision based partly on differences between myself and my attorneys. As my appeals process is just beginning it is more convenient and beneficial for everyone involved to have satisfactory counsel appointed now rather than at a later date when the process has actually begun.
>
> My two currently appointed attorneys, Alexandra Yates and Sapna Mirchandani, are Jewish and Indian respectively. It is therefore quite literally impossible that they and I could have the same interests relating to my case.
>
> It is also a barrier to effective communication. The lawyer appointed to represent me at my federal trial was David Isaac Bruck, who is also Jewish. His ethnicity was a constant source of conflict even with my constant efforts to look past it.
>
> Trust is a vital component in an attorney client relationship and is important to the effectiveness of the defense. Because of my political views, which are arguably religious, it will be impossible for me to trust two attorneys that are my political and biological enemies. The difficulties during my trial are evidence of this.
>
> My intentions are to have the appeals process for my case go as smoothly as possible—and to be as effective as they can be, the

---

23. United States Attorney's Office, "Full Dylann Roof Confession," 13:04–14:05.

appeals should be worked on and written by lawyers with my best interests in mind. I am confident after meeting my current attorneys that they will be unable to represent me in an efficient manner.

For the reasons stated above I ask that the court remove and replace my current counsel.

Respectfully Submitted, Dylann S. Roof[24]

The Honorable J. C. Nicholson Jr. (retired), a judge who presided over some of Roof's hearings in the Tenth Judicial Circuit Court, answered a questionnaire sent to him. In his reply, the judge expressed a belief that Roof's beliefs about race were shaped by the fact that he was not accepted by his peers, but white hate groups accepted him. Judge Nicholson does not believe Roof's faith history affected his actions at Mother Emanuel. The retired judge also does not believe that Roof's faith and belief intersect with his beliefs about race. Nicholson states that Roof chose Mother Emanuel Church in particular, explaining in his manifesto that he intended to start a race war.[25] That manifesto can be read in full in appendix A.

CURRENT LIFE

Regarding Roof's current spiritual life, as of January 28, 2020, his spiritual care provider, Father John Parker, had visited Roof weekly for two years, and they had spent approximately one hundred hours together. The Orthodox priest declined a phone interview, citing confidentiality concerns, but communicated via email, stating the following: "Because of my ongoing pastoral relationship to Dylann, it is important that I not take part in the survey/interview. I have intentionally kept very, very quiet publicly about the Mother Emanuel tragedy for this reason—apart from denouncing the unspeakable crime. I believe the only public record is my deposition in his second competency hearing."[26]

In contrast to Father Parker's testimony, in December 2017, a reformed white supremacist named Christian Picciolini reached out to Roof to offer him an alternative way of thinking. In response, in December 2017, Roof wrote back to Picciolini, lambasting him for his change in views. Roof

---

24. United States v. Dylann Storm Roof, "Pro Se Motion." See appendix H.
25. J. C. Nicholson Jr., reply to questionnaire from author, Dec. 11, 2020.
26. John Parker, e-mail to author, Oct. 6, 2020.

accused Picciolini of "undermining your own race" and basing his findings on emotions rather than facts. Roof closed his letter by saying, "One of the unforgivable sins is to know the truth and deny it. I'm unable to understand how you are able to live with yourself. Have fun beating a dead horse" (appendix C).

WRITINGS AND STATEMENTS

In addition to Roof's manifesto, he left notes to both his parents in his car on the evening of the shooting. They were handwritten and read, "Dear Mom, I love you. I'm sorry for what I did, but I had to do it . . . I know that what I did will have repercussions [sic] on my whole family and for this I truly am sorry. At this moment I miss you very much and as childish as it sounds I wish I was in your arms. I love you, Dylann." The second read: "Dear dad, I love you and I'm sorry. You were a good dad. I love you" (appendix F).

Roof has been prolific, both in writing and verbally, explaining and expounding on his beliefs about race and where he learned these beliefs. He did not learn them in church, but rather in online white supremacist groups. Roof also did not learn anti-racism theology in church. Roof wrote that he was stirred to action after reading about the Trayvon Martin case and searching out "black on white crime" statistics. About six weeks after the shootings, Dylann Roof wrote extensively in a journal. He displayed no remorse, grief, or religious reflection in his writings.[27]

Roof continues to correspond with admirers from prison. Since his arrest, Roof has completed a number of drawings from prison. Several were presented in court as evidence during a hearing for an appeal. Four drawings in particular showed religious symbolism combined with racist imagery. Included were a picture of eight weeping ghosts, a tilted cross, and a demon-type figure. Another shows a cross with "In God we trust" written near it and teardrops surrounding it. One includes a cross with "14," "88," a swastika, other imagery, and "DSR" (Roof's initials) on it, and another is simply of Jesus with his hand outstretched (appendix E). According to the Anti-Defamation League, 14 and 88 are symbols of the white supremacist movement. The 14 represents the movement's 14-word slogan: "We must secure the existence of our people and a future for white children." The 88 stands for the eighth letter of the alphabet, h. The 88, therefore, means

27. United States v. Dylann Storm Roof, "Brief of Appellant," 48.

HH, which stands for "Heil Hitler." Variations exist, including 1488, 8841, and 14/88.[28] Roof's white supremacy beliefs, by his own admission and as evidenced in his writings and artwork, extend beyond African American people. His user name on lastrhodesian.net, where he posted his manifesto, was rtf88, and the "88" looks to be intentional. Anyone who is nonwhite, other than perhaps Asian people, is reviled by him.

SUMMARY

Dylann Roof, though raised in an ELCA church, did not learn about racism, pro or con, in the church of his childhood. It was not part of his childhood Sunday school classes or his confirmation curriculum, nor was there a particular course of study or discussion about violence or racism anywhere in his home church. Roof's psychological evaluation, presented in court, states, "With Dylann's disordered thinking and autistic focus and concentration, along with lack of exposure to competing points of view, racist thought became the most important thing in his life."[29] No racist, anti-racist, violent, or anti-violence views were presented to Roof in his religious socialization. The only direction Roof was receiving regarding racism and violence was through the white supremacist forums he had discovered online. When you're listening for direction and hear only one voice, there's only one voice to follow.

To put this into context, Rozella Haydee White, a Black ELCA church member and leader in the predominantly white denomination, said this after the killings at Mother Emanuel: "It hit me like a ton of bricks: I am a part of a church that raises racist white people who then kill people of color who are educated in our institutions. That may seem like an oversimplification to some, but this truth broke what was left of my heart and I plunged into despair."[30] Rozella Haydee White decries a mainline American denomination that has failed to address its racist past and present. Institutional racism within churches does not simply exist. It is thriving, and churches need to address racism with parishioners of all ages.

Regarding the shooting in which Roof was the perpetrator, two thoughts stood out in an interview with Rev. Dr. Tony Metze, Roof's childhood pastor. In that discussion, Metze explained that he'd told two

28. Anti-Defamation League, "1488," paras. 1–2.
29. United States v. Dylann Storm Roof, "Brief of Appellant," 10.
30. White, "Truth," para. 13.

particular stories to reporter after reporter, but no one would publish them. Metze says these stories need to be told, and he was assured they would be included in this project. The first involves the abundant grace shown by another church family shortly after the shootings. This church's reaction is something many families of faith strive for, but not all can achieve. In Metze's own words:

> The shooting occurred on a Wednesday, and we were in crisis mode. I went in my office on Friday morning. The secretary said there was a call on the line from the pastor of the AME congregation in Pomaria, South Carolina. My initial thought was, well, I didn't know. Was he going to say, "What are you guys doing there?" Or "What's going on?" I picked up the phone, and he said, "You don't know me. We may never cross paths, but I want you to know that I and my congregation are praying for you and for the Roof family and for your congregation."
>
> And I couldn't speak. I literally could not speak. I was struck dumb. He said, "Are you there? Are you okay? Is there something I've said?" And finally, I said, "Hold on." I got my composure and I said, "That's the most amazing, beautiful thing I've heard in a couple of days, so thank you for that." So, there were lots of miracles, lots of wonderful works of grace, the outpouring from people. That's the story that needs to be told.[31]

Metze's second story involves Rev. Clementa Pinckney, the pastor at Emanuel AME church, who was Roof's first victim. Even though I interviewed Metze six years after Roof killed the Bible study participants in Charleston, his voice was quiet and his demeanor was humble as he discussed his memories of Clementa Pinckney. Metze said his congregation had two members who were in the state senate in 2015. One of them, whom Metze identified as Paula, contacted Metze in the spring of 2015 and said she had a friend, Senator Pinckney, whom she was sending Metze's way. Pinckney and his church were interested in learning more about what both pastors called "high church" practices during the season of Lent. Pinckney had questions about the use of ashes and ways to prepare them for Ash Wednesday, and Paula told her Metze was "the guy to ask."[32] The two pastors agreed to meet, and Metze says they just hit it off. He said Pinckney was on the other side of the political spectrum, but the issue never came up. The

---

31. Tony Metze, interview by author, Jan. 6, 2021.
32. Tony Metze, interview by author, Jan. 6, 2021.

senator and pastor came to Metze's office, and they had a great conversation. Mere weeks later, a man who had been seated in the very pews as Metze preached every week murdered his new friend, Rev. Pinckney.

It is not an understatement to say that my interview with Rev. Metze was pivotal in both the doctoral project this book is based on and, in a different way, this book itself. His factual information was helpful, of course. But much more so, his words of hope, faith, and encouragement changed the project's focus. Rev. Metze is a large part of why the focus changed from fear to hope, from protection to prevention, and from anger to compassion.

Chapter 8

Who Is Emanuel Kidega Samson?

INTRODUCTION

COMPARED TO DYLANN ROOF, Emanuel Samson is almost a mystery. Volumes of study have been completed on Roof, whose past and present have been evaluated from every imaginable angle. Academic and mainstream articles continue to regularly appear about Roof, his beliefs, and his shooting at Mother Emanuel. As of this writing, about 3,700 academic articles have been written about him and the actions he took on that awful day in 2015. In contrast, 10 scholarly articles were found that mention Samson. An overdue exploration into the background of Emanuel Samson follows. Sources include court records, social media records, and statements from family and acquaintances.

BACKGROUND

Childhood

Emanuel Kidega Samson was born November 11, 1991, in Khartoum, Sudan. Court documents explain that Samson said his middle name is spelled Kigda, but for consistency, Kidega is used throughout all legal proceedings.[1] A public records search lists him as "Emanuel K Samson."[2] When he was three months old, to escape the ravages of war, his family first left

---

1. State of Tennessee v. Emanuel Kidega Samson, "Appeal," 2.
2. BeenVerified, "Emanuel K Samson."

South Sudan and fled to Egypt. They eventually arrived a few years later in Nashville, Tennessee, as legal immigrants through a refugee program in 1996. Samson was five and a half years old. He has vague memories of war-related violence before leaving Sudan and knows family stories of relatives being burned to death in the conflict.

Soon after arrival in the United States, Samson's parents separated, then divorced the next year, 1997. Samson's older sister, Christina Samson, testified that their parents fought "like cats and dogs, always fighting, verbally and physically." She said that during a fight, her father once broke a glass bottle on her mother's forehead, leaving a scar. The mother had anger problems as well.[3] Samson, who witnessed the domestic violence, lived primarily with his mother until he was fourteen, then lived with his father, Vanansio, until the father tried to return to Africa, leaving Samson without support.[4]

Samson says his father was an overbearing parent and that he did not have much freedom growing up. He was not allowed to go outside or invite friends over, go to other people's homes, or go to the movie theater. His mother, he says, was emotional and unpredictable. Samson says his birth was unplanned by his mother, who was seventeen or eighteen when she had her first child. He says his mother was verbally abusive, telling him that she wished he had never been born and that she regretted having him. Samson was substantially older than his three younger half-siblings and he resented having to take care of them while his mother worked an evening shift.[5]

His sister, Christina Samson, explained in court that after the father was out of the picture, the mother used Samson as a surrogate for her anger.[6] She corroborated the reports of extreme physical abuse by his parents, adding descriptions of the mother throwing an iron at him and of him being beaten with a belt buckle by his mother so fiercely that it left marks. The mother regularly told Samson she wished she had aborted him. In Christina's opinion, the mother was channeling anger that she had for their father at Samson. At one point Samson reported abuse to the Department of Children's Services, who interviewed him and his school counselor but did not visit his home or speak with his parents. This abuse resulted in issues later in life.

3. State of Tennessee v. Emanuel Kidega Samson, "Appeal," 27.
4. State of Tennessee v. Emanuel Kidega Samson, "Appeal," 3.
5. State of Tennessee v. Emanuel Kidega Samson, "Appeal," 5.
6. State of Tennessee v. Emanuel Kidega Samson, "Appeal," 27.

Samson's older sister also described Samson as being bullied in elementary and middle school by other students over his skin color, his appearance, and his immigrant status. In high school, he began working to defend himself from bullying. During that time, their mother worked from 3:00 p.m. to 11:00 p.m., leaving Christina and Emanuel Samson to care for their three younger half-siblings. For this reason, they were unable to participate in after-school activities or have friends over to visit. Christina also testified that at the age of thirteen or fourteen, her brother began getting into trouble at school and having drastic mood changes.

Young Adulthood

Samson's Facebook account lists his name and a nickname, Bulda. It says he is from Khartoum, Sudan, and graduated from Smyrna High School (Tennessee) in 2010. He told the court that he became interested in guns as a hobby sometime in 2012 or 2013.

Samson lived in Murfreesboro, Tennessee, and was twenty-five at the time of the shooting. He worked at both Papa Johns as a pizza delivery driver and at Taylor Farms as an unarmed security guard. His first day at Taylor Farms was the day before the event at Burnette Chapel. Samson's father told the court that about a month before the shootings, he noticed a change in his son and believed him to be dealing with job-related and financial stressors. Samson's girlfriend, Maya Hill, testified that Samson had rapid mood changes and suffered sleep problems in the month leading up to the shooting. Samson told the court his sleep issues had been going on for years. Hill said that on some days Samson was happy, but some days he was really, really sad and expressed a desire to kill himself.

Though Hill related an incident in which Samson punched a hole in a wall during an argument, she described him in court as caring, compassionate, and patient, and said he never hurt her or her children. After the shootings, Hill and Samson remained in contact, and some of their telephone conversations from when Samson was in prison were used as evidence in court. Samson did say he did not wish to talk about events surrounding the event and did not enjoy the notoriety he was receiving.

RELIGIOUS HISTORY

Samson has an African cultural religious history that leans heavily on the belief in the existence of shadow people. His mother vocally spoke about shadow people moving around the house, a belief from their unspecified African cultural spiritual tradition. Samson testified that a month before the shootings he hallucinated a dark figure reaching toward him while he was in bed as well as in the bathroom. He was already having sleep problems before this shadow figure showed up to torment him, so he was unsure if the presence of the shadow figure impacted his ability to get good sleep. Samson's sister Christina testified that he had trouble sleeping because he saw "shadows or something is coming for him" and that he would go "two or three weeks without sleeping, just wandering." She testified that he would occasionally "space out" with a "blank stare."[7]

Shadow people feature in many cultures and folklore from all over the world. There is a wide variety of opinion as to whether these figures are helpful or harmful among those who believe that shadow people are paranormal/spiritual entities. Experiences with shadow people have been reported from people who suffer from sleep apnea and paralysis. In the former, sleep apnea can cause the sufferer to see shadows moving in the corner of their eyes. During sleep paralysis, sufferers may see shadow figures looming in corners of the room while they are simultaneously unable to move their bodies. Shadow people have also been reported by people who take the antihistamine diphenhydramine (Benadryl). Methamphetamine addicts have reported seeing shadow people as well. Schizophrenia and bipolar disorder can also cause visual hallucinations of shadow people. It is unclear exactly what belief system that involves shadow people the Samson family espoused. In a nonreligious sense, however, sightings of shadow people can happen to people with severe sleep disturbances,[8] which both Samson and Hill say he had. It is possible that the combination of his early religious upbringing, sleep disturbances, mental illnesses, and experience with methamphetamine-related drugs (such as bath salts) combined to cause hallucinations.

During either 2013 or 2014 (accounts vary), Samson attended Burnette Chapel with his three cousins. There are differing records on whether Samson was ever a member of Burnette Chapel Church of Christ.

7. State of Tennessee v. Emanuel Kidega Samson, "Appeal," 22.
8. Horsnell, "Hypnagogic," para. 4.

Regardless, he went to church there regularly before the shooting and had been active in the life of the church, according to a church social media post from September 27, 2017. As recently as 2012, Samson posted on his Facebook page, "Rise and shine, it's church time!" He regularly shared posts about his church and his faith on social media. Samson invited others to attend church with him.[9] He had attended Burnette Chapel multiple times, between one and two years before the shooting, according to church members, but had not attended recently.

Because he enjoyed the church, he encouraged his older sister and her children to come as well. Samson had helped with the church's Sunday school program, teaching and mentoring children. Pastor Joey Spann testified at trial that the members of Burnette Chapel "thought the world" of Samson and his cousins when they attended services there. Spann said that they attended services faithfully, and there were never any problems or anything out of the ordinary with them as churchgoers. Pastor Spann said, "They were great, great guys." Confirming the testimony Samson gave in court, Spann said he was not aware of any animosity between Samson and anyone at the church.

Samson also spoke highly of the church during his testimony. In court, he said, "They were very receptive, kind, warm, compassionate. They let us in, and they let us in on beyond the church. They let us into the unity in the community within the congregation and they were good to us." Samson said no one there did anything that made him mad or upset, and he had no reason to be angry or resentful toward the congregation. He testified that the congregation at Burnette Chapel was predominately white, "sprinkled with a couple of Hispanics, maybe some Asians, and some Blacks."

In stark contrast to those statements, Samson's girlfriend, Maya Hill, testified that Samson hated organized religion. In recorded phone calls from jail, Samson explained to Hill that the reason Pastor Spann said kind things about him in news reports is that the pastor remembered Samson from years ago when he was more interested in Jesus and religion. He and Hill agreed he no longer felt that way.

---

9. Stephens, "Shootings," para. 6.

FAITH LEADER STATEMENTS

Minerva Rosa-Gonzalez

In court, church member Minerva Rosa-Gonzalez stated that she worked with Samson at vacation Bible school at the church and felt betrayed by his actions. Samson participated in that children's program three to four years before the shooting.[10]

Gloria Riches

Burnette Chapel church member Gloria Riches said Samson and other Sudanese men were very active with vacation Bible school before changing to a different church.[11]

Joey Spann

The pastor of Burnette Chapel, Spann, spent three months after the shooting recovering from his wounds. In court, Pastor Spann said that the church thought the world of Samson and that there was no animosity toward the church and Samson prior to the shooting.[12] Pastor Spann's words upon his return sought to unite all worshipers in the church universal. "When he attacked Burnette Chapel, he attacked every body of worshippers, wherever they may be. That's why I think so many people are touched by what took place at Burnette Chapel. When we were attacked, you were attacked."

Florence Koks

Samson's aunt (sister of his father), Florence Koks, testified in court that Samson visited her home and taught her children from the Bible. She said the Bible was his favorite book, and he frequently mentioned Scripture in conversations. Koks expressed shock at Samson's actions, stating, "He's not the kind of kid that would do that. It kind of makes me speechless. It's like a dream, and I don't believe that he did it."[13]

10. Shelton, "He's Killed Me," paras. 2–4.
11. Tamburin, "Personal Turmoil," para. 27.
12. Shelton, "He's Killed Me," para. 3.
13. Tamburin, "Personal Turmoil," para. 22.

Who Is Emanuel Kidega Samson?

MENTAL HEALTH

As part of his trial process, Samson was interviewed by Dr. Stephen Montgomery, a forensic psychiatrist, for about three hours. The doctor also studied Samson's medical records and documents related to the shooting. Dr. Montgomery noted that in April 2014, Samson reported to his primary care physician that he felt "stressed out." Samson was diagnosed with bipolar II disorder and prescribed an anti-psychotic medication and mood stabilizer. At a visit three weeks later, Samson reported to the doctor that he had improved significantly. The doctor doubled Samson's medication dosage. Samson did not return to follow up.

His father, who had arranged and paid for treatment, returned to Africa. In June of that same year, Samson visited a therapist. He told of having a temper issue for which he was seeking counseling that was "precipitated by a spiritual awakening." Samson's history of extreme childhood violence and abuse, Dr. Montgomery testified, led to a rewiring of his brain and the onset of schizoaffective disorder. Samson has a family history of mental illness, as his grandfather had been diagnosed with schizophrenia. Samson also testified that he has been diagnosed with post-traumatic stress disorder (PTSD) because of childhood abuse.

Dr. Montgomery concluded that Samson was experiencing disassociation symptoms at the time of the shooting. The psychiatrist explained his belief that Samson was likely hearing voices at the time of the shooting. Samson believed he was famous at times, that people were persecuting him, that his cell phone had been hacked, and that he had telepathic powers. The voices Samson heard and the hallucinations he saw were always deprecatory, telling him to kill himself. However, Montgomery testified that there was not enough evidence to show that Samson was unable to form intent.[14]

While in jail, Samson's mental health records show he was initially put on suicide watch, but that level of personalized supervision was reduced over the ensuing weeks. Samson said he had chronic depression, thoughts of suicide, mood swings, chronic insomnia, distractibility, rapid speech, racing thoughts, increased energy, decreased need for sleep, social isolation, visual hallucinations of shadows, and auditory hallucinations of voices saying negative things to him. Despite these issues, he declined medication.

After his second visit with mental health providers at the jail, he was diagnosed with bipolar disorder, and he was in a manic phase without

14. State of Tennessee v. Emanuel Kidega Samson, "Appeal," 6–7.

psychotic features. Samson was started on a low dose of lithium. This treatment was successful in treating his mania. In August of 2018, Samson told of having visual and tactile hallucinations, which he attributed to spiritual phenomenon that are within the beliefs of his African culture about shadow people.[15]

DRUG USE

Samson described using bath salts (synthetic cathinones) in 2015, which is a stimulant and mood-altering type of synthetic drug that is sometimes used to mimic the effects of cocaine and methamphetamine. He also said he has used cannabis on and off throughout his life, and that he had last used cannabis the morning of the shootings. Cannabis causes anxiety and/or panic attacks in about 30 percent of users. In his courtroom testimony, Dr. Montgomery said that cannabis use can exacerbate the mental illness symptoms from which Samson suffered.

CRIMINAL HISTORY

Prior to the Burnette Chapel shootings, Samson had no criminal history.[16] However, police previously had contact with him on multiple occasions. In January 2017, Samson's then-girlfriend Jeanna Ambrose summoned police to Samson's home in Murfreesboro, Tennessee. Ambrose told police that Samson had punched her television and broken a small figurine. Their dispute arose out of his belief that she was cheating on him, she said. Two months later, in March 2017, police were called to the same home. Samson told police he had broken up with Ambrose but that she was harassing him, and he was afraid of her. Ambrose argued that she was simply picking up belongings. Police helped her retrieve her items and told them not to have further contact with one another. Three months later, in June 2017, Samson's father called 911 and said Samson was making suicidal threats, saying he had a gun to his head. Police located Samson, who said he was fine. Police determined he was not in danger.

---

15. State of Tennessee v. Emanuel Kidega Samson, "Appeal," 4.
16. BeenVerified, "Emanuel K Samson."

MOTIVATIONS

On the day of the shooting, Samson left writings in his vehicle explaining that he sought to kill ten white people as revenge for Dylann Roof's killing of nine Black people.[17] No other motivation has been suspected or voiced. Samson claims he does not remember the shooting.[18]

WRITINGS AND STATEMENTS

Before his arrest, Samson was active on social media, particularly on Facebook. Though his account has been deleted, screen captures of his posts were taken before the page was removed. Samson also reposted videos from Ankh Ma'at Ra and Sa Neter, self-identified Black nationalists who are popular in social media and on YouTube. According to the Southern Poverty Law Center, these videos encourage a swath of black nationalist and pan-African ideology, part of which is linked to the New Black Panther Party, Black Hebrew Israelites, Moorish Nation, the Nation of Islam, and other radical black nationalist groups.

In May 2010, Samson posted on Facebook that he would "pursue to do what the Lord has called me to do. I'm aiming at psychologist," he said, "but also becoming a preacher."[19] Three months prior to the shooting at Burnette Chapel, Samson texted his father a note of distress, saying, "I have a gun to my head, have a nice fucking life." Vanansio Samson told the court he asked police to take his son's guns away from him in June of 2017, but said the police told him Emanuel had the right to own his guns.[20]

On the day of the shooting, Samson's last Facebook post came at 10:26 a.m., about thirty minutes before the shooting. Samson posted: "Everything you've ever doubted or made to be believe as false, is real. & vice versa, B." Another post from the same day read, "Become the creator instead of what's created. What you say, goes." His posts from the Sunday morning of the shooting included pictures of Samson, a bodybuilder, lifting weights, captioned "unrestricted paroxysm."[21] About an hour before the shooting,

---

17. State of Tennessee v. Emanuel Kidega Samson, "Appeal," 18.
18. State of Tennessee v. Emanuel Kidega Samson, "Appeal," 44.
19. Tamburin, "Personal Turmoil," 34.
20. Tamburin, "Emanuel Samson's Father," para. 4.
21. Rau, "Before Antioch," para. 3.

Samson sent a note to work colleagues at Crimson Security Service, saying he would no longer be coming to work.[22]

During the trial, jurors read jail phone call transcripts to the jury. Samson told Hill, his girlfriend, that he heard "some funny shit" while he was on the floor after the shooting and referred to people at the church as "wack asses" during jail phone calls. Less than a month after the shooting, Samson laughed while speaking to Hill and talked to her about being able to "look at the humor in any situation," including the shooting, according to transcripts of phone calls played in court. Prosecutors played Samson's jail phone calls in an effort to contradict Samson's testimony when he said he had not laughed or joked about the shooting. In one call, Samson said to Hill:

> You feel it, you feel it. No no where they coming from is a time back when I was a Christian I told you that, remember that so they are still hanging on to that image of "mmhm Jesus" that sh[-]t, they still hanging on to that . . . That is what they mean by he loved the Lord and by loving life, look at what everybody who don't know me was thinking. Listen listen listen I just got off the phone, I was talking to my dad earlier. My dad has always bragged on me, if there is one thing he has always bragged on me and that I have always loved life is the fact that I know how to *undecipherable* people so I may come off and confuse people that is why to even this day even the psychiatrists they just can't see or understand why I put three bullets in my chest but people like you and I do because we understand how our minds work. These people only see the external sh[-]t. They see me always laughing, joking, smiling, cracking up. You see what I am talking about? Them two things together that's why they got you thinking and saying what the f[-]ck is y'all on? You know what I am saying? But yeah.

CURRENT LIFE

Emanuel Samson is an inmate at Riverbend Maximum Security Institution in Nashville, Tennessee. He is serving a life sentence without parole.[23] There is no public information as to whether Samson currently has a chaplain or pastor.

---

22. Tamburin, "Personal Turmoil," para. 5.
23. Tamburin, "Jury Sentences," paras. 1–2.

SUMMARY

The shooting in which Emanuel Samson opened fire at Burnette Chapel Church of Christ uncovered many important stories. Reverend Joey Spann is the pastor of Burnette Chapel Church of Christ. Spann was one of the victims of Samson's shooting who survived. He lost an index finger, was shot in the torso, and still carries the bullet inside him.[24] His testimony about how he and his wife, Peggy, realized there was a shooter in the building and rushed to get people out was extremely moving.

In a sermon broadcast in August 2019, Pastor Spann preached an emotional sermon titled "Time Sure Is Precious" which included the words "Do not wait until another funeral to tell that person how much they meant to you."[25] The service was rebroadcast on August 16, 2020. The minister did not specifically mention the name of Melanie Crow Smith, but he emphasized that life is brief and unpredictable, and to let those we love know of our feelings for them. To conclude the service, he moved into a discussion of forgiveness, using Jesus's forgiveness on the cross as an example to which we should aspire.

---

24. WKRN, "Newsmaker: Joey Spann."
25. Burnette Chapel, "Sunday, August 16th, 2020."

Chapter 9

Who Is Devin Patrick Kelley?

INTRODUCTION

ONE OF THE MOST chilling demonstrations of red flags that were ignored in a potentially (and inevitably) violent person is Devin Kelley. Kelley is the young man who unleashed terror on Sutherland Springs, Texas, a tiny (population six hundred) community southeast of San Antonio, Texas, putting the town on the map in the worst way possible. As word spread that Kelley was the perpetrator in a mass shooting, those who knew him were not surprised. Kelley's murderous outrage was the deadliest of the shootings described in this book, and one of the largest mass shootings our nation has seen. He was a powder keg about to explode for years. When the explosion finally happened, he destroyed many lives, including his own.

Because there is no court testimony from Devin Kelley about the events leading up to, during, or after the shooting at First Baptist Church in Sutherland Springs, Texas, a broader view of Kelley's troubled life is taken here. Kelley died at the end of the event, so other sources were drawn upon to gain information about his background and personal life leading up to November 5, 2017. Reports by governmental agencies, both military and civilian, were used for this research. Documentation with survivor testimony from the federal trial brought by families of victims and survivors against the United States Air Force was used, as well as a transcript from his 2012 court martial hearing. Interviews and mass media reports round out the information.

Kelley was a troubled, violent person who was fixated on harming himself and other people and, in at least one case, an animal. His story is a cautionary tale for churches, law enforcement, mental health care providers, and the United States military. Anyone with a disturbingly violent family member, colleague, or acquaintance can learn from Kelley's tragic and too-brief life. In his short twenty-six years, he was repeatedly suspended from high school, dated two thirteen-year-olds when he was seventeen and eighteen, was court-martialed by the US Air Force for abuse of his wife and stepson, escaped a mental health facility, killed twenty-six people, and wounded twenty more before killing himself.

Warning signs were addressed only to an extent with brief hospitalizations and treatment with medications that left him as troubled, if not worse, than before he was admitted. The ball was dropped and clues were missed on many occasions. Kelley himself recognized how problematic his issues were and repeatedly told others that violence was imminent. For example, after being convicted of fracturing his stepson's skull, he confessed to the assault in a self-recorded video. In that recording, he said, "The whole world is going to know, I'm a child beater. I am a wife beater." He continued, "We all suffer the consequences for the mistakes we make, and I happened to make one. This is not the first mistake, and this is not the last mistake of probably many to come."

In June of 2013, a woman signed a complaint against Kelley, alleging he sexually assaulted her. The victim was not given a physical examination, which she reported three days after the alleged assault happened. The sheriff's department had difficulty contacting Kelley, so the matter was not pursued, even though they were in contact with Kelley for a separate domestic violence issue in 2014. The sheriff's department has given conflicting answers for why the sexual assault charge was not pursued.[1] If the signs he exhibited and the statements he made had been addressed appropriately and promptly, he and twenty-six others might still be with us.

BACKGROUND

Childhood

Devin Patrick Kelley was born on February 12, 1991, in San Marcos, Texas. He grew up in New Braunfels, Texas. The town of about twenty-eight

---

1. Associated Press, "Sheriff Didn't Pursue."

thousand (at that time) is about thirty-five miles north of Sutherland Springs. His parents, Michael and Rebecca Kelley, had been high school sweethearts, and they have now been married for over forty years. When Kelley was two years old, his parents bought twenty-eight acres of land on which they quickly erected a barn. For a few years, the parents, Kelley, and his older sister lived in the barn and a pop-up camper while their new home was being erected. Kelley has two sisters, Lillian and Lauren.

Kelley's father, Michael, testified that there were many animals on their property when Kelley was a child, and he was very good with them. Michael described Kelley's close family relationship with him and especially his younger sister. Kelley was also active with his father in Cub Scouts, Webelos, and Boy Scouts. Two aunts testified independently at Kelley's 2012 court martial hearing that the Kelley family had a loving home with no abuse. In contrast, his first wife, Tessa, said that Kelley told her that he had killed a dog at age ten by snapping its neck and thought it was very funny.

Kelley graduated from high school in May of 2009 and ranked 260th out of a class of 393. While that sounds typical, it was anything but that. Kelley had multiple suspensions from New Braunfels High School from December 2006 until February 2007 for falsifying records, insubordination, profanity, and a drug-related charge.[2] During one suspension, Kelley enrolled in an unnamed alternative school, then returned to New Braunfels High in time to graduate. Ryan, a classmate at the public high school who chose not to give his last name, said Kelley had a "Columbine feel to him. You know that kid that wears a trench coat to school?" Ryan said. "He was kind of like that. I would acknowledge him and say, 'Sup?', because if he were to bring a gun to school, I didn't want to be on the list."[3]

Kelley took karate lessons during those years and earned a black belt after four or five years of training. His martial arts instructor said Kelley signed up for karate to defend himself against bullying. Kelley was described by classmates as a social outcast, and many had deleted him from their phones and social media because of his habit of sending inappropriate and/or aggressive messages. One classmate wrote, "I was close with Devin Kelley from middle school through high school . . . and I had always known there was something off about him." She continued, "He used to be happy at one point, normal, your average kid. Over the years we all saw him change into something that he wasn't." While speaking of the Sutherland

2. Rosenberg et al., "Who Is Devin," paras. 11–12.
3. Shugerman, "Columbine Feel," paras. 4–5.

Springs mass shooting, she added, "To be completely honest, I'm not really surprised this happened, and I don't think anyone who knew him is very surprised either."

Young Adulthood

At seventeen, Kelley met Danielle, who was thirteen at the time. Danielle had a difficult childhood. She said in federal court that she was abused by her biological parents and that they burned her with boiling water over 80 percent of her body. She was put into a new home by Child Protective Services and says her adoptive father sexually abused her for years. With these experiences, Danielle longed for someone to hear her without judgment. Kelley felt like a safe place for young Danielle to talk about what he was doing to her. Kelley joined the air force on January 5, 2010. He completed training at Goodfellow AFB in San Angelo, Texas. He served overseas and earned the Global War on Terrorism Service Medal.

When Kelley was eighteen, he also dated another thirteen-year-old girl, Brittany Adcock. Adcock says he pressured her to have sex with him. She was quoted in an NBC article as saying, "At the time I didn't think much into it being so young but now I realize that there's something off about someone who is eighteen with someone who is thirteen." She also said that after she broke up with him, "He somehow would always find out my number although none of my friends talked to him and he would constantly call me until I blocked his number. Then I'd get calls from an unknown number, so I've had to change my number quite a bit." She also stated that Kelley offered her money for her company. She said, "There has been one point that I called the police because he was just calling me so much, I wanted to report harassment. One time he told me I should move in with him and his wife and that he would take care of me as long as I walked around topless. Not long after that his wife messaged me and asked why I'm talking to her husband, and I told her what he was saying and sent her screenshots and she then apologized and then I was blocked from speaking to her."[4]

In the summer after his junior year of high school, Kelley met Tessa Brennaman when they worked together at a fast-food restaurant. Tessa went on to a relationship in which she had a son, but she and Kelley reconnected and married in April 2011. According to his father, Kelley did

---

4. Stelloh et al., "Who Is Devin," paras. 17–19.

not inform his family about his marriage because he knew they would say he was too young. His parents did welcome Tessa and her son into their family. Tessa and Kelley's marriage was brief and lasted just over a year. She described physical and sexual abuse and controlling behavior from her husband during that time. She said she was not allowed to look at his phone during their relationship and found out later that he had been exchanging various sexually explicit messages with other women. At the same time, he and Danielle kept in touch through letters.

After he entered the air force, Kelley's troubles increased. As his time in the military progressed, so did his disciplinary actions. Between July 2011 and March 2012, he received thirteen military reprimands. Offenses included using his cell phone in places that weren't allowed, failing courses, doing his job incorrectly, missing meetings, wearing headphones while in uniform, disrupting the work of other people, lying to a supervisor, losing his military identification documentation multiple times, and not reporting to his duty station after being ordered to do so.

According to Staff Sergeant Jessika Edwards, Kelley had a fascination with mass murders. He admired mass murderer Dylann Roof, who killed nine people in a church in 2015, and wished he could do what Roof had done. Edwards said that Kelley would joke about wanting to kill people, and eventually threatened to harm himself. Curiously, the latter threat garnered him a referral for mental health treatment, but somehow the former did not. A government report said he had been sneaking weapons onto the air force base in an effort to carry through on a threat to harm his military supervisors. Edwards further shared that in Facebook messages, Kelley discussed acquiring dogs from the online site Craigslist so that he could shoot them.

In October 2012, after his court marshal and dismissal from the US Air Force, Kelley's first wife, Tessa, divorced him, and he reconnected with Danielle. They married each other on April 4, 2014, when Danielle was nineteen and Devin was twenty-three. During this time, Kelley lied on applications to obtain a license from the Texas Department of Public Safety to be a security guard. He worked for the grocery store chain HEB for two months in 2013 but quit that position. In 2017, he worked for five weeks as a night security guard at Schlitterbahn Waterpark Resort in New Braunfels, Texas, but was fired in July, which is peak tourist season for the park. He worked for a little over a month at Summit Vacation and RV Resort, also in New Braunfels. At Summit, coworkers described him as hardworking but somewhat unfriendly. Kelley also ran a billing software company out of his home called Dilloware, Inc., which operated out of the home on his parents' twenty-eight-acre property. His mother, Rebecca, worked as art director for Dilloware.

Meanwhile, on that same property, his wife Danielle endured regular beatings, social isolation, and rape for years. During her testimony Danielle described the horrific abuse she suffered at the hands of Kelley after their marriage. He kicked her in the stomach while she was pregnant, resulting in the loss of the baby. She stated that he did not allow her to have friends, and he cut off her contact with family, especially her mother, Michelle. Michelle had recognized Kelley's abusive behavior toward Danielle and had encouraged her to leave him.

Kelley dictated what Danielle wore, what makeup she could use, and how to use it. He even went so far as to develop a series of hand signals that he used to describe punishments for looking at other men in public or speaking out of turn. She also said she wasn't allowed to leave the house because Kelley would keep their garage door shut with cinder blocks and place heavy furniture in front of windows, and he could hear if she opened their heavy front door. During her testimony, she explained, "He said if I ever left him, I would have to pay for it, and the only way of leaving this marriage was one of us is going to end up in a body bag."[5] Danielle was not permitted by him to go anywhere alone, including church.

At the time of the shooting, Kelley, Danielle, and her two-year-old son lived on his parents' property. A neighbor who lived across the road, Doug (who declined to give his last name), said that he didn't know the family despite living on the same road for eleven years. "The only time I see them is when they're going out and they don't even look my way." After seeing a picture of Kelley, he still didn't recognize him. Doug said he regularly heard gunshots coming from the Kelley property, which caused commotion for his dogs, but he otherwise thought little of it.[6] Another neighbor, Mark Moravitz, said he frequently heard gunfire from the Kelley residence at 10:00 or 11:00 p.m. "We hear a lot of gunfire," he explained, "But we're out in the country."[7]

---

5. Conrad, "Wife," para. 20.
6. Rosenberg et al., "Who Is Devin," paras. 15–17.
7. Rosenberg et al., "Who Is Devin," paras. 18–19.

MENTAL HEALTH

As early as September 2011, twenty-year-old Kelley voluntarily sought out mental health treatment at his air force base's mental health clinic. He cited high stress, both at work and home. Between September 7, 2011, and February 22, 2012, Kelley was treated seventeen times at the clinic and was prescribed atomoxetine, ibuprofen, albuterol sulfate, fluticasone, and omeprazole. On February 21, 2012, Kelley initiated a clinic visit, telling staff his wife left him and told the military he had assaulted her. He returned the next day, still upset. He told staff he would likely go to a psychiatric hospital for help because he didn't think he could help himself as an outpatient. The following day he followed through on that, staying as an inpatient for two weeks in the psychiatric facility until March 8, 2012. Upon dismissal, he was told to follow up with the clinic, which he did. He was seen there seven times in six weeks. On his last visit, he expressed that he was having more difficulty than ever.

In the summer of 2012, during and after his court martial and while in military confinement, Kelley attended and completed various treatment classes. These included Dialectical Behavioral Therapy, Victim Impact, Substance Abuse Education, Substance Abuse Training Program, Anger Management, and Crossroads. Because Kelley's confinement at Naval Consolidated Brig was not long, he did not have enough time to enter violent offender treatment, a program only for inpatients.

DRUG HISTORY

In both 2009 and 2010, Devin Kelley stated that he had never used or experimented with marijuana. However, he had a history of possession of marijuana as a minor while in high school. Kelley had no other history of illegal drug use or arrests. In a memorandum written by Kelley for his court martial hearing, he refers to struggles with the overuse of alcohol.[8]

CRIMINAL HISTORY

Kelley's criminal-related history includes several unremarkable, minor traffic offenses in addition to:

---

8. United States Air Force, "Proceedings," 392.

- November 29, 2006: Misdemeanor juvenile marijuana possession arrest.
- June 9, 2011: Charged with assault on a child. The victim was his stepson. Kelley cracked his skull, and the child spent time in an intensive care unit. A second hospitalization revealed a handprint-shaped bruise on the child's cheek. The child was eventually placed into foster care for his safety.
- February 2012: Issued a no-contact order on his then-wife Tessa.
- April 23, 2012: Charged with communication of a threat and assault.
- June 7, 2012: Kelley left the Peak Behavioral Health facility in Santa Teresa, New Mexico, without permission from the staff and without notifying anyone. This was treated as a charge of being absent without leave.
- June 8, 2012: Kelley was recognized at a Greyhound bus station in El Paso, Texas, handcuffed, and returned to the military health clinic.
- On the same day, Kelley's commander prepared a pretrial confinement package, including a memorandum stating that Kelley's commander was "convinced" that Kelley was "dangerous and likely to harm someone if released."
- June 13, 2012: Escaped from a mental health clinic in Santa Teresa, New Mexico. Local police report stated that he had attempted to sneak weapons onto the air base and "carry out death threats" against his chain of command.
- June 25, 2012: A military protection order was issued in an attempt to prevent Kelley from abusing Tessa Kelley and her son any further. Interviews conducted by the military of three witnesses and four former girlfriends affirmed Kelley's abusive actions and nature.
- July 26, 2012: Court martial from air force on two charges of assault. Pled guilty and was convicted of fracturing his stepson's skull and assaulting his first wife, Tessa. The child was younger than two years old. Assault against Tessa included pulling her hair until some came out, choking her, and hitting and kicking her multiple times in 2011 and 2012. Assault against the stepson included slapping and pushing the child until he fell over. This occurred on multiple occasions. In

one incident Kelley caused a subdural hematoma, and in another, his actions led to the child falling and sustaining a fractured clavicle.[9]

- November 6–7, 2012: Court martial sentence served of twelve months' confinement and demotion to rank E-1. This sentence was upheld on appeal on December 3, 2012.

- December 18–20, 2012: Kelley was incarcerated at Naval Consolidated Brig as a suicide, assault, and escape risk. After being released into the general population, he accumulated seven write-ups for violations of rules.

- August 1, 2014: Kelley was cited for animal cruelty to a dog. Court records say four people saw Kelley strike a dog several times with his fist on its head and chest, pick it up by the neck, throw it into the air, and drag it to his camper. This offense was a misdemeanor, and he received deferred probation and paid $368 and restitution.

Kelley had multiple accusations over the years of assault that were either not corroborated or dropped before charges were filed. For example:

- June 2013: A woman signed a complaint alleging Kelley sexually assaulted her three days prior. The investigation, according to the Comal County Sheriff's Department, was inactive because of their inability to contact Kelley, as they believed he had moved. Comal County Sheriff Mark Reynolds said, "This was an error on the part of the sheriff's office."

- September 30, 2016: Kelley's former Forty-Ninth Logistics Readiness Squadron supervisor received a threatening message from Kelley on Facebook. The message stated, "Hey you stupid b****. You should have been put in the ground a long time ago. Better hope I don't ever see you. You can't face facts, you fat piece of s***." This was a misdemeanor case and was dismissed by the air force.

Kelley does have a minor criminal record in Comal County for various traffic offenses, which include driving with an expired registration, speeding, failure to stop at a stop sign, and driving without insurance.

In December 2018, the Department of Defense Office of Inspector General (DoD OIG) issued this statement, recognizing the US Air Force's failure to prevent the harm that Kelley eventually caused:

---

9. United States Air Force, "Proceedings," 37.

Report of Investigation into the United States Air Force's Failure to Submit Devin Kelley's Criminal History Information to the Federal Bureau of Investigation DODIG-2019-030

On November 5, 2017, a former Air Force member, Devin Kelley, shot and killed twenty-seven people (including himself) and wounded twenty-two others at the First Baptist Church of Sutherland Springs, Texas. Kelley was able to purchase a firearm from a federal firearm licensed dealer, even though he had a disqualifying conviction while in the Air Force. He had been discharged from the Air Force in 2014 after being convicted of assault. Because of that conviction, the Air Force should have sent his fingerprints and final disposition report to the FBI, which should have prevented him from legally buying a gun. However, the Air Force did not submit his fingerprints or a final disposition report documenting his conviction to the FBI for inclusion in its criminal history databases, which allowed him to purchase the weapons he used in the shooting.

The DoD OIG conducted this exhaustive investigation to determine Kelley's actions while in the Air Force, and to examine why the Air Force had not provided his fingerprints to the FBI, as was required.

The DoD OIG determined that the Air Force had four opportunities to submit Kelley's fingerprints to the FBI but did not. On four occasions, Kelley purchased firearms from stores that were Federal Firearms Licensees and completed the Bureau of Alcohol, Tobacco, Firearms, and Explosives Form 4473, which is required to obtain a firearm license. Since the Air Force did not submit fingerprints to the FBI prohibiting the sale of firearms to Kelley, he was able to purchase the firearms.[10]

RELIGIOUS HISTORY

Two of Kelley's aunts testified in court that the Kelley family was a "Christian home." In 2011 Kelley recorded a video in which he confessed to beating Tessa and her son, and in that video, he tells his parents, "I still love God." In that video (shown in the court martial trial), Kelley referred to God giving him Tess and her son, and he hopes God forgives him.[11] This

---

10. Department of Defense, "Report."
11. United States Air Force, "Proceedings," 197.

presumes that Kelley believed in God at this point. Further, in November 6, 2012, he wrote a memorandum for the sentencing hearing at the court martial trial. In that memo, he expresses love for the Bible, Jesus, and God, and says that after high school he had ambitions of becoming a missionary.

Devin Kelley attended First Baptist of Kingsville, Texas, for about two months in the summer of 2014. During that time, he volunteered for one day to help in vacation Bible school, a children's program often held by churches. The pastor, Jack Willoughby, said Kelley was not at the church long enough for anyone to know him well.[12]

Kelley's uncle, Dave Ivey, posted on Facebook about his nephew multiple times. Ivey posted, "He believes in his rights as a human. . . . He is an atheist . . . Non Believer. . . . He has had several domestic cases with his new wife who is a member of the church." Danielle Kelley, widow of Devin, says her husband grew up believing, but later became a self-proclaimed atheist. When she could convince him to go to church, he would laugh throughout the service. She says Kelley believed that a God wouldn't let them go through the troubles and face the cruelties that they had.

MOTIVATIONS

As Kelley is deceased, there is only speculation as to his true motives. Dave Ivey also believed Kelley had a grievance as his motivation and posted on Facebook that "Devin was angry with the government" but did not explain why. The FBI has said the shooting was neither religiously nor racially motivated, but some, including the Sandy Hook Project, believe it was an anti-religious hate crime.[13] It's possible Kelley was reacting to an argument with his mother-in-law, Michelle, who had received threatening text messages from him before the shooting. Danielle and Michelle did not attend First Baptist that morning, but Michelle's mother (Danielle's grandmother) Lula White did, and was one of the twenty-six Kelley shot and killed. Danielle believes her husband committed the shootings to punish her for wanting a divorce. Another theory posits that Kelley was angry at the members of First Baptist because he felt they treated Danielle poorly when she accused her adoptive father, a parishioner of the church, of sexual assault. Danielle testified in court that a family in the church told her she deserved to be molested, and one person said she was promiscuous. She was so distraught,

12. Christenson and MacCormack, "Gunman in Church Attack," para. 15.
13. Sandy Hook Promise, "Gun Violence Facts," para. 5.

she says, that she tried to kill herself after she reported the abuse. She said some of the families of those killed or injured by Kelley blame her for the massacre.[14]

WEAPON HISTORY

During his time as an inpatient in the military mental health facility, Kelley was discovered multiple times to be looking at guns on the internet. Counselors discussed the inappropriateness of this with him at the time. At the time of the shootings and Kelley's death, his Facebook page had a picture of an assault-style rifle. According to the United States Air Force, Kelley bought six firearms from licensed stores between 2014 and 2017. Each time he completed the appropriate forms, and each time a background check was completed. Because the air force had failed to submit documentation of his arrests, he cleared all background checks each time. Three of these firearms were used at First Baptist Church.

WRITINGS AND STATEMENTS

Kelley's social media posts include Facebook posts classmates found "depressing," but also screeds assailing religion and a LinkedIn page that claims he cares about animal welfare. This is contrary to the above-referenced Facebook message and a 2014 court case claiming Kelley abused a dog. He also claimed to care about children, though he shot children at First Baptist Church. He posted that he was passionate about civil rights. While expressing care for people, he also displayed contempt. In the months leading up to the attack at First Baptist Church, Kelley would add people from Sutherland Springs to his list of Facebook friends, then pick fights with them.

SUMMARY

The red flags and alarm bells could not have been more visible and audible than they were with Devin Kelley. Beginning early in his life and throughout early adulthood, he waved his own flags and sounded his own bells. As time progressed and help was not forthcoming, others threw up alerts in a desperate attempt to help mitigate the oncoming disaster: there were

---

14. Conrad, "Wife," paras. 27–30.

multiple alerts, varied, and often. "He went to a psychiatrist and just got a five-minute type of visit with a prescription and wasn't able to get the help that he was seeking. He wasn't able to access it," said Lisa Krantz, a photojournalist who spent weeks in Sutherland Springs with survivors.[15] An abundance of data, testimony, and experience pointed to a problem, but time after time, treatment was ineffective, or results were fleeting. Time after time, evidence of his troubled behavior grew.

The legal safety systems that are supposed to stop dangerous people from purchasing weapons failed. Because the USAF failed to report Kelley's violent history, he was able to pass every background check he underwent. This enabled him to do everything from working at a grocery store to purchasing six guns in four years from licensed dealers. The air force has admitted their multiple errors in this scenario. In 2022, a federal judge ordered the air force to pay $230 million to families of victims and survivors of the shooting at First Baptist Church. That judgment came too late for the nearly fifty people killed and wounded in a little Baptist church in Sutherland Springs, Texas.[16]

---

15. Lisa Krantz, interview by author, May 24, 2024.
16. United States Air Force, "Proceedings," 595–97.

Chapter 10

What Are We Doing as Churches?

INTRODUCTION

AFTER NINE CHAPTERS OF diving deeply into the history of mass shootings in churches, three specific incidents, and three perpetrators of mass shootings in churches, you may be wondering: What are we doing to help? How are churches actively working to make the world a safer, less violent place? The answer is: probably not enough. We can do so much more.

Churches are in a unique position in American society. Historically, the church has shown that it can and does affect positive change on an incredibly large scale in society. Going back to the early eighteenth century, the church changed higher education in the United States. The first Great Awakening gave us evangelical movements with ministers trying to help people experience the Spirit of God outside of the church, out in the world. There were preachers like John Wesley and Jonathan Edwards and sermons like "Sinners in the Hands of an Angry God." Great religious fervor swept through the colonies by way of the New Light Christians. Their opponents, the traditional Old Light Christians, strongly opposed the evangelical uprising. Protestantism underwent a split in the colonies.

The fruits of that Spirit awakening, though, included the founding of new educational institutions that would ultimately shape both the American educational system and society at large. A lot of colleges began not just as teachers' colleges, but also as theological colleges. In 1746, a group of New Lights, all Presbyterian ministers, decided to start a college that could educate young ministers. As a result of their work, King George II chartered the College of New Jersey, which became Princeton University. As a result of Christian churches working together, a new era of education began.[1]

In a more modern instance, the church transformed American society through the civil rights movement of the 1950s, 1960s, and beyond. Before the work of Rev. Martin Luther King Jr. and so many others, segregation was legal and acceptable in our country. Sunday morning is still one of the most segregated times in our country, but that, too, is slowly changing. Racial tensions were extremely high in my hometown of Detroit, Michigan, during the early decades of the civil rights movement. Segregation, bussing, and interracial relationships were the hot topics of the day. In the white, suburban church my family attended, guards were posted at the doors to prevent any Black people from trying to come in and worship with us. Civile rights leaders organized powerful events like the Montgomery bus boycott, the march at Selma, sit-ins in public spaces, the March on Washington for Jobs and Freedom, and other nonviolent protests. Reverend King and other church leaders moved the country forward by creating the Southern Christian Leadership Conference (SCLC), which, together with the NAACP, led protests against Jim Crow laws. The fight for racial justice in America continues, but the civil rights movement is a prime example of the church working for positive change.

On the opposite end of the spectrum are instances where the church affected extremely negative change. When Christians try to legislate Christianity, it can go very badly. Some people truly believe that passing Christianity-based laws is a good way to run a government, but historically that has been disastrous. For example: from 1920 to 1933, Prohibition was the law in the United States. The American Temperance Society, the Women's Christian Temperance Union, the Anti-Saloon League, and the United Methodist Women were influential and successful in making the production and consumption of alcohol illegal in the United States. On January 16, 1919, the Eighteenth Amendment was ratified in the hope that legislating Christian morality would be successful.

The proponents of the amendment surely had good intentions. They had seen firsthand the damage that can be done by the culture that had built up around saloons and the devastating effects of alcoholism on families. However, Prohibition led directly to the rise of organized crime. The manufacture of alcohol went underground, and gangsters became very

---

1. Glass, "Princeton," paras. 1–12.

wealthy through alcohol sales. Bootlegging and rum-running, illegal ways to transport alcohol, thrived. Making things illegal to match Christian values did not thrive and did verifiable harm. The amount of damage humans can inflict on one another in the name of religion is staggering, but so is the amount of good we can do. Let us err on the side of positive change, rather than simply attempting to legislate religion.

WHAT HAS THE CHURCH DONE?

All three shooters profiled in this book were either raised in a church or attended one for a period of time. Though all three churches taught people to love each other, actual discussions about nonviolence were not a regular part of any sort of programming, teaching, or preaching in these churches. Nonviolence is taught throughout Scripture, especially by Jesus. The Beatitudes include "Blessed are the peacemakers, for they will be called the children of God" (Matt 5:9). Jesus taught his disciples, "But to you who are listening I say: Love your enemies, do good to those who hate you, bless those who curse you, pray for those who mistreat you" (Luke 6:27–28). This has always been a difficult concept for humans to grasp, from long before Jesus's time until now. Our instinct is to return evil for evil, but our Lord urged another way: a loving way, which is to help prevent others from committing violence. It is incumbent on churches to spread Jesus's message.

As evidenced by Roof, Samson, and Kelley, proactive anti-violence training for both youth and adults is desperately needed in faith communities. What Dylann Roof did learn about Christian belief is summarized in a journal he kept in prison.

> Christianity, I cannot agree with the form of Christianity most modern preachers preach. It seems to me that this form of Christianity says, "Leave it to God. There is nothing you can do about it." Okay. Well, maybe we can do something but don't because it's not your place. And I can't agree with this. I see some people who seem to use Christianity as an excuse for not doing anything. They tell themselves they are being pious, but they are really being cowardly. Their pity is their excuse. But Christianity doesn't have to be this weak, feeble, cowardly religion. There is plenty of evidence to indicate that Christianity can be a warrior's religion.[2]

---

2. United States v. Dylann Storm Roof, "Brief of Appellant," 48.

From Sunday school classes to youth group discussions, from confirmation classes to Sunday morning sermons, change can start within congregations. From there, however, the church can and must move its message out of its walls and into broader society. Efforts are being made in that direction, but there is an opportunity for so much more. Recognizing the biblical basis and the urgent need, what has the church done to affect change? Some examples of efforts made by various Christian denominations follow.

Public Statements

When Christian churches make public statements promoting nonviolence, they tend to be geared toward world peace, with personal and inter-relational violence taking a back seat. For example, in 2017, Pope Francis gave a World Day of Peace message, in which he recognized the global crisis of violence. "To be true followers of Jesus today also includes embracing his teaching about nonviolence," the pope said. He continues to use the term "nonviolence" in interviews and other public statements.[3]

The United Church of Christ (UCC) issued its Just Peace Pronouncement in 1985 and reaffirmed it in 2015. The pronouncement states, in part, that "Just Peacemaking expresses our commitment to engage practices to resolve conflict at every level—in ourselves, in our families, in our communities, and in our world—without violence whenever possible; when it is not possible, to then restrain, contain and reduce violence; and finally, to work actively to bring it to a swift, sustainable, and just conclusion."[4] Specifically, the document outlines steps for governments to take to ease world tensions.

Similarly, the Presbyterian Church (USA) encourages its congregations to commit to being "peace churches," with a nonviolence stance that focuses mostly on the problems of war and militarism. The denomination offers customizable curriculum and resources "to engage in study and discernment around the challenges of violence, militarism, and war."[5]

Racism is a form of violence, and some denominations have made anti-racism statements to show that their tradition is actively working against racism. As recently as 2018, then-presiding bishop Rev. Elizabeth A. Eaton

---

3. Rynne, "Pope," para. 10.
4. United Church of Christ, "Nonviolent Direct Action," para. 1.
5. Presbyterian Church (U.S.A.), "Becoming a Peace Church."

of the Evangelical Lutheran Church in America (ELCA) "named the reality of institutional and structural racism" within their denomination. The bishop and the ELCA made this statement in response to the Charleston shooting in the hope that talking openly about the truth would lead to transformation. The ELCA has officially and publicly worked to end the practices and beliefs that comprise this racism. The ELCA acknowledges they cannot do this work alone and vows to work ecumenically and with interfaith organizations to accomplish that goal.[6]

The Southern Baptist Convention, the largest body of Baptists in the United States, has issued anti-violence resolutions over the years. The most recent is from 2018, entitled "On Gun Violence and Mass Shootings." This document affirms that all life is sacred and gun violence is escalating. The resolution specifically mentions the massacre at Sutherland Springs Baptist Church. It expresses solidarity with victims and calls on the government for change, but stops short of advocating for change from within.[7]

Formally and publicly, at least some branches of the Church of Christ espouse non-racism as a doctrine, explaining that all persons are made in the image of God, and they therefore reject discrimination.

A multitude of denominations have participated in anti-violence and anti-racism demonstrations and marches. For example, in 2015, the Episcopal Church participated in Pilgrimage to Ferguson to embody their baptismal covenant through work on racism and criminal justice reform.[8]

Discussions

In 2013, the group Women of the ELCA began a discussion about the history of race relations within their denomination.[9] The conversation acknowledges that without recognizing the ELCA's past participation in racist practices, forward movement cannot happen. The document also begins to include the Black Lives Matter movement.

Regarding actual practice, at least some Churches of Christ in the United States are taking active steps to open discussion on issues of racism. During the summer of 2020, Harpeth Hills Church of Christ in Brentwood, Tennessee, hosted weekly discussions on the topic. Other church bodies

6. ELCA, "Presiding Bishop," para. 7.
7. SBC, "On Gun Violence."
8. Korkzan, "Episcopalians," para. 3.
9. E.g., Davis, "Justice."

and organizations within the Church of Christ in the United States have recently opened dialogues around the topics of violence and racism, working to combine concepts found in Scripture (which is vital to this denomination) with anti-racist messages.[10]

Bishop Elizabeth Eaton of the ELCA issued a statement calling for an end to racism in response to the murders committed by Roof. The Church of Christ has hosted summits to teach skills of active listening and meditation in order to bridge racial divides.[11] In theory, each of these denominations espouses anti-racist platforms. Traditionally, however, neither has put large-scale, practical efforts into practice to change the racist structures of their churches.

Publications

In 2018, publications were calling for the ELCA to unlearn racism and to redirect its focus from retaining membership of young people to teaching those same people to be actively anti-racist. As part of a Lenten series in 2016, the Episcopal Church's Office of Government Relations published "Engaging the Beloved Community," which promotes listening, relationships, and action.[12]

Appeals to Mass Media

Benjamin L. Corey is a self-described "cultural anthropologist, public theologian, author, international speaker, faith-related consultant, and commentator." Author of the book *Undiluted: Rediscovering the Radical Message of Jesus*, Corey says:

> One of the most difficult Christian doctrines to accept is the doctrine of Christian Nonviolence. The reason why it is among the most difficult Christian beliefs to embrace is because it directly contradicts what American culture has taught us from day one.
>
> However, the teachings of Jesus were always radical. They were in conflict with culture from the first moment he uttered them, and remain so today. This is because we all live submersed into

---

10. International Churches of Christ, "Racism Dialogue Response."
11. Camp, "Response."
12. Office of Government Relations, "Lenten Series."

kingdoms of men. The invitation Jesus brings is to forsake these earthly kingdoms and to begin living in the Kingdom of God ... a kingdom that does things very differently than anything you'll experience here on earth.

One of these principles is that the Kingdom of God is nonviolent, and the hallmark of the kingdom is a nonviolent love of enemies. Early Christians understood this, but ultimately violent principles of earthly kingdoms were reintroduced to the Christian community and over the course of time, Christians assimilated to this new position.[13]

Corey has used his time in the spotlight to speak on mass media about faith-based nonviolence. He has been interviewed by *TIME*, CNN, and *Huffington Post*. If one has access to such a wide audience as these media outlets, using that access to open conversations and spread the message of nonviolence is a positive, responsible contribution.

Apologies—Do They Help?

On June 5, 2020, I interviewed Rev. Sharon Washington Risher. The topic of mass murder is close to her heart. She has a deep, emotional connection to the murders at Mother Emanuel, as three of her family members and a friend were killed that day by Roof. I asked her thoughts about Roof's theological socialization regarding race. Her brief remarks on the issue are as follows:

> Not too long ago there was a Lutheran person I ran into, and they wanted to apologize to the whole damn denomination for Dylann Roof, and I'm looking at that woman like, whoa, that's a heavy thing to take upon yourself. I understand where she was coming from, and I accepted that. But no matter where you come from, people grow into who they are. You can sit by somebody in church every day and not know what goes on in the psyche of their brains. So, it's hard.[14]

---

13. Corey, "Common Objections," paras. 1–3.
14. Sharon Washington Risher, interview by author, June 5, 2020.

WHAT HAS THE CHURCH LEFT UNDONE?

Limited Views on Racism

In 2020, the ELCA was identified in a Boston University study as having "white, elite cultural forms in its journey from immigrant religious tradition to American mainline Protestant denomination." The author of the study urged the ELCA to expand its views regarding racism.[15] In courtroom transcripts, Rev. Dr. Tony Metze explained that he knew Roof from a church youth group and confirmation classes in 2007. Nowhere in court documents does Metze mention discussing violence or racism with Roof, or the church hosting classes or events regarding racism.

Exclusivity

Lewis Rambo, editor of *Pastoral Psychology*, was raised in the Church of Christ tradition from the age of about five. Rambo describes the denomination as "very committed to the Bible," but also as "somewhat rigid, conservative, and exclusivist." In the 1960s, Rambo attended Abilene Christian College, an institution that, at the time, had a large population of Church of Christ students. Rambo remembers that there was a racist practice of enrolling African students but not African American students.[16] The college changed its practice, but the structural and institutional foundation had been laid.

Preaching

After the assassination of Martin Luther King Jr., Rambo wanted to preach a sermon in his Church of Christ congregation about racism but was talked out of it by his wife, who said the congregation would not welcome such discussion. Instead, he offered a prayer that addressed the killing of King. In turn, the church asked him to leave.[17]

---

15. Carlson, "Practices of Belonging," 19–20.
16. Carlin, "Preface," para. 4.
17. Carlin, "Preface," para. 6.

What Are We Doing as Churches?

Introspection and Acknowledgement

Both the ELCA (in which Roof was a member) and the Church of Christ (where Samson attended) acknowledge, at least officially, their past history of racism and prejudice against African American persons. Exploration of the depth of white supremacist roots, particularly in fundamentalist traditions (including the Church of Christ), is severely lacking. An examination of the violence that white Christians have traditionally committed in order to affirm their supremacy is missing in Christian tradition.

When asked what his understanding is of the ELCA's official stance on racism is, Metze replied: "I think the ELCA's statement, what I've read in the past, has been very clear that we just simply will not tolerate treating people differently based on their skin color."[18]

In an interview with this author, he said:

> I'm not sure I've actually read the official statement. My stance comes from, which I think for a lot of folks in the South, at least in my appearance and my mother in particular who drilled into my head that people are people and followers of Jesus are followers of Jesus, period. And what you look like on the outside does not reflect what you are on the inside by any means. So my mother, I think, is more my foundation than any political or not political but any statement by a church. I think the ELCA's statement, what I've read in the past, has been very clear that we just simply will not tolerate treating people differently based on their skin color. My understanding comes from growing up in the South. In my early years, there were a lot of things done that were racist, and it wasn't till I was in college that I realized how maybe systemic, I guess is the word, it was in the stuff we did and said without realizing it. And that in contrast with what my mom had tried to teach me, I thought, "I need to listen to Mom."

Considering his local church's views on racism and race-based crime, Metze said,

> I think that the best way to sum it up is that when Dylann did what he did, there was just tremendous shock in the congregation that I serve. Now, what the church was forty years ago, I can't speak to. But I know the church that I serve now felt deeply hurt because of course there's this expectation, or not expectation. That's the wrong word. Sort of the image that we would be a church that

18. Tony Metze, interview by author, Jan. 6, 2021.

grew this kid who was mentally ill, but that's been ignored, because he fought that anyway.¹⁹

Metze said it's been a long road, but the church is healing.

Curriculum

A 2024 visit to Cokesbury.com, an online Christian bookstore, revealed seventeen results for books that address nonviolence, but yielded no results for curriculum on the topic of violence, nonviolence, or how to avoid violent events. Christianbook.com had 141 book titles that included the topic, but there was no nonviolence curriculum to be found. A deeper dive reveals a few excellent publications aimed at preventing violence through churches, including *Youth Ministry as Peace Education: Overcoming Silence, Transforming Violence*, by Elizabeth W. Corrie. That author envisions a type of youth ministry that overcomes violence.

SUMMARY

Dylann Roof was not taught about nonviolence or racism in the church of his childhood. The hope of both his family of origin and his spiritual/church family was that their own examples of how to live would prevail. They hoped that through what they considered to be their own lack of overt racist or violent actions, Roof and others in his age group would avoid racist ideology. Clearly, the results show that this practice was not successful.

What would happen if the same teenagers, from Dylann Roof to Lee Boyd Malvo and others, who have access to both in-person and online radicalization also had access to anti-racism and pluralistic thinking? Roof's early internet search for information on Trayvon Martin began to lead him down the path that eventually led to the demise of nine African American parishioners in South Carolina. What was needed was theological education to combat those messages of racism and violence he was receiving.

Besides spiritual anti-violence education to balance outside messages, though, proactive anti-racism training for both youth and adults is desperately needed in Sunday school, in youth groups, in confirmation classes, and on Sunday mornings. This is an issue that permeates our society, and

---

19. Tony Metze, interview by author, Jan. 6, 2021.

in the cases studied in this project, the results of a lack of education were deadly.

Our communities of faith possess the ability to make real, positive change for the mitigation of violence. This will benefit our churches, of course, but will extend far and wide into the world outside of our faith communities. Let us take notice of the historical examples of change the Christian church has made in the world, and intentionally work to effect positive change. It's time for a new approach. What we've done and what we've left undone as the church in the United States has not stemmed the tide of violence. Our resources are great, and our actions must match our abilities. We can follow God's directives and move past our differences, joining together to find a new and better way that centers itself on hope rather than fear.

Chapter 11

The Racial Component

THIS BOOK HAS ITS foundations in a doctoral project that had the pinpoint focus of racially motivated mass shootings in churches. Issues of racism that specifically targeted African Americans and mass shootings were the focus of that project. I recognize that racism and hate crimes target people of many races, not only African American people. Violence that targets American, Asian, Hispanic, and other people is very, very real. Doctoral projects are geared to have a very narrow focus, though, so this project focused on racially motivated mass shootings in churches, specifically with two cases that involved African American/white dynamics. The broader racial element cannot be ignored, however, and is important to study, learn from, and act upon it. This chapter, though, with its roots in that doctoral project, explores only African American/white interconnections.

Two of the three case studies included in this book that were racially motivated were the focus of the doctoral project: the shootings perpetrated by Dylann Roof and Emanuel Samson. Of those, one was an attack on a historic African American congregation, and the other was in retaliation for that shooting. Many shootings in houses of worship are not race based, but the component of racially motivated hostility cannot be dismissed. This chapter delves into this particular angle of the mass shooting problem.

For some, this section will be difficult to read and might even cause them to put the book down. Racial issues are more relevant to mass shootings than one might think, though. Since racism and mass shootings so often intersect, it is vital to consider our country's past, present, and future in regard to the intersection of racism and violence. The previous chapter examined the history of violence in the United States, but our history of race-based animus is just as dire. Despite any potential discomfort with the topic of racism, please consider the following with an open and analytical mind.

Author Isabel Wilkerson, Pulitzer Prize and National Humanities Medal winner, describes systemic racism in the United States by comparing the United States to an old building. In an aged edifice, there can be myriad hidden problems that are unseen by both the casual observer and even by the person living in the structure, unless that person does the deep, exhaustive work of exploring underneath the surface. Faulty wiring, water damage, infiltration from animals, and innumerable other problems with infrastructure can be present in what appears to be a strong, stable, and even beautiful building. The United States, Wilkerson explains, is similar to an old building. Our racial constructs (which the author extends to include a deeply embedded caste system) exist barely under the surface, oftentimes bubbling up to the surface in disastrous ways.[1]

Dylann Roof and Emanuel Samson are both products of our country's old building with its faulty racial system, but from opposing angles. To simply call out the racial implications of Roof's shooting and the reaction of Samson is not sufficient to prevent further similar situations. To point at the problem of race being ignored in white Protestant churches in the United States is not enough to stem the tide of violence. Instead, the systems that produced these people must be examined, called to task, and given tools to change.

Roof, a white male, is a member of the ruling class (the group that sets the rules in society—in this case, white people) in America's social order. He was raised in a white Protestant church. Samson is both an African immigrant and Black, giving him a double membership in the group ranked the lowest in our country. Immigrants of Samson's type are not white, often have language barriers, and frequently have trouble finding employment. These challenges, while working to learn a new culture, put African immigrants like Samson at a disadvantage. From a religious standpoint, Samson was raised in a mixed-race Protestant church. Both immigrants and nonimmigrants attended the church. The institutional systems that contributed to the formation of both these men are deeply embedded in American society, not insignificantly by our churches.

---

1. Wilkerson, *Caste*, 14.

To get us started, this chapter is an elaboration on four major studies in the fields of violence in the United States, socialization by Christian churches, and the role that the church in the United States has historically played (and must play in the future) regarding socialization. These studies are not an exhaustive examination of the issue. As racism is both systemic and pervasive in the United States, the problem infects every aspect of American life. Much work has been done with quality research conducted in the field, but the four books that follow cover four specific angles of the issues in-depth.

WILLIE JAMES JENNINGS: *THE CHRISTIAN IMAGINATION: THEOLOGY AND THE ORIGINS OF RACE*

Jennings uses a historical, theological, and educational exploration of race within the Christian context in this historical book. Jennings's work reveals the white foundational roots of Christianity in the United States and traces the roots of American notions of whiteness. White men wrote Christian history, translated Christian Scripture, and created modern Christian theology. The colonialist roots of racial enmity by whites from the fifteenth century forward have created a "whiteness landscape."[2]

Socialization within and by white Christianity has succeeded in maintaining segregated societies. This cultural divide, Jennings explains, is created by the white Christian social imagination and driven by imperialism, colonialism, and racism. The measure by which all things socioeconomic and sociocultural are judged to be good or bad is how closely they align to whiteness. The author dives deeply into the topics of land and culture and slavery and emphasizes that the goal of white American Christianity has always been to keep Black persons in a suppressed, oppressed state.

Possibly of most value, though, is that first, Jennings recognizes that Christianity has failed in its attempt to repair divisions in society. But second, Jennings also imagines a Christianity that recognizes its Jewish connections and moves into a future in which Christianity is less centralized. He believes this can be accomplished through reworking our theology, reworking our racial identities, and changing our racial boundaries.

---

2. Jennings, *Christian Imagination*, 202.

In 2015, Jennings also wrote an article titled "Dylann Roof Was Wrong: The Race War Isn't Coming, It's Here," published in Religion Dispatches. In this piece, Jennings encapsulates the problem of white persons claiming ownership of land and people.[3] Jennings's work is of great value because he combines such a large group of disciplines in his study: history, theology, geography, ecology, and other disciplines. He employs Native American history, postcolonial studies, and more. His work regarding white Christianity's failure to actively work to heal racism, as outlined above, is invaluable.

ROBERT P. JONES:
WHITE TOO LONG: THE LEGACY OF WHITE SUPREMACY IN AMERICAN CHRISTIANITY

Jones draws on history, surveys, and personal experiences in his book. Whereas Jennings explored the history and current practice of racism in the United States, Jones zeroes in on racism within white Christianity. His work includes important historical and theological information regarding the eschatology of white Christianity with a particular focus on fundamentalism. Jones was raised in a Southern Baptist tradition. This denomination, the author explains, was created in the mid-1800s when the group split from other Baptists over the issue of slavery. Southern Baptists were on the pro-slavery side of this divide. However, Jones attended Southwestern Baptist Theological Seminary and was among the first group of seminarians from that institution to learn this historical information.

There is undeniable historical information in Jones's work, both statistical and anecdotal, regarding how white Christianity has historically explained, encouraged, and even celebrated chattel slavery and Jim Crow laws. As the founder and CEO of the Public Religion Research Institute, Jones has access to surveys done by the organization regarding race, Christianity, and the intersections therein. Through these surveys, Jones determined that racism and white Christianity are deeply intertwined. In the surveys, white nonreligious persons polled were less likely to be racist than white persons who self-identified as Christians. The work of white Christianity from this point forward, Jones has determined, should be to recognize its racist roots, take responsibility, and work for repair.[4]

3. Jennings, "Roof," para. 4.
4. Jones, *White Too Long*, 157.

White Too Long is only the most recent example of Jones's deep and valuable work regarding racism, religion, and politics. From articles in the *New York Times*[5] to another book, *The End of White Christian America*, his study in this field moves the topic forward greatly.

EBOO PATEL: *ACTS OF FAITH*

Eboo Patel is an American Muslim who promotes religious pluralism and gives us a view from outside Christianity. His observations are important to this work because, as a non-Christian, his long view of the problems in white American Christianity is both helpful and hopeful. One area in which Patel focuses is the importance of spiritual formation in younger persons, particularly in the middle school age range. Middle school is an incredibly formative time in a young person's life. As his introductory example, Patel describes Eric Rudolph who, between 1996 and 1998, detonated bombs four times in Atlanta, Georgia, and Birmingham, Alabama. His attacks killed two people and injured hundreds. Rudolph, who did not trust anybody, hid in the mountains of western North Carolina for five years. He was captured by the FBI in 2003.[6]

Rudolph was raised in the Church of Israel, a Christian Identity group that believes in "serpent seed doctrine." This ideology promotes white persons as superior to other races. Rudolph was unrepentant at trial, going to great lengths to explain the reasoning behind his actions, which he believed were sanctioned by the Christian God. Also, in high school, Rudolph wrote an essay about his belief that the Holocaust never happened. In contrast, Patel presents a group of teenagers who gave tours of a Holocaust museum and explained the horrors that happened in a railcar there. The author compares the differences in experiences and outcomes of these two distinctly different ways of learning.[7]

Acts of Faith is one of seven books published by Patel since 2006. *Sacred Ground: Pluralism, Prejudice, and the Promise of America* expands on the concepts brought forward in *Acts of Faith* and proposes hope for the future. Patel's work on the intersections of racism and religion are significant and far reaching, particularly in the study of violence that stems from such racism.

5. Jones, "Rage."
6. FBI, "Eric Rudolph," para. 1.
7. Patel, *Acts of Faith*, 1.

A. R. HILTON: *A HOUSE UNITED*

Jennings gave us the history of the problem. Jones explained the current problem and gave a vision for the future. Patel helped us see ourselves from the outside looking in. Finally, Allen Hilton's work is where bright hope for the future enters the picture. Hilton posits that allegiance to political parties is a bigger problem in the United States than racism, and believes it is imperative that the Christian church lead major societal change. He differs from Jennings, using a shorter historical approach and more of a modern one. He believes religion is not inherently divisive but recognizes that white Christianity has certainly driven a wedge that further polarizes races in the United States. For example, he believes that Karl Barth (1886–1968) would call for unity if he were able to view our churches today.[8]

Hilton extends the racial divide into a political one, which is helpful for this study, as violence and religion are often intertwined with politics in the United States. Hilton's vision for Christian churches leading the way to healing speaks to the heart of this study. "God built the church to save the world, after all," Hilton says, "And if God is calling us to a new way to do that, you're in."[9] The author believes people of all political leanings in America are honestly seeking to do good and promotes the idea that humility can help each side better understand the other. This book so expertly weighs the problems on the sides of both conservatives and liberals that by the end of the book, the reader is still not certain which way the author falls politically. The hope that the church can affect positive change in the country, and by extension the world, is inspirational as we work toward violence prevention.

These three authors show us an overview of our country's history and the church's past, present, and potential future regarding violence. Let's take a deeper dive into how that has played out. Systemic racism within the United States and specifically within white Christian religious organizations exists, and racism's unchecked existence, proliferation, and continuation have affected society as a whole. That systemic racism influenced the actions of both Dylann Roof and Emanuel Samson.

Though race-based domestic terrorism by way of mass shootings has increased in recent years, the concept is far from new; this is a country that was founded on the very concept. Four national racial landmarks can be

---

8. Hilton, *House United*, x.
9. Hilton, *House United*, xi.

seen that have led us to the point in history in which we now exist. Vital to the conversation about established race-based terrorism in our country, both individually and corporately, is the fact that Christian churches, particularly white Protestant churches, largely signed on to the ideals that dehumanized Black persons. It becomes evident that throughout the history of the United States, the norm has not been to seek justice. As Christians saw themselves as God's chosen people, the notion of being elevated became cross-applied to race by white persons.[10]

First, chattel slavery came to the United States in 1619. This is an enterprise in which men and/or women are purchased or simply taken against their will, brought to the United States, forced into slavery, and treated as nonhuman.[11] In 1619, when the first group of twenty kidnapped and enslaved Africans arrived in Jamestown, Virginia, the practice began in the United States.[12] The entire practice was race-based terrorism, and it certainly did not end in the seventeenth century. It still hasn't ended.

Second, the deputization of white men continued the race-based domestic terrorism in the country. As early as the eighteenth century, posses became an integral part of law enforcement in the United States. White men who were physically able completed compulsory service in posses, for which they received no financial compensation. Slave patrols stemmed from posses, but slaveholders added financial incentives in order to recapture slaves who had escaped slavery.[13]

This form of race-based domestic terrorism was legally reinforced in 1842 when, incredibly, the United States Supreme Court ruled in *Prigg v. Pennsylvania* that the Fugitive Slave Act of 1793 was constitutional. In that case, a slave named Margaret Morgan had escaped slavery in Maryland and fled to Pennsylvania, a state that had passed a statute in 1826 forbidding recapture of slaves. Edward Prigg had captured Morgan and pled guilty to kidnapping charges. The case was escalated to the Supreme Court, which ruled in Prigg's favor. Included in the court's decision was:

> The owner of a fugitive slave has the same right to seize and take him in a State to which he has escaped or fled that he had in the State from which he escaped, and it is well known that this right to seizure or recapture is universally acknowledged in all the

---

10. Hill Fletcher, *Sin*, 5.
11. Bales, *New Slavery*, 123–24.
12. Rein, "Mystery."
13. Rao, "Federal Posse," 10.

slaveholding States. The Court have not the slightest hesitation in holding that, under and in virtue of the Constitution, the owner of the slave is clothed with the authority in every State of the Union to seize and recapture his slave wherever he can do it without any breach of the peace or illegal violence.[14]

The reinforcement of chattel slavery by the ruling white men was clear and succinct. Black persons were not considered human. They were thought of as property to be owned. Similar to livestock, if escape happened, recapture by owners or other citizens was completely legal and encouraged.

After slavery was abolished in 1863, many southern states passed Black Codes in a successful effort to limit freedom for Black people. The laws made it illegal for Black persons to own land or work as independent farmers and made it legal for white persons to force a Black person into involuntary servitude. The codes legalized wage theft, kidnapping, and servitude of Black children, and a $100 "head tax" in some states. The codes varied between states, but all involved race-based domestic terrorism and dehumanizing of Black persons.[15]

Third, in 1866, a Confederate group was formed for veterans of the Civil War called the Ku Klux Klan. Formed in the early years of reconstruction in Pulaski, Tennessee, the group unified around their hatred for Black freedom. By 1868, the group had become well known. Its members "terrorized former slaves, raped women and attacked anyone too closely associated with the Republican Party and its political allies. They demanded that whites alone should govern the United States in general, and southern states in particular."[16] The group grew and morphed to oppose immigration, Mormons, the Catholic Church, all Jewish persons, and nonheterosexual persons. The Ku Klux Klan is perhaps the most well-known race-based domestic terrorist organization in the United States. Lynching of Black persons, which involves hanging a victim from a tree for simply existing, was committed and endorsed by the KKK. The practice of lynching peaked in the nineteenth century but has continued to the present day.[17]

After an Indiana KKK Grand Dragon named David Stephenson was found guilty of murder of a white woman, membership in the Klan fell

---

14. Prigg v. Pennsylvania, 41 U.S. 539 (1842), 40.
15. Middleton, "Repressive Legislation," 1.
16 Guard, "Origins," 13.
17. Bledsoe, "Silence Is Complicity."

sharply. The Klan still exists, however, and had a resurgence during the civil rights movement of the 1960s.[18]

Fourth, further in the nineteenth century, Jim Crow laws successfully enforced segregation of Black persons from the rest of society in multiple ways, but especially physically and regarding voting rights. Physical separation of Blacks and other races in public places was enforced, including in schools and on public transportation. Interracial marriages were outlawed.[19] The Ku Klux Klan experienced a resurgence in the 1920s, and Jim Crow laws and practices remained in place until the Civil Rights Act of 1964 and the Voting Rights Act of 1965.[20]

White Christians have created and sustained a system where white persons are the dominant race since the founding of our country.[21] Data comparing white evangelical Protestants (the types of churches Samson and Kelley attended) and white mainline Protestants (Roof's tradition of origin) vary little in either their historical or current experience with racism. For example, both evangelical and mainline Protestants have similar opinions regarding the appropriateness of Confederate flags and monuments (with between 70 percent and 85 percent finding them symbols of southern pride rather than of racism). Similarly, between 60 percent and 70 percent of both groups disagree with the statement that "generations of slavery and discrimination have created conditions that make it difficult for blacks to work their way out of the lower class."[22] Racism remains a deep, festering wound that crosses denominational boundaries in American Christianity.

ROOF AND SAMSON

Dylann Roof and Emanuel Samson both had the experience of being involved in a Christian church. Before each committed a mass shooting in a church, both expressed clearly the reasons for their actions, and in each of their minds, their reasons made sense. Racial animus was pervasive in both Roof's and Samson's religious/faith experiences but was neither recognized nor addressed in either shooter's faith or religious settings. Both shooters had goals and objectives in mind that they felt needed to be accomplished.

18. Guard, "Origins."
19. Clark, "Religion and Race," para. 32.
20. Jones, *White Too Long*, 191–92.
21. Feagin, *Systemic Racism*, 5.
22. Jones, *White Too Long*, 98.

Neither Roof nor Samson was rational, but both had drawn conclusions and wanted as many people as possible to know about those conclusions.

Prior to his murderous rampage, Roof wrote a manifesto outlining in detail (but without a spellchecker) his white supremacist views. After the shootings, Roof told investigators he had intended to start a race war. In this self-published manifesto, Roof stated his reasons plainly. In part, his statement includes: "I have no choice. I am not in the position to, alone, go into the ghetto and fight. I chose Charleston because it is the most historic city in my state, and at one time had the highest ratio of blacks to Whites in the country. We have no skinheads, no real KKK, no one doing anything but talking on the internet. Well someone has to have the bravery to take it to the real world, and I guess that has to be me" (appendix B).

Samson, in a note left on the dashboard of his vehicle during the shooting, explained that his goal was to retaliate against Roof's actions and to kill one more person than Roof had. The note said Roof was "less than nothing" and referenced vengeance (appendix A).

According to his own statements, Dylann Roof had decided to murder African Americans while they worshiped in church to resist racial integration and to avenge wrongs committed against white people—and chose Mother Emanuel as his target because of its national prominence as the first independent African American congregation in the South. Mother Emanuel comes from a history of being racially oppressed. As part of the African Methodist Episcopal Church (AME), they are a member of a denomination that originated during the anti-slavery movement predating the Civil War. The very Charleston church that Roof attacked started with a large percentage of its members being enslaved, and over time has had a long history of working for racial justice.[23]

After the shootings, Roof told investigators he intended to start a race war. Court documents explain the premeditation involved in the shooting, as well as the outcomes. In his police interview immediately after the shooting, Roof unequivocally explained why he chose Mother Emanuel Church. Spelling and grammatical issues are untouched, as this is the official court record.

> DR: You see what I'm saying? I thought about going to like a black festival or something like that but then you got security and stuff and you got to wait for the day, you know you can't do it whenever you're ready, so.

23. Frazier et al., *We Are Charleston*, xv.

CJ: So I'm, so we're understanding you correctly, you specifically, you did your homework obviously, cause you were quoting statistics earlier, you, you did research and you, you specifically chose and area where there would be all African Americans there, is that correct?

DR: Yes

MS: Are you, are you in any type of, of. Well earlier you made, and you mentioned like the Neo Nazis and . . .

DR: Yeah. . .

MS: . . . the KKK and the skinheads.

CJ: The skinheads.

DR: . . . yeah, well there are no skinheads. I wish they were but there aren't.

MS: Are you, so you're not into any. Are you in any groups like that?

DR: No

MS: I guess what I'm asking is do you have other associates or friends that are well, let me back up. Would you consider yourself a white supremacist? I know sometimes that's a, a but that the white people are superior.

DR: I consider myself a white nationalist . . .

MS: A white nationalist.

DR: . . . rather than a white supremacist.

MS: Okay

CJ: What's, what's, what's your definition of the two then? Because you said you're not a white supremacist, you're a white nationalist. What's, in your mind, what's the difference?

DR: Well no, but I all this I do consider myself a white supremacist, sure.

MS: You . . .

DR: White people are superior, if that's what you mean.

MS: Yeah, that's what I'm asking, right, you know, that, that, the white race is superior to all the other races, is what, and so you're . . .

The Racial Component

DR: No, no, no, I don't think there's like for example, you know you've got East Asian people, they've got higher IQ's than white people and I don't have a problem admitting that, it's just the facts.

MS: So you. So as white supremacist it's only to certain races?

DR: Right, well look, white people are superior to blacks or you know, Hispanics you know. But then you got white Hispanics, you know. There're Indians, you know, Arabs, South East Asians, you know. The only other races probably you know about equal to white people would be like East Asians, you know like Chinese, Japanese and Koreans, people like that.

CJ: But as a white supremacist do you still think that you're, do you still think the white race is superior to East Asians even though they have a higher I, you said the higher IQ than Caucasians?

DR: I think in general, yes, I mean because we've invented a lot more stuff than them. But they're good at they're good at improving on our inventions.

CJ: Sure, but in your mind, the white race is, is the dominant race?

DR: (laughs) No, I don't think the white race is the dominant race. I wish it was though. You know I think it should be.

MS: Do, do . . .

DR: That's the problem.

MS: Do you think, like, what you did last night, do you think that helps to, to maybe. Were you, I guess were you trying to start a revolution to where other people say, "hey, it's time to stand up," if everybody does this? You know what you, you understand what I'm saying?

DR: I'm not delusional, I don't think that you know, that something like what I did could start a race war or anything like that, you know, but.

MS: But I know would you like that? I mean, would that be. Would that help?

DR: Well a race war would be pretty terrible, you know.

MS: Yeah

DR: People dying all the time.

MS: Yeah, yeah it would.

DR: But you know I'd rather just, you know, just be able to like reinstate segregation or something like that, you know, without there having to be a race war. But, you know, I there probably will be a race war, eventually.

MS: But just segregation, correct, I mean is all?

DR: I mean that would be okay with me for right now but like I said, you know, that's, that's really unrealistic, you know. The black people just aren't going to allow themselves to be, to go back into segregation. Not that segregation was bad, you know, it wasn't, but.

CJ: How long have you um, how long have you felt this way? I mean did, I guess my question is were, was there ever a time where you?

DR: Right well I can tell you . . .

CJ: Yeah

DR: . . . the first thing that, I guess I would say, I would say that woke me up, you know, would be the Trayvon Martin case. You know, I mean that was a while back.

CJ: Right

DR: What was it two years ago? And you know, I'm, I'm, I kept hearing about this kid you know and I'm like, eventually I decided to you know look, look his name up, just type him into Google, you know what I'm saying? And then I read the Wikipedia article about Trayvon Martin, and I couldn't understand what the big deal was, you see what I'm saying? And then, for some reason after I read that, I, I, I typed in uh, for some reason it made me type in the, the words black on white crime and that's, that was it, every since then.

CJ: So prior to that you really didn't think too much about black and white relations or white and black relations?[24]

SUMMARY

When factors that contributed to racial violence are revealed, learned, and understood, subsequent actions should be taken. Upon googling the death of Trayvon Martin, the first results that Dylann Roof was shown were white supremacist organizations. This introduction ultimately resulted, at least in part, in his radicalization and the murders of nine innocent people as they exercised their right to worship freely.

24. United States Attorney's Office, "Full Dylann Roof Confession," 30:10–32:33.

The Racial Component

As much as people of faith hope and pray that their places of worship are safe from such tragedy, it is necessary for church congregations to address issues of race and white supremacy in their own communities of faith. Perhaps the precedent for these discussions could be Google's own response to Roof's research that utilized their platform. In a 2016 blog post, a product management director of search at Google posted that the search engine had changed the format of their algorithm to prevent such an event from occurring again.[25]

As of this writing in 2024, the teaching of critical race theory is being hotly debated. While this academic theory is primarily taught in law schools and graduate programs, the debate has extended to whether school children should learn the history that is outlined in the first two chapters of this book. Some Americans believe that not talking about racism is the same as treating everyone equally, and therefore the correct answer. Others recognize that without reconciling our past societal racism, change is not possible.

Whatever is decided in cultural circles, churches can forge their own way and, as Eboo Patel in *Acts of Faith*, Jurgen Moltmann in *Liberation in the Light of Hope*,[26] and A. R. Hilton in *A House United* posit, show the way for a society to recognize our issues and make positive change. White Christian churches are in a place of power in the United States and are uniquely positioned to facilitate that change. May it be so.

---

25. Yehoshua, "Google Search," para. 2.
26. Moltmann, *Liberation*, 413–29.

Chapter 12

Moving Forward: Recognition

THERE'S SOMETHING ABOUT TEENAGERS. I'm not a person with any sort of specialty in youth ministry, primary or secondary education, or anything to do with kids, really. My experience with people this age is largely academic with small bits of anecdotal evidence mixed in. My limited exposure to people in this demographic has taught me that there's a certain quality in many of them that I really admire. It seems that they're old enough to reason and contemplate, inexperienced enough to still be hopeful about the world, and young enough to lack some of the filters that adults tend to use in communication. A teenager seems, to me, to be more likely than an adult businessperson, for example, to just speak their mind, particularly if they know they're in a safe space and there won't be negative repercussions for doing so.

As research for this book, I spoke about mass shootings with countless adults, but also with groups of teenagers. If we're concerned with preventing mass shootings before they happen, young people will be a large part of our target audience, both as helpers and those who may need help. They're not our only audience, but leading people to find nonviolent resolutions to issues is vitally important. Part of finding those resolutions is recognizing when people exhibit warning signs for potential violence. Young people are inherently part of this conversation.

Dylann Roof was raised and confirmed in the Evangelical Lutheran Church in America (ELCA) and was twenty-one when he picked up guns and went to Mother Emanuel church. Emanuel Kidega Samson had been a regular attendee at the church he attacked; he was twenty-five years old when he shot people at Burnette Chapel. Devin Kelley had been active in Baptist churches and was twenty-six years old when he killed dozens at First Baptist Church. In all three situations, people who encountered each of these men recognized that they were dealing with a troubled person. What more could have been done before each attacked these churches?

Hopefully, when you picked up this book you were interested in (or quickly became interested in) helping the church and society move toward prevention of violence. But . . . why? Why should we focus on prevention rather than on outlawing guns or building stiffer security? It's because God has called us to care for the world, after all. It's because it's the right thing to do. This can save lives. The work is not easy, and it isn't instinctive. When we're startled or scared, the fight or flight instinct kicks in. Choosing to find out what we can do to be startled or scared less often takes intentionality.

It's difficult to learn what warning signs we should look for and what course of action we should take when we recognize red flags. We tend to be afraid to ask too many questions, and maybe one question is too many. It's also incredibly difficult to hear a person explain that they're considering harming others, particularly if that's a person we know, love, and trust—but we must. It is incumbent on us to watch and listen and interact with people rather than to hold them at a distance. The alternative is to shush people or to downplay what they're trying to communicate to us and to act as if it's not a real issue. When a person is angry enough to be violent, denying that the anger exists, or giving a "There, there, it'll be fine, take a few deep breaths"–type answer only serves to intensify their grievance and make them angrier.

One example of a time when pushing warning signs aside resulted in tragedy was the Marjory Stoneman Douglas High School shooting in Parkland, Florida. That shooter, Nikolas Cruz, had just been expelled from school and then came back to public school. He had transferred schools six times because of behavioral issues. After expulsion, he came back, killed seventeen, and injured seventeen. This is not a problem we can avoid, push away, or move to another locale.

Yes, God calls us to this task. There are some people, however, who may not be convinced to embark on this work because of God's desire for us to take care of each other. Personal stories may not sway them, and data may not be convincing. If none of that helps sway parishioners and church boards to take their focus off security and gun control and move that attention to preventative action, it may be time to remind them of the Crumbleys.

In March of 2024, James and Jennifer Crumbley became the first parents in the United States to be convicted of involuntary manslaughter when they ceased to act to prevent their son, Ethan, from committing a mass shooting. On November 30, 2021, Ethan, fifteen, killed four fellow students and injured seven (six students and one teacher) at Oxford High School in Oxford Township, Michigan. His parents not only purchased the weapon for him, but they also neglected to keep it properly stored. The court found that the Crumbleys ignored warning signs that, if heeded and addressed, could have prevented this tragedy. In April of 2024, both parents were sentenced to fifteen years in prison and are eligible for parole after ten years.

The presiding judge, Honorable Cheryl Matthews, said, "They [the parents] are not expected to be psychic. But these convictions are not about poor parenting. They concern acts that could have halted a runaway train. Opportunity knocked over and over again, louder and louder, and it was ignored." Judge Matthews's expanded sentence of ten to fifteen years was "to act as a deterrent" and reflected the parents' failure to stop the attack.

Fear of lawsuits and financial ruin are not why we should act preemptively. We should do it because it's the right thing to do. However, some people are motivated by finances, and the Crumbleys' story is real. Relating it could change the minds of even the most jaded in your church and help them understand the need to recognize likely problematic behavior.

WARNING SIGNS

After an incident of mass violence, have you heard the expression "he/she just snapped"? It's a common phrase that is used by citizens and law enforcement officials alike. The problem is that it doesn't work that way. In nearly all cases, there is not one event that sends a person into an instant rage that immediately culminates in a mass shooting. Warning signs almost always abound. For example, Broward County, Florida, Sheriff Scott Israel said his department had received twenty-three calls about Nikolas Cruz (mentioned above) in the decade prior to that shooting. Public records show that during that decade, forty-five calls were made to the Sheriff's Department about Cruz or his brother. The calls started when Nikolas was just nine years old. Law enforcement records show that the calls included domestic disturbances, a report of a mentally ill person, child/elderly abuse, missing person, fights involving Nikolas and his brother, and assault on his mother by Nikolas. There was ample warning that Nikolas's behavior was escalating.[1]

Countless researchers have studied violence and its causes and have determined that committing a murderous act starts with the idea that hurting or killing others exists as an option to fix a problem or correct a perceived wrong. Mass shooters nearly always feel like they have been mistreated or aggrieved in some way. They also nearly always display troubling behaviors, make threats, or otherwise give clues as to their potential actions. In a sense, they self-report, whether intentionally or not. It's not that those of us around them see and hear the clues but don't listen—it's that we don't want to hear. Many of us lean toward positivity and hope that a troubled person will work things out, or that enough time will pass that the person will find a better answer on their own. It's easier to walk away and hope for the best than it is to build relationships with potentially violent people. But in order to help them not commit a horrendous act, we can connect with them and help them find another way.

The Nebraska Emergency Management Agency and partners produced a program called Disrupting the Path to Violence. In that program, they explain that violence can be either reactive (in response to a perceived threat) or targeted (aimed at a particular person or group). Potential shooters with targeted goals are the most likely to give clues, hints, and warnings regarding their planned violence. The identified pathway to violence begins with a grievance. Thoughts about violence and justification for it follow, which leads to research, planning, and preparation of the event. Finally, the act itself is carried out.[2]

This is the exact path followed by Dylann Roof, Emanuel Samson, and Devin Kelley. All three had a grievance, then studied and plotted, made a plan, and followed through with their plan. At each step in this process, warning signs were evident. In particular, as Dylann Roof learned and developed his ideas about racism and the idea that Black persons were a threat to the country, he shared those ideas with others. He was not listened to by people who recognized the troubling signs. Rather, his comments were met with offense, so he quickly stopped discussing the issue.

---

1. Devine and Pagliery, "Sheriff Says," paras. 1–2.
2. Nebraska Emergency Management Agency et al., *Disrupting the Path*, 15.

Recognizing Warning Signs

Both the FBI and the Nebraska Emergency Management Agency's Disrupting the Violence program have lists of red flags to watch for in people capable of mass violence. The FBI's list focuses on youth. Studies from both organizations have shown that when a mass shooter communicates (in writing, verbally, etc.) their motives, they are likely to kill more people than a shooter who has not communicated motives. Dylann Roof, for example, had made racial comments to friends and documented his beliefs in both online and paper journals. Emanuel Samson had made social media posts.

Below is a combined list of warning signs from these two resources. Let's use this combined list and compare each potential warning sign to each of our shooters and see how many of the FBI's cautionary signs each shooter displayed. As shown, no shooter displayed every warning sign, but all three had most of the signs. Comparatively, there are twenty-eight signs listed here. Dylann Roof displayed at least sixteen of them, Emanuel Samson displayed at least twenty, and Devin Kelley displayed at least twenty-one of the warning signs.

WARNING SIGN	DYLANN ROOF	EMANUEL SAMSON	DEVIN KELLEY
Past violent or aggressive behavior	Yes	Yes	Yes
Increasing violent or aggressive behavior	Yes	Yes	Yes
Access to weapons	Yes	Yes	Yes
Bringing a weapon to school (or work)	?	?	Yes
Past suicide attempts or threats	No	Yes	Yes
Family history of violent behavior or suicide attempts	No	Yes	Yes
Blaming others and/or unwilling to accept responsibility for one's own actions	Yes	Yes	Yes
Hostile feelings about recent experience of humiliation, shame, loss or rejection	Yes	Yes	Yes
Bullying or intimidating peers or younger children	Yes	Yes	Yes
A pattern of threats	No	Yes	Yes
Being a victim of abuse or neglect	No	Yes	No
Witnessing abuse or violence in the home	No	Yes	No

WARNING SIGN	DYLANN ROOF	EMANUEL SAMSON	DEVIN KELLEY
Themes of death or depression repeatedly evident in conversation, written expressions, reading selections, or artwork	Yes	Yes	Yes
Preoccupation with themes and acts of violence in TV shows, movies, music, magazines, comics, books, video games, and internet sites	?	?	?
Distancing from friends and colleagues	Yes	No	No
Changes in work or school performance	?	Yes	Yes
Mental illness, such as depression, mania, psychosis, or bipolar disorder	Yes	Yes	Yes
Use of alcohol or drugs	Yes	Yes	Yes
Disciplinary problems at school or in the community	Yes	Yes	Yes
Past destruction of property or vandalism	No	Yes	Yes
Cruelty to animals	No	No	Yes
Setting fires	No	No	No
Poor peer relationships and/or social isolation	Yes	Yes	Yes
Involvement with cults, gangs, or other dangerous groups	Yes	?	No
Little or no supervision or support from parents or other caring adult	No	Yes	No
Internet searches for weapons, mass shootings, or extremist web sites	Yes	No	Yes
Social media posts that include weapons, threats, or views that endorse violence	Yes	Yes	Yes
Communication of motivations	Yes	Yes	Yes

THE PATH TO VIOLENCE

The Nebraska Emergency Management Agency (NEMA) worked to determine a general path that is followed on the way to mass violence. During each of these phases, warning signs usually arise. As the steps progress, so should the concern.

First is the grievance stage, which is the motive or reason behind the violence. In this stage, a person feels like someone, some group, or some other entity has wronged them in some way, and they want to do something about it. A person may speak to someone else about their issue. Social media posts, emails, letters, journals, and essays may be ways that the person vents these feelings.

The second stage involves thoughts about violence or justifying violence as a solution to a problem. In the potential perpetrator's mind, the idea that violence is the answer begins to take root. More subtle approaches may be sharing or reposting violent social media posts or frequently talking about groups or people that have a history of violence.

Third is the research and planning stage: planning how, when, and where the violence will happen. A person in this stage may spend a lot of time online learning about groups or causes that promote violent beliefs. They may spend an unusual amount of time online researching weapons, their prices, and how to obtain them. They may study when and how their target would be most vulnerable to attack. This research may be done online, in person, by phone, or through conversations with others. Any research into how to get around security systems or protective practices is cause for concern.

Fourth, the potentially violent person typically moves toward preparation, or taking steps to make the violence possible. Weapons and ammunition are obtained and stockpiled. All shooters profiled in this book used multiple weapons in their attacks. Often, a shooter will invest in tactical gear such as a bulletproof vest.

The final step is the carrying out of violent acts towards oneself and/or others.

The shooters highlighted earlier in this book followed these steps.[3]

- Dylann Roof put a great deal of research into what his target should be. He posted a manifesto online explaining his racist views and opinions about how violence was justified. He aligned himself with white supremacist groups. He chose his target, Mother Emanuel Church, and intentionally attacked a Bible study group.

- Emanuel Samson used guns he had been holding onto for a relative. He emailed a resignation letter to his employer before he attacked Burnette Chapel. Samson chose clothing with depictions of human targets. He left a note on his dashboard explaining his motives. His actions were deliberate and targeted a church he knew well. Knowing he would be recognized, he wore a mask.

---

3. Nebraska Emergency Management Agency et al., *Disrupting the Path*, 9–15.

- Devin Kelley researched guns even when ordered not to by the military. He voiced his thoughts of violence loudly to nearly anyone that would listen and often acted on those thoughts. Kelley purchased a gun a year, building up his own reserve of weapons. He posted about death on social media and posted photos of himself with a gun and called family members to say goodbye. He wore tactical-type gear.

DISCUSSION

To an adult, the FBI's red flags and NEMA's general path toward violent behavior might seem obvious. However, interviews with multiple teenagers showed that, almost universally, youth do not know what to recognize as a warning sign for potential violence. They're not ignoring the problem—it is very much an issue that's on their minds and is part of their everyday reality. Some of the students I spoke with attend schools that have active shooter drills. Annie, a sophomore, said she has a recurring dream about a school or church shooting. In the dream, she says, "I attack the shooter, and I beat him up, and I win." Students think about what they would do in a shooter situation. Annie continued, "First thing I would do is try to get out, but if I couldn't get out, then I would go hide in the drama closet because I've been in there before, and I was thinking to myself, and I was like, this would kind of be a good space to hide because no one would expect it." Violence is never far from the minds of students.

I asked the groups two specific questions:

1. What would you recognize as a red flag in a peer as a sign that they could be violent?
2. If you saw those signs in a person, what would you do?

In response to the first question, the answers were varied but still nebulous. Out of dozens of teenagers—not a scientific sampling, but still a broad range of age and experience—none could definitively say what would cause them alarm and point to potential violence.

Aaron, a high school junior, said he would be on the lookout for people who are easily angered and don't know "how to take a joke . . . too sensitive." He also said he watches out for people who are very shy and don't interact with others. Lyle, seventeen, said it's nothing he can put his finger on, but danger signs are "just a feeling."

Abigail, twelve, said, "Interactions of either isolation, the absence of all interactions, or particularly negative interactions. I'd probably have to think before anything what their home situation might be . . . How they interact with others and how they interact, their parents have interacted with them, how the people around them are, maybe in response to how they act. I do think you have to go a little bit beyond the stereotype of the quiet kid in the black hoodie or the trench coat or whatever."

Ben is a fourteen-year-old who had just completed middle school when interviewed. His uncommon perspective is that he has attended public school, a Catholic parochial school, and a military academy. At the academy, he had fellow students from many other countries, which changed his perspective somewhat. He realized that mass shootings are particularly a United States problem.

When he considered what he would see as red flags of potential violence in a fellow student, he thought that peers who had difficult home lives were more at risk, as well as those without many friends who may endure bullying. On the other hand, he knows plenty of kids who live in poverty or have incredibly difficult home lives, and "They're good kids." They do well in school and show no signs of wanting to hurt others.

Guy, an eighteen-year-old high school senior, said that what a peer mentions in conversation can matter. "I just think some kids have a disgruntled look in their eye. It's an attitude towards everything they do is they kind of push back. They don't always put the most effort into it, but there's always just a nonconformist kind of air to everything they do."

AFTER THE RECOGNITION

In response to the second question, "If you saw those signs in a person, what would you do?," there was nearly unanimous agreement that there was nothing to be done. The young people I spoke with came from varied backgrounds and experiences, but one thing they had in common was that if they did see what they perceived as troublesome behavior or warning signs for potential violence, they would do nothing. "There's nothing really you can do until it's too late, you know?" said Ben. "Unless they can put him in another home or I guess some kind of mental facility or something else, they can't do anything. You can't change a person. When the damage is done, the damage is done. It's like cracking an egg and putting it back together. You can't do that. Once the egg is cracked, it's cracked."

Moving Forward: Recognition

As Ben, who is particularly well spoken if not somewhat fatalistic, gave his ideas, other young people in the vicinity agreed. "The media makes it sound like there's so many ways to handle stuff like this and so many ways to make sure this doesn't happen. That's just not the reality in most situations. Like all the ads to prevent bullying or smoking, those don't do anything. They don't do anything because you can't stop people from doing awful things or doing things."

Common responses to this question included "Nothing," and "Try and be nice to them so I'm not on a list." Those answers received broad agreement. Every group I spoke with talked about a fellow student who had a list of names of some sort, but nothing ever came of it. They believe the vast majority of people with a "hit list," as one teen called it, are just trying to get attention and will never act on any threats made. Abigail thought that troubling behavior might be referred to a school counselor, but Guy is concerned about the lack of trained staff to recognize troubled youth. He said:

> I do know that our school has the people that are in charge of discipline. The kids that are in trouble all the time and getting disciplined all the time, there's no set standard by the school for anyone up high that they should be intervened with on a personal, face-to-face level. The two discipline workers at our school, they do talk to the kids on their lunch when they're eating with them, but that's just on their own merit. They don't do that because it's part of their job. So, I think if that was in place and if schools . . . If it's noticed a kid is slowly moving away from the herd and doing his own thing . . . or hers, I guess . . . and hardening up and getting bitter, no one has to ask what's wrong. They will if they think it's the right thing to do, but it's not part of the job.

An administrator at a high school explained that while resource officers, counselors, and other staff are in place to help teenagers, the trained professionals are stretched thin. Their time and resources are used on those who are unhoused, have food insecurities, and other issues. There is simply not the time or the hands on deck to handle potential problems while they're busy putting out fires for survival.

Youth aren't alone in not being entirely sure what to watch for, but they did have some more solidified ideas for recognizing potential violence in people. Rather than particular actions, adults tend to notice how people treat others. Bill has been a coach for various sports for decades and told a story about a time when a coach colleague recognized something "very dark" about one high schooler. "He had no moral ground. He had no feelings about regret, about how people should be treated, or about how he treated people. I remember that this kid would challenge both me and Coach Glen, but he knew we couldn't touch him. He would cuss us out and say, 'Go ahead and hit me!' I remember Coach Glen saying, 'He's a kid that will go into a school and shoot it up, or he will murder someone somewhere down the road, and it won't bother him a bit.'" Indeed, a few years later, this young man shot and killed two people and set their home on fire. It didn't bother him a bit.

Sometimes there are noticeable behaviors in people. Bill, a person of faith, believes that he recognizes those signs because the Holy Spirit helps him discern to be cautious and observant because something's not right.

When we hear what we think might be troubling and potentially violent ideas from a person, we should keep listening. We should listen in a nonjudgmental way for motives and targets. Thinking about hurting someone isn't a crime—this isn't the movie *Minority Report,* in which people were arrested and convicted before they committed a crime because technology showed that they *might* commit a crime.[4] Thoughts, when vocalized, should be heard so that we can help. From a Christian perspective, church should be the safe place where a potentially violent person can recognize that they have a problem and come seek help.

---

4. Spielberg, *Minority Report.*

Chapter 13

Taking Action Before Trouble Happens

MY POINT IN THIS book is this: there is good—no, great—news: we can do this! Finally, we can move beyond theory and data and examples. We, as churches and as people of faith, can move away from the mentality of hiding from shooters and shift to a mindset of healing and hope. The church—much as it's done throughout history—can lead to change both in churches and in society. If we were to sum up the answer to the "How can we help?" question, it would be one word: relationships.

As Christians, one of our goals is to not only follow Jesus but also think and act like Jesus (Phil 2:5–11). Jesus flipped the script that we tend to use. He didn't hide from those who wished him harm, and he didn't try to take away their implements of harm. Instead, he reached out to troubled people and built relationships with those who needed him. The lives of those with whom he connected were improved every time.

Avoidance is not a tactic that will work. It won't help if we just recognize warning signs and then shun the person or shuffle them off somewhere else in the hope of solving the problem. This is a strategy that's been used for eons: if a person is problematic, send them elsewhere. The excuse is that perhaps a new environment will fix the person's issues, but the environment is rarely the problem. Recoiling from potentially violent people does not make the people feel less violent.

Another tactic that won't work is talking at people. A lecture from an authority is unlikely to help a person who is on the verge of acting out their violence. Consider your own experience with people who want to talk to you and convince you of something. Have you noticed that people who want to share their beliefs with you rarely ask you to share your religious beliefs with them? Conversations that go in at least two directions are more useful and long lasting than one-way screeds. How can we know what a person is going through unless they tell us? Until we learn to hear, we've not earned the right to be heard, no matter what our message is.

The answers are not simple. Catastrophes quickly get our attention and cause us to want to react even more quickly. Working towards the start of a real solution, however, isn't quick or exciting. It's hard, serious work. But as Dr. Martin Luther King Jr. famously said, "The arc of the moral universe is long, but it bends toward justice." The following proactive, rather than reactive, resources are for use in your church or organization.

The concepts of violence prevention must be woven into the fabric of everything a church does, rather than offering a one-off seminar or class and only mentioning the topic annually. This chapter offers actionable ideas—all based on relationships, both with God and one another—to help churches first to take a proactive approach and, second, to recognize potential issues and mitigate violence.

MENTORSHIPS

A proven solution has been relationships and connections. No person was ever created to be in isolation. Through authentic connections, we make each other better. When we work together, pray together, serve together, and ask God's guidance as we keep moving forward, God will lead us. What we do together matters, and whatever we're doing, if we go to God first, we'll hear the voice of God. Together, we move closer to what God intended humanity to be. Together, we hear the Holy Spirit better. Together, we know by what power we do this: in the name of Jesus.

The God who created us in God's own image and, somehow, loves us all, wants us to love one another. The Son who came into the world not to condemn it, but to bring healing and salvation, wants us to help those of us who are in the direst straits. And the Holy Spirit, who inspires and challenges us, can spur us along this path. That is a power that cannot be thwarted.

The Christian church is in a uniquely advantageous position to do great anti-violence work both in the church and in society. We can also learn much, though, from entities outside of church that are working towards similar goals. Christianity is not alone in its desire to use its position in the world for the goal of nonviolence. Schools are institutions that spend more time with young people than virtually any other organization. Educators are in contact with students more hours per day than anyone else, apart from parents or guardians. Some schools and community organizations have worked together, recognizing the need for mentorships for students. These efforts are building strong, positive, life-changing connections with great success.

Example 1: Children and Youth in Church

Children and youth are not the future of the church; they are the present of the church. If you are blessed to have students in your congregation, the church is as much theirs as it is a person's of any other age. When we relegate church participation to children's church, youth groups, or an annual "youth Sunday," we tell young people that they're on a different level than adults in God's estimation. What we know to be true from Scripture, though, is the opposite. "Jesus said, 'Let the little children come to me, and do not hinder them, for the kingdom of heaven belongs to such as these'" (Matt 19:14). Jesus didn't say to silo the children off by themselves. He didn't say if they keep coming to Sunday school and worship services they can inherit the kingdom of heaven. Jesus said the kingdom of heaven is already theirs, and to bring the children to him. This suggests mentorship: children pairing with trusted adults to bring them closer to him.

Consider the committees or groups that exist in your church and whether a child or teenager could possibly be involved. My own church has adopted a practice of having a child or youth greeter each Sunday so that if a young visitor comes, they are greeted by another young person. That greeter also serves as an usher (always with an adult mentor), helping to collect the offering and then bring it forward for a blessing. In my experience, there are few things that make joy spread across the faces of a congregation than a child assisting in worship.

Children can also be involved in worship teams, Scripture reading, prayers, or multiple other ways, depending on your tradition's practices. In one church, a nine-year-old happened by the room where the designated people were counting the offering, and they asked her if she'd like to help. She agreed and was given the task of counting envelopes for the special mission offering that was collected that day. She wasn't privy to how much any one person or family gave and didn't have access to financial spreadsheets. Rather, she just counted envelopes. She's invested now, though, and cares more about how the offering works than she ever did before. The involvement of children in church, especially when visible in worship, is a delight for adults and reminds the younger person that this is their church too. If a person invests in their church at an early age, that investment in involvement in a faith community can last a lifetime.

Example 2: Bible Buddy Program

First Presbyterian Church in Mexico, Missouri, has a robust program that connects adults and children who are not related to one another. The initiative has been successful, is heavily used, and has resulted in long-term relationships between children and their mentors.

The program began when the church's Children's Committee discerned that children should learn and understand certain fundamentals of the faith by certain ages. Each child is paired with an adult by the child's family with help from the Children's Committee. All volunteers pass appropriate child protection training and background checks. The child and their adult buddy meet together once a week, typically after worship, but other times can be arranged that are convenient for all participants. Again, all child protection policies are followed, and an adult is never alone with a child.

Each time a "benchmark" is achieved—that is, assigned tasks are completed—the child gets a star on a chart. When a grade level is completed, the child receives a framed certificate, and the child and their buddy take part in the twice-a-year Bible Buddy presentations that occur during the church's worship services. The young person's accomplishment is celebrated, and the community of faith is drawn closer. The congregation is reminded of the existence of the program, leading both new children and adults to become involved.

Recognizing that children learn at different paces and that children come from a wide variety of religious experiences, the program is easily adaptable for each child. For example, one child didn't enter the program until third grade. Her family could have opted to start her with third-grade benchmarks, but instead, they decided to back up to the prekindergarten benchmarks. The girl attends a parochial school and has strong religious training at home, so she quickly worked her way through the earlier grade levels and caught up to her current grade.

Each grade level contains seven categories of education: memorization, Bible skills, prayer, worship, sanctuary, Presbyterian identity, and service. This variety of topics helps children understand what we do, why we do it, and how to practically put our faith into action. The goals at each level are age appropriate. Any faith tradition could easily adapt this for its own use. The program has two valuable benefits: the child gets valuable religious education, and they develop a long-term relationship with a mentor who is a positive influence. The following are the educational benchmarks for each level.

Educational Benchmarks

Prekindergarten

1. Memorization: The names of the four Gospels
2. Bible Skills: Find the four Gospels in the Bible
3. Prayer: Be able to answer the question "What is prayer?"
4. Worship: Learn the worship songs "Gloria Patri" and "Doxology"
5. Sanctuary: Identify and know the purpose of the pews, Bibles, hymnals, worship bags, offering plates
6. Presbyterian Identity: Know we are First Presbyterian Church
7. Service: Learn ways to treat people and place of worship with respect and love

Kindergarten

1. Memorization: The Lord's Prayer
2. Bible Skills: Find the Lord's Prayer in the Bible
3. Prayer: Understand the Lord's Prayer
4. Worship: Identify and know the purpose in worship of the Lord's Prayer and Children's Time
5. Sanctuary: Identify and know the purpose of the lectern, pulpit, and front steps

6. Presbyterian Identity: Identify leaders at church—pastor, elders, deacons, teachers
7. Service: Learn the names of everyone in your Sunday school class and at the Children's Time; learn what it means to treat one another with respect

First Grade

1. Memorization: Recite five Bible verses and where they are found
2. Bible Skills: Find the five verses in the Bible, learn the context and meaning
3. Prayer: Understand and participate in Prayers of Thanksgiving in worship and in personal prayer
4. Worship: Identify in the worship bulletin the various unison prayers and know their purpose
5. Sanctuary: Identify and understand the purpose of the narthex, front porch, bathroom, and six exits
6. Presbyterian Identity: Understand the concepts of love God, love neighbor, love yourself
7. Service: Send cards to people who do good things—parents, teachers, neighbors

Second Grade

1. Memorization: Recite the Ten Commandments
2. Bible Skills: Find the Ten Commandments in the Bible, learn the context and meaning
3. Prayer: Understand and participate in Prayers of Intercession in worship and in personal prayer
4. Worship: Identify in worship the Cares & Concerns and Passing of the Peace and know their purpose
5. Sanctuary: Identify and understand the purpose of the sanctuary windows, lights, cross, and flowers
6. Presbyterian Identity: Understand the symbols of cross, Presbyterian seal, cup/grapes and bread/wheat

Taking Action Before Trouble Happens

7. Service: Send cards to people on Cares & Concerns and others they know in need

Third Grade

1. Memorization: Recite Psalm 100
2. Bible Skills: Find Psalm 100 in the Bible, learn the context and meaning
3. Prayer: Understand and participate in Prayers of Adoration in worship and in personal prayer
4. Worship: Identify in worship the hymns, songs, and anthems and know their purpose
5. Sanctuary: Identify and understand the purpose of the choir loft, organ/piano, musical instruments, sound system, and balcony
6. Presbyterian Identity: Understand the emphasis and interaction of Scriptures, preaching, and praying
7. Service: Share in the worship by singing, reading, and passing the offering plates (as a participant in the pews, as well as being a leader in worship)

Fourth Grade

1. Memorization: The twelve disciples, their calls, and their occupations
2. Bible Skills: Learn the overview of the New Testament and be able to recite the names of the books of the New Testament
3. Prayer: Understand and participate in Prayers of Confession in worship and in personal prayer
4. Worship: Identify in worship the sacraments of baptism and the Lord's Supper and know their purpose
5. Sanctuary: Identify and understand the purpose of the table and font
6. Presbyterian Identity: Understand the concept of calling—as pastors/elders/deacons/teachers/committee members/congregational members. Understand the words "session" and "board of deacons."
7. Service: Understand the concept of care for the Earth. Participate in bringing used gallon milk jugs, plastic bags, and beverage cans to recycle at church.

Fifth Grade

1. Memorization: The major and minor prophets
2. Bible Skills: Learn the overview of the Old Testament and be able to recite the names of the books of the Old Testament
3. Prayer: Learn about the importance of prayer from Paul's letters
4. Worship: Identify the church seasons and holidays
5. Sanctuary: Identify and understand the purpose of seasonal colors, paraments, banners, stoles
6. Presbyterian Identity: Understand the concept of connections—to other Presbyterians, other churches, and other faiths
7. Service: Learn all the missions our church supports; go with your parents to see what one of our missions looks like; do one thing to help that mission.

Example 3: The Lunch Buddy Program

Dr. Sarah Gooch understands connections and their value. She has taught in the Missouri public school system for thirteen years. She is involved in an umbrella of an organization called Bright Futures, and one of that organization's programs is called Lunch Buddies. In concert with an advisory board, community members, school leadership, the local chamber of commerce, parents, and guardians, Gooch leads this mentoring program. Enduring, high-quality, and effective mentoring experiences are associated with more school engagement, a greater tendency for youth to view their futures positively, and higher academic achievement, so this program is incredibly valuable.[1]

After noticing a large percentage of students who lacked a home support system, Bright Futures launched the Lunch Buddy program for elementary, middle, and high school students. The program enables responsible adults in the community to make relationship connections with students who may need an adult in their life to help encourage and support them in their educational, emotional, social, and employment journey. It's a simple model: an adult from the community, always prescreened and intentionally matched with a child or teenager, is paired with a student and

---

1. Gooch, "Recommendations to Solve," 13.

they have lunch together once a month. High school cadets at the local military academy have also served as mentors for children in kindergarten through fifth grade. If the cadets became lunch buddies for high schoolers, the dynamic would be changed to a peer mentoring program.[2]

Typically, at-risk and underserved students with academic and social needs are chosen to participate in the program. Similar mentoring programs have had success attracting mentees through social media advertisement channels and mailing lists. Diversity committees engage in recruitment and retention of racially and ethnically minoritized students through improved program climate by valuing and respecting diversity.

Before matching a mentor and mentee, both mentors and mentees complete an application process to determine their appropriateness for the program and to help pair them with an optimal partner. This process involves a criminal history check for the mentor and a volunteer interest assessment form. The matches must be made by a human rather than a software program.

Training of the mentors is important in the program. Trained mentors tend to achieve better results with their mentees than their untrained peers, and trained mentors show better retention in the program. In the Lunch Buddy system, mentors and mentees sign a contract that outlines decision-making (who will decide what activity they do), time commitment expectations, and goals for the relationship between the Lunch Buddy and the student. These factors help both parties maintain a focus in their lunch meetings.

The Lunch Buddy program has not always had smooth sailing. Program organizers have found it more difficult to enlist mentors for high school students. Funding the program and training for mentors can be problematic. Also, as children grow, their needs change, and they may find a need for a different mentor with new areas of expertise than the one who served them well in their earlier years.

On the other hand, success stories from the program are plentiful. Susan, a long-time lunch buddy, posts social media updates each week after she meets with her young friends. She's been posting since at least 2016, and the stories are refreshing, fun, and inspiring. Her insights also show the dire need for adult mentors. Her Facebook post from March 14, 2017, is shared here with permission.

2. Gooch, "Recommendations to Solve," 12.

Lunch Buddy Report, Star Date: Pi Day, 2017.

Today was taco salad day. It was cold outside so recess was inside. We had a talkative table today. One girl had to go to the dentist today, so that had everyone talking. Besides that girl and me, no one had ever been to the dentist! What the what? Nope. Never been. We discussed how important that was and that maybe the dentist would come to the Back To School Fair. No one had ever heard of the Back To School Fair. Nope. Never been. What the what? Then we started talking about that one girl's brother is getting married. So it came up that no one had ever been to church. I must admit that I am not a big fan of the institutional church, but I am thankful that my mom took us every Sunday and exposed us to the option of spirituality. I have relied on my faith and its expression ever since. I cannot imagine not having that solace and source of support throughout my life. I encouraged them to find a church home whatever faith they followed. So there you have it. More needs that require attention. So maybe you are not a lunch buddy, but you are a dentist. Maybe you are not a pastor, but you could help with the Back To School Fair. You are so running out of excuses with me.

On a lighter note, because my posts have gotten a little preachy... I did make a mess by spilling my salad. We did have a laugh when that one girl said she was going to be in a wedding and the bride's colors were white and brown. (Nobody does that.) The other girl is getting to wear white and purple at that wedding.

This type of in-school support system works. Mentoring has been shown to increase not only academic achievement but also involvement by students and a tendency for youth to see their futures in a more positive way.[3] Social needs are met through the program, and negative outcomes decrease.[4]

CURRICULUM

Educational materials for diverse cultures to live together in peace exist in abundance. Christian bookstores and online retailers can help you find a fit for your context. However, the need for churches to invest and actively engage in specifically anti-violence discussions, classes, and activities

3. Beltman et al., "I Really Enjoy."
4. Mentor, "Mentoring Impact."

is evidenced by the increase in violence over the past few decades. Some resources exist, but there is room for much more.[5] Christians of all ages can learn about violence prevention in their church and in our country and can be involved in recreating a new theology with an anti-violence approach.

Further, more curriculum that specifically addresses violence related to supremacy issues is needed. Dylann Roof hated persons in many groups, not just African Americans. Roof did not learn the fallacy of these ways of thinking in church. Before curriculum can be created, however, training and educating of curriculum writers need to take place. Before writing the curriculum, the authors must be aware of the history of violence in our country and its past and current effects, as well as the role Christian churches have played. Without an understanding of both the historical and current implications of Christianity's role in violence in the United States, the curriculum will inevitably fail to effectively address the issue.

Appendix G contains the outline of a curriculum titled *Unity in Conflict*. The course includes the structure of a six-week or six-session course that can be taught in your church. Since church and other worship contexts vary greatly, it is a highly adaptable course, open for interpretation based on context by the leader. Books are recommended to accompany the course. The goal is to teach people how to avoid violence by addressing conflicts and grievances in productive ways.

SERMON OUTLINES

Preaching about nonviolence is the least interactive of the suggestions listed here. In the moment that it is delivered, a sermon usually does not allow for questions or discussion. However, those of us called to preach are called to preach all of the word of God and to apply those principles to our current lives. We are called to be united as one. Jesus calls us to love people, not to shun people.

While the concept of loving our enemies seems easy enough to preach in theory, the reality is that the preacher is likely to get pushback from his or her congregation. I've heard comments such as "That's all well and good, pastor, until your enemy has pushed you too far. Then we'll see how much you love your enemy." There is no New Testament Scripture that calls us to violence, though, in any situation. Instead, Jesus repeatedly encourages

---

5. See https://nationalcouncilofchurches.us/anti-racism-resources/.

peace. Below are some sermon outlines that may spur you to occasionally, or even regularly, preach about nonviolence.

Sermon Outline 1: Loved People Love People (Rev. Micah McNeal)

"Fathers, do not embitter your children, or they will become discouraged" (Col 3:21).

This is an outline for a sermon that tightly focuses on the importance of parents practicing their faith in the home. The church can say to love and care for others, but the support starts at home. One thing I say a lot as someone working in student ministry is that we do not know what goes on behind the closed doors of a child's home. While a pastor cannot dictate to their parishioners how they are to treat their children it is important that it is talked about.

1. The Context:

    12 Therefore, as God's chosen people, holy and dearly loved, clothe yourselves with compassion, kindness, humility, gentleness and patience. 13 Bear with each other and forgive one another if any of you has a grievance against someone. Forgive as the Lord forgave you. 14 And over all these virtues put on love, which binds them all together in perfect unity. 15 Let the peace of Christ rule in your hearts, since as members of one body you were called to peace. And be thankful. 16 Let the message of Christ dwell among you richly as you teach and admonish one another with all wisdom through psalms, hymns, and songs from the Spirit, singing to God with gratitude in your hearts. 17 And whatever you do, whether in word or deed, do it all in the name of the Lord Jesus, giving thanks to God the Father through him. (Col 3:12–17)

    a. A call to harmonious living

        i. Summed up: "And over all these virtues put on love, which binds them all together in perfect unity" (Col 3:14)

2. The Verse

    a. A word to those in relationship to others

        i. A parent who should love their children

    b. A word to those in control of others

Taking Action Before Trouble Happens

        i. A parent who directs their children where they should go

    c. "Start children off on the way they should go, and even when they are old they will not turn from it" (Prov 22:6)

3. The Command

    a. Do not provoke your children

        i. Children need love, care, compassion, and support

        ii. Treating children harshly does not equal perfect children, it can create perfect shells

    b. Encourage Children

        i. In order for them not to lose heart, encouragement is not just important. It is necessary.

        ii. Encouragement and support do not create weak children. They create loved children

Loved People Love People.

Sermon Outline 2: Nonviolence: It's Not Just a Good Idea, It's a Commandment

Key Text: "You shall not murder" (Deut 5:17).

Introduction: Most people know at least a few of the commandments, but this one, the sixth commandment, is arguably the most well known.

1. To talk about murder, we should first talk about what murder is not

    A. Self-defense

    B. Defense of others

2. Then we can talk about what murder is

    A. The unjust taking of another person's life

3. God is the God of life

    A. All life is authored by God

        i. Nothing that is alive chose to be; it is alive because God instilled it with life

  ii. Parents take action and the result is a baby, but none of us make fingers and toes appear in the right place or cause lungs and heart to operate in a way that brings life

 B. First John 2:6 is one of many Scriptures that say we should walk in the same way that God walks: "Whoever claims to live in him must live as Jesus did."

 C. It logically follows, then, that we should work to preserve, protect, and promote life

4. People are made in God's image

 A. Injuring others causes injury to God

 B. We are created to reflect God, to be God's image

 C. "All people were knit together in their mothers' wombs, and are fearfully and wonderfully made" (Ps 139:14)

5. All life has a purpose

 A. The Lord works out everything to its proper end—even the wicked for a day of disaster" (Prov 16:4)

 B. When we stop a life, we stop God's purpose for it from happening

Summary: All of God's creation is beautiful, but life is the most incredible. We are to uphold it at every opportunity.

Useful quotation: "We are accordingly commanded, if we find anything of use to us in saving our neighbors' lives, faithfully to employ it; if there is anything that makes for their peace, to see to it; if anything harmful, to ward it off; if they are in any danger, to lend a helping hand."[6]

Notes: This sermon may include a discussion of the Hebrew text and an explanation of the difference between the KJV "Thou shalt not kill" and other interpretations that translate the Hebrew as "murder."

Depending on your theological context, just war may not be considered murder. There is also a discussion to be had about whether capital punishment is murder.

---

6 John Calvin, *Institutes of the Christian Religion*, as quoted in Tallman, "You Shall Not Murder," para. 4.

Sermon Outline 3: Fruit That Works Together

Key Text: "But the fruit of the Spirit is love, joy, peace, forbearance, kindness, goodness, faithfulness, gentleness and self-control. Against such things there is no law" (Gal 5:22–23).

Introduction: The different iterations and understandings of "longsuffering" (KJV), "forbearance" (NIV), and "patience" (NRSV).

Example: In modern American English dialects, "longsuffering" might bring to mind something like a person whose spouse is embarrassing in public, but they deal with it silently for years with grace and in silence. "Forbearance" might refer to the longsuffering spouse showing restraint and not commenting on their partner's behavior. "Patience" could mean that the longsuffering spouse is able to show forbearance by accepting their partner's behavior.

1. This is not the "waiting in bad traffic" type of patience. This is a deeper, longer-range type of patience. It goes beyond the immediate moment and thinks about the bigger picture.

2. This is the type of patience of someone who is horribly wronged. Someone has sinned against them in an incredibly awful way. This person would have the right, the reason, and the understanding of their peers and probably governing authorities if they chose to take vengeance and justice into their own hands. Instead, though, this wronged person chooses not to act on their hurt. That's the type of patience listed in the fruit of the Spirit.

3. When one part of the fruit of the Spirit is exhibited, the others flow from it. When that type of patience is shown, there is love, there is joy. Peace in relationships begins to happen. Kindness, goodness, faithfulness, gentleness, and, especially for the purposes of the topic of nonviolence, self-control are all produced.

4. When someone is horribly wronged, it's very human to want revenge. We want the person who harmed us (or someone we love) to feel the pain we felt. The fruit of the Spirit takes us in another direction.

5. Don't let revenge be the default. Instead, default to the law of love. Instead of taking the course of revenge, follow the course of God's love for the world.

6. The Spirit is already at work in the world. Just pay attention and follow.

Useful quotation: As Craig Blomberg says, "The true test of genuine Christianity is how believers treat those whom they are naturally inclined to hate or who mistreated or persecuted them."[7] Patience doesn't come naturally to most of us, but through prayer and discipline, it is a skill we can develop.

PRAYERS

Perhaps the thing we can agree on the most readily is that we are in a situation that needs prayer—fervent, honest, continual prayer. Below are some prayers written by people of faith from varying denominations, religious experiences, vocations, cultural backgrounds, and ages. They were all written specifically for this project, to assist in your study or worship planning.

Prayer of Lament

Dear God,

I can no longer keep track of all the shootings. In a school, in a club, at a concert, in a church, in a synagogue.

I feel like I should grieve each one equally, or perhaps in proportion to the number of people killed, or maybe there is a complex formula that takes into account the number of children, or the square root of the total seconds spent in abject terror. I do not know how to grieve so many.

Somehow, proximity matters. The shootings in my own city leave me hollow inside. But then again, the shootings in cities where I have friends or family are also terrifying. And sometimes when reports arrive from a town I've never heard of, I look at a map and realize I once spent a weekend in the same county, and familiarity of the terrain makes the event more heart wrenching.

My children were in elementary school when the shooting at Sandy Hook happened. I was teaching in a college classroom when one of the undergraduates noted there were thirty-two people present, the same number who had been killed the day before at Virginia Tech. I, too, have smiled to the unknown visitor in Bible study, gesturing toward an empty seat.

The unfathomable calculus of grief makes palpable the connections between each of us.

---

7. Blomberg, *Matthew*, 114–15.

To survive the weekly, sometimes daily, death tolls, I pretend the invisible spider web strands that weave each of us together are not real. Otherwise the grief would bury me.

This, too, is violence. A denial of our interwoven humanity.

God, I do not know how to grieve so many.

Amen.

—Rev. Dr. Shannon Craigo-Snell

Prayers for the Church

Father,
>Quiet us in this moment.
>Slow our breathing... slow our hearts.
>Bring us to hear Your still, small voice.
>And in that, remind us of all
>You have taught us with gentleness.
>Vengeance is Yours, Lord, not ours.
>You know what perfect justice is.

Liberate us from the chains of anger, fear, and hatred that hold us back from finding relationships forged in peace and the hope for a better world, country, city, neighborhood, house... a better us.

Bless us with the ability to bring Your Word and Your wisdom into every problem in our lives,
>and encourage others to do the same—
>To see Your kingdom ever before us:
>built in gentleness, endurance, faith, and love.
>This we ask in Your Holy Name... Amen.

—Rev. Harry "Max" Hazell II, CHC, USN

Mighty and Gentle God,

Help us to see that You have called us to also be the same: mighty and gentle. Help us create the church to be a place where people can be safe and secure. If we have a place called a sanctuary, we should probably be that. Help us to work with a confidence that builds sanctuary, not just within our churches, but to also go beyond the church walls and show others that your presence is a sanctuary. A place that does not tolerate violence, that makes sure the vulnerable are cared for, that speaks life and hope into the hearts of people who feel they have none.

At the same time, let us be graceful. Help us to remember that fear and anger and pain lead people to speak and act in ways that they normally wouldn't. Let our words be courageous but gentle, powerful but humble, words that confront evil and show tender mercy, both corrective and graceful.

Help us meet people exactly where they are and then love them way too much to let them stay that way. You know, just like you have done for us.

Amen.

—Rev. Zane Whorton

Prayers for Those Considering Violence

Oh God to Whom is known all the secrets of our hearts, we grieve that bloodshed is even a possibility in the world that You created and called "very good." Even so, from Adam and Eve's children spun a never-ending cycle of violence begetting more violence. As we deplore these wicked actions we remember that Christ Himself was a victim of extreme violence. Yet in the midst of His suffering He still held compassion for those who killed Him.

In the example of our Lord we pray for those who feel that the only option left for them is a path of destruction. Still their hands from taking the life of another, oh God, that they may not be burdened with the weight of wielding death as a weapon. Open their eyes that they may see and understand that all people, including themselves, are Your beloved children. Guide their steps, that they may walk in ways that build up their community, rather than destroying it.

Lord, we have no way of knowing how even our smallest of actions might impact another's life. May all that we say and do remind the people around us that they are loved and valued beyond measure. May we be the spark of hope that soothes an angry soul.

We pray all these things in the Name of Jesus Christ, our wounded and risen Lord.

Amen.

—Rev. Sarah Dierker

Holy God,
    Something's up.

You know that, of course. You know all of your children, and you know what is on our hearts before we can even admit it to ourselves. I'm admitting now that I need help.

Someone I care about is in turmoil, God, and I don't know what to do. Someone is struggling. They're on a path I don't understand, and I'm afraid about where it's leading.

I don't want them to be hurting, but they are.

I don't want them to hurt others, but they might.

I don't know how to fix things, but I don't have to know everything. You do.

You are with me, God. You don't leave us, even when we're feeling lost, and I am feeling lost now. Center me in your presence and ground me in your truth.

Almighty God, help me with the courage I need to start hard conversations. Give me the patience and compassion to listen. May I find resources and community to help bridge the gap between this person and a good future. I lift their name up to you, asking for your help and mercy . . .

Loving God, spur me into action. May I work to protect others and care for all of your people. I'm asking you these things because I know we all need you, and I know you are with us. Thank you for your ever-present love and the hope of your transforming grace. Amen.

—Rev. Katie Styrt

Prayers for Those Who Want to Help

Jesus,
I am doing my best.
I see me for who I am, as You see me too.
I struggle. I feel lost. I feel broken.
And I struggle my way through what feels like a lost and broken world, seeking You.
Jesus,
I know You can fix this, because You know, like I do, it wasn't always this way.
Give me the gift of Your presence, and the presence of Your children in this church.

Remind us constantly that no one is meant to feel an outcast in this family,
for we are all one in You.
Through this, lighten my load with the help that this body can give.
Ease my struggle, put me on right paths, and heal my brokenness.
Renew me, Jesus, and strengthen me—
So, when I see one who has struggled like me, I know how to help.
Help me be the bearer of Your light by giving this body and all Your Church,
that healing.
This I pray, Jesus. Amen.

—Rev. Harry "Max" Hazell II, CHC, USN

You know, God,
Loving others is hard. Thanks for calling us to do it anyway.
Amen.

—Rev. Zane Whorton

God,
You called us to live a life of Hope, Love, Joy, Peace, Grace, and Change.
Help us remember that fear and anger are not listed there.
Amen.

—Rev. Zane Whorton

Prayers to Be Prayed by Those Considering Violence

Heavenly Father, thank You for the privilege of entering Your throne room today. I come before You with a heavy heart, seeking guidance and strength in this challenging time. I ask for clarity and calmness to fill my mind and heart. Please help me see the value of every life and respect all beings' inherent worth and dignity. Please grant me the wisdom to understand that violence produces only more violence, and that true strength lies in compassion and forgiveness. I pray for healing and transformation within myself, that love may replace any anger or aggression. May I learn to resolve conflicts peacefully and to communicate with kindness and understanding. Father, guide me to address my inner struggles and external challenges peacefully. Please help me find healthy outlets for my emotions and seek support from those who can help me navigate this journey. In Jesus's name, Amen.

—Pastor Rich Neeley

Heavenly Father, thank You for the privilege of entering Your throne room today. I come before You with humility and a heavy heart, seeking Your guidance and grace in my inner turmoil. I acknowledge the darkness within me and the violent impulses that stir my spirit. I ask for your divine intervention to calm the storm raging within me, to soothe the anger and aggression that threaten to consume me. Father, help me see the humanity in others, even in moments of intense emotion. Please grant me the strength to resist the urge for violence, to choose compassion and understanding over hatred and harm. Please fill me with the wisdom to recognize the consequences of my actions and the courage to seek peaceful resolutions instead.

Father, may your light illuminate the path toward healing and transformation within me. Please guide me to resources and support to help me confront and overcome these destructive impulses. I pray for forgiveness for any harm I might have caused. In Jesus's name, Amen.

—Pastor Rich Neeley

Heavenly Father, thank You for the privilege of entering Your throne room today. Father, I'm struggling with a deep anger and lingering hatred toward those who have caused me so much pain and abuse. The weight of this anger feels overwhelming at times, and I feel like I'm on the brink of losing control. Despite my efforts, I haven't been able to tame this anger. It's clear that I need to address the root of this issue. Father, I humbly ask for Your help. I understand that the only way to confront my anger is by redirecting my heart and thoughts towards You. You carried the burden of all my sins, anger, and resentment. I also realize that true forgiveness towards those who have hurt me is essential. Father, please guide me to imitate Your words on the cross, "Father, forgive them," and keep my focus on you. I confess my anger and ask for your forgiveness. In Jesus's name, Amen.

—Pastor Rich Neeley

OPPORTUNITIES FOR FUTURE STUDY

Current literature explains the problems and hopes for the future, but there is a lack of literature that compares the distinctives and commonalities regarding faith and religious experience of mass shooters in general, and specifically church shooters. Although most sources recognize the problem of both racism and violence within ecclesial bodies, the literature tends to ignore the religious socialization process.

There is also a distinct and racist imbalance in the gathering and reporting of violent crime, particularly mass shootings, that involve African American persons. When certain types of mass shootings are omitted from results, such as in the Stanford criteria referred to earlier, the data becomes skewed. The reporting is one sided and neglects to recognize data regarding the deaths of Black persons. Additionally, study in general on mass shootings has been hampered by federal laws limiting researchers' efforts.[8] In order to move forward in anti-violence efforts, a full picture of the situation must be attainable.

Another area that deserves more attention is the examination of programs and other efforts that have been successful in the prevention of violence. A few examples are given in this book, but a deeper dive could be extremely beneficial. What other initiatives have documented successes? How can churches and organizations beyond faith communities learn from, emulate, and expand on those programs? This field is ripe for further study.

SUMMARY

Besides spiritual anti-violence education to balance outside messages, though, proactive anti-violence training for both youth and adults is desperately needed in Sunday school, in youth groups, in confirmation classes, and on Sunday mornings. This is an issue that permeates our society, and in the cases studied in this project, the results of a lack of education can be deadly.

Despite all these preventative measures, if you begin to see warning signs in a person, the next chapter is for you.

---

8. Breck, "Northwestern Study," paras. 5–6.

Chapter 14

Taking Action After We Spot Trouble

DESPITE OUR BEST EFFORTS, not every person is going to be moved off the path to violence by our efforts. If an unfortunate situation occurs in which you discover a person displaying the red flags discussed earlier, this chapter has resources regarding how to help prevent a person from acting out on any urges they may be having.

Jillian Peterson and James Densley are two professors who studied mass shooter profiles to know if a shooter could be recognized before they picked up a gun. The pair published their findings in an evidence-based study called *The Violence Project: How to Stop a Mass Shooting Epidemic*. The research showed that when we see danger signs in a person, we must pay attention to them. Most mass shootings begin with a person having a grievance, and pushing the person away only makes them angrier. Not hearing them serves to convince them that whatever they're angry about has merit.

An eighteen-year-old California student planned for months to carry out a large mass shooting at his high school. His goal was to do this on April 20, 2024, the twenty-fifth anniversary of the Columbine High School shooting. That shooting, in 2019, left fifteen dead, including the two shooters. In his home, the California student had access to at least ten weapons, including rifles, revolvers, and a shotgun, and over one thousand rounds of ammunition. The young man had no criminal history and was not being bullied or harassed, which are situations that would have given school officials reason for concern. The reason the shooting didn't happen is because another student noticed the potential shooter's obsession with mass shootings, knew he had access to weapons, and alerted authorities. One student spoke up—just one. The student who spoke up, according to police, definitely saved lives.[1]

You can help, of course, if you put the suggestions here into practice in your own life. However, you can make an exponentially more positive change if you share the information with others. This can be done one-on-one or in a group. Consider leading a class or seminar in your church or in your community. The more people share information, the more like-minded people can work together, supporting and encouraging one another in their efforts. The following is a list of actionable measures that can be taken by people of all ages.

SPEAK UP AND MAKE CHANGES

If you notice that someone is showing signs that they might be on a pathway to violence, it would be easiest to simply do your best to stay out of the person's way and, as the teenagers spoken with earlier in this book noted, to try to stay off their hit list. That might keep you safe, but it doesn't solve the problem; complacency can be as deadly. Talk to the person if it's safe and appropriate to do so. Find out what kind of help they're getting, and if the answer is none, help facilitate that for them. Talk with their family if possible. Find out if the person has access to weapons. Involve authorities if appropriate (see below). Above all, do not stay quiet. Simply noticing someone is troubled doesn't help anyone; step in and get involved.

When factors that contribute to violence are revealed, learned, and understood, subsequent actions should follow. Upon googling the death of Trayvon Martin, the first results that Dylann Roof was shown were white supremacist organizations.[2] This introduction ultimately resulted, at least in part, in his radicalization and the murders of nine innocent people as they exercised their right to worship freely.

As much as people of faith hope and pray that their places of worship are safe from such tragedy, it is necessary for church congregations to address issues of violence in their own communities of faith. Perhaps the precedent and inspiration for these discussions could be Google's own response to Roof's research that utilized their platform. In a 2016 blog post, a product management director of search at Google posted that the search

1. Farberov, "Student 'Obsessed.'"
2. Shaffer, *Data Versus Democracy*, 14.

engine had changed the format of its algorithm to prevent such an event from occurring again.[3] God calls us to improve the world. When we see an area where we can improve, we should seize the opportunity.

TRAINING CLASSES

Consider holding regular—such as annual—training classes for your congregation or group. This is not an exhaustive list of elements that could be included in such a session and can be supplemented with other material. PowerPoints can be created, or existing resources can be used, such as those distributed by the Nebraska Emergency Management Agency in their Disrupting the Violence program. A class structure could look like the following.

Introduction: An explanation of the problem and the fears that people have around the issue can be given. It should be stated early that this class is not about gun control or security systems, but rather about prevention.

1. Prayer

   Everything we do should start with seeking God's will. Consider opening your meeting with one of these prayers or a similar one: "God who guides us, we are about to embark into a time of learning and discussion about a topic fraught with preconceived opinions and heightened emotions. Calm the disquiet in our spirits that arises when another's beliefs unsettle our own. Remind us that our desire to be correct should never take precedence over the love we have for our friends and neighbors. When we disagree, may we disagree respectfully, remembering that we hold in common our discipleship to Jesus Christ our Lord, in whose Name we pray. Amen."—Rev. Sarah Dierker

   "Good and gracious God, thank you for bringing us together today. We are here to follow in your way and to do our best to take care of your beloved children. Help us as we learn to keep fear at bay. Guide us by your light as we seek to follow Jesus's commandment to love one another as ourselves. We pray this in Jesus's name. Amen."

2. Why are we here?

   We're here because we can and must help, and the goal is to help people get off the pathway to violence. We who do not work in law

---

3. Yehoshua, "Google Search," para. 2.

enforcement can intervene when we become aware of potential violence. Knowing which resource to contact can increase the speed and effectiveness of intervention. In the most drastic cases, if a person expresses that they are planning to harm themselves or someone else, it is appropriate to call 911 immediately.

3. What do they believe are red flags?

   Invite the class to share what they would consider to be warning signs that a person might be considering violence. Affirm those replies that are accurate, but do not judge any answers; let the attendees speak their minds.

4. What should we avoid doing?

   Let your class members know the importance of not interrupting the person who's sharing their grievances and plans. We should not assume we know what they're about to say. We should try to understand them and repeat what they've said back to them, reworded, to make sure we understand correctly.

5. What is listening?

   Give a description of effective listening to the class. Remind them that while the reasons a person gives us for wanting to commit violence may not make sense to them, they make sense to the speaker. After those explanations, pair the participants up (preferably with participants they don't know well, if possible) and have them role-play a conversation. Assign one person to be the aggrieved party and the other to be the listener who is watching for warning signs. The listener should work to be reassuring, supportive, and clear that they are there to help, not to judge. When the class reconvenes, have them share their experiences.

6. What action should I take?

   From the discussions in step 2, move to instructions about when it is appropriate to keep listening, when it would be appropriate to alert health or mental health care authorities, and when calling 911 would be the appropriate course of action.

7. What should I say?

Have the participants pair up with a new partner to practice making a report. The Nebraska Emergency Management Agency offers sample sentences to say when reporting. For example, "I would like to report behaviors that might be on the path to violence. I am concerned about [name] and want to get them help. Here are the behaviors I am concerned about: [then list what you saw or heard]."[4]

8. What organizations can help? Discuss what helping groups are available, both in your community and virtually. Have handouts with contact information for the resources available for the attendees. Keep your resources lists updated regularly; make sure phone numbers, email addresses, and websites are working before each class convenes.

9. Help your class participants leave the session invigorated, empowered, and eager to help minimize violence in their community.

TELEPHONE AND ONLINE RESOURCES

We live in an age where communication options abound. Make sure class participants are aware of multiple forms of resources, including phone calls, text messaging, websites, and online chat options.

1. If a person is in immediate physical danger, call your local 911.
2. The national Suicide & Crisis Lifeline is 988. Users in distress can call or text that number or chat online at 988lifeline.org/chat and be connected with a trained crisis counselor.
3. If a person in distress needs an LGBTQ+-affirming counselor, text the letter q to 988, or call 988 and press 3.
4. If the caller to 988 is a veteran, they can press 1 for a counselor trained to work with veterans. The person can also text a message to 838255 or chat online at https://www.veteranscrisisline.net/get-help-now/chat/.
5. The Health Resources and Services Administration keeps an active list of teleconsultation phone lines categorized by state, including resources for people on native lands. Google the name of that

---

4. Nebraska Emergency Management Agency et al., *Disrupting the Path*, 15.

organization or go to https://mchb.hrsa.gov/programs-impact/programs/pmhca-awardee-teleconsultation-phone-lines.

6. People struggle for many reasons, and struggles intersect. A website called www.findhelp.org connects people with resources in their area for food, housing, financial assistance, health care (including mental health), and more. Simply type in a zip code, and a plethora of resources will appear.

7. Physicians and other primary care providers can access psychiatric telephone consultation programs for referrals for psychiatric care. These exist in most US states and help healthcare providers locate appropriate mental health care for their patients. Doctors are very used to talking to other doctors and frequently consult one another, but the simplicity of calling up and talking to a psychiatrist about a patient quickly, rather than waiting six weeks for an appointment for the patient, can expedite treatment.

8. Project Semicolon is a mental health care organization that gives resources and connects people that are experiencing mental health issues: www.projectsemicolon.com/.

CARE FOR SURVIVORS

We don't always win. Sometimes we miss cues and tragedy happens. Other times, even when we recognize cues and act on them, we are unable to avert disaster. Devin Patrick Kelley was recognized, even by himself, to be on the verge of a major violent event but ended up being the perpetrator in one of the largest mass shootings in the country. After the Sutherland Springs shooting, survivor David Colbath says that counseling and help with PTSD were valuable tools in his recovery.[5] Those affected by his actions, and the actions of any mass shooter, need love, care, and support.

Sherri Pomeroy

Sherri Pomeroy is the mother of Annabelle Pomeroy, fourteen, one of Kelley's victims. She is married to Frank Pomeroy, who was the pastor of Sutherland Springs Baptist Church in 2017. (He retired in 2022.) In a

---

5. Petrie, "Survivor," paras. 10–15.

2024 interview with me, she spoke from an angle of hope, but wanted to acknowledge the darkness that survivors go through after such an event.[6] I asked Sherri what she would say to someone who is in a very dark place after having been affected by such a terrible event. In her warm, kind voice, she explained and said that she had been in her own dark place for a very long time, and that she had even been suicidal while just going through the motions of life. She wants people to know that healing and working through grief is not a one-time event, but for many like her, it can be a slow, slow process. Two to three years ago, Pomeroy had a breakthrough of sorts and was finally able to not just say she was okay, but to really know she's going to be okay. She attributes this to many things, including:

- Prayer
- Medication
- Meditation
- Therapy
- Prayers of people who would pray for her even when she couldn't pray for herself or didn't want to pray for herself

Pomeroy's work now includes advocating for the destigmatization of mental health care. In her own words: "I am very vocal in talking about mental health because now I've been there, and it's about place. I advocate for the stigma of mental health; we need to do something about that. It's not shameful to ask for help. It shouldn't be shamed upon to discover someone's on medication for their mental health. It shouldn't be shameful for someone to find out you're seeing a therapist. I want to change that stigma." EMDR (eye movement desensitization and reprocessing), group counseling sessions, personal counseling sessions, and writing have all proved helpful for her, as has being open about her healing process in an effort to help others. She has shared her struggles interpersonally, has given talks to women's groups, and uses social media as an outlet as well.

When people go through traumatic situations, they rarely remember what people say to them unless it's extremely helpful or extremely hurtful. The suffering person nearly always remembers those who were there, but the details of what was said often become a blur. For Sherri, she remembers the worst thing that was said to her very clearly. A chaplain said, "Well, at least you have other children." Pomeroy doesn't remember where she was

6. The following section is from Sherri Pomeroy, interview by author, June 22, 2024.

when that was said to her, but she certainly remembers the feeling she had, which was devastation. The chaplain surely meant well, but the idea that children are replaceable by their siblings is not a helpful thing to say to a suffering parent.

The other side of that coin, though, is that Sherri remembers two incredible things that were said to her. Both comments talk about how, though the shooting was awful, good somehow also came from it. Kris Workman was the worship leader on the day Devin Kelley shot so many people in that worship service. As he hid under a pew, Kelley shot him in the spine, partially paralyzing him. Workman told Pomeroy, "If my legs are the only thing I had to give up for one person to come to Christ, it was well worth it." Pomeroy says that spurred her on to hope then and still does today.

The other story she remembers is that someone said, "I am so sorry that this happened to your family, but because of this, me and my family found Christ." She says she knows that many, many people came to Christ because of this event.

I asked Sherri what she would say to people who are afraid in churches. Her thoughtful reply is as follows:

> God didn't give us a spirit of fear and you can't live in that. We can't live in fear. If you live in the "what ifs," you'll never be okay. It's okay to visit there but it's not okay to live there. That's what I had to learn. At some point I've had pity parties.
>
> If we live in the what ifs, we're never going to get better. At some times I just had to . . . it made me very angry in the beginning at my husband and some others that said it's a choice to heal. That angered me because I felt like they were telling me I'm doing this on purpose. In a sense, yes, that was right, but you can't tell someone who's in that that. It's like telling somebody on the street, "I hope you find some clothes," and go on your way. No, you stop and help them.
>
> I had a lot of anger and I had to work through that anger. I couldn't just flip a switch and be over it. I had a lot of work to do on myself to get over the anger. I think one thing that helped me was in talking to other survivors of tragedies, one thing that I didn't have to deal with was facing our attacker because he did commit suicide. On a level of myself, I don't know that I could have faced that, so I was glad that one obstacle was taken out of my control. God knows exactly what you can handle, and my handle was broke right there, so I didn't have to deal with that. I am glad;

after talking to other survivors, I didn't have that extra component to deal with.

God can work good out of terrible, Pomeroy explained. "Yes, God is working in and around us, but he also requires us to do some of the work as well. I can't just lay in bed for seven years and say, 'God, heal me.' I have to get up and do the work. For a long time, I didn't want to get up and do the work and didn't care if it got done. I wanted to die right along with her." And she did get better. She described the moment she knew she was better. It was in the early 2020s, she was driving, and a news story came on the radio. It was about the lawsuit (that Sutherland Springs Baptist Church was not a part of) against the United States Air Force. The announcer said that the government had found that the air force was 60 percent responsible for the twenty-six deaths. The sudden jolt back to that day sent Pomeroy into a panic attack. She was driving over a bridge at that moment and couldn't breathe. But she knew she was getting better because in that moment she prayed, "God, just get me home safe." She realized she was better because not too long before that, if she had heard the same news story, she would have said, "I can just drive off this bridge and end it now." But instead, she prayed for God to keep her safe. That's when she knew she had turned the corner.

Sherri Pomeroy works long weeks with FEMA in Texas, helping other people after disasters. She wears a semicolon ring and is part of Project Semicolon, a mental health organization, and that ring and what it stands for help keep her grounded. Even during the FEMA work project she was on while I spoke with her, she had been able to connect with other mothers who had lost their children. She knows that if she can make it, others can too. "My battle cry is never stop sharing your story," she said. "Somebody needs to hear your story to keep them alive."

Clyde Smith

Clyde Smith, whose name has been changed at his request, spoke with me in June of 2024. In 2022, he was an employee of the Uvalde, Texas, Consolidated Independent School District, working in a supportive role. What happened at Robb Elementary School in Uvalde on May 24, 2022, was not a church shooting, but the lessons about aftercare of survivors and those affected by such a tragedy are universal. That day, eighteen-year-old Salvador Ramos shot and killed nineteen students and teachers and injured seventeen. It was well over an hour before law enforcement entered the school to stop the shooter. Because of the difficult circumstances surrounding that mass shooting, much hurt, anxiety, anger, and tension still exist in Uvalde and the surrounding area.

As Smith spoke of how things are now, two years later, he wanted me to know that he couldn't speak for all of Uvalde, but he was willing to share his own observations. Smith said that though he was not a teacher, Uvalde is a small town (about fifteen thousand), and the teachers who were involved had taught some of his relatives. He knows the families of some of the students who were killed and injured. On the law enforcement side, he has neighbors and family who were part of the events that unfolded that day.

Smith said, "There is still a lot of pain for a lot of people here. Things are getting better, but there's still a lot of blame going around, and you have to be careful of what you say to certain people as you don't want to hurt feelings further or get them upset again. Anyone that talks or tries to help the people directly involved will see some of the dark places and hurt these people are bound to be carried for a long time if not for the rest of their lives. That can't help but affect the people around them."[7]

The effects of that mass shooting are so far reaching that even Smith, who is neither a teacher nor student at Robb Elementary, has changed his life as a result of that day. He didn't have a family member killed or injured in the shooting, but he's affected. He said that he knows how important it is for people to be able to talk about their feelings, yet he can't even speak with his friends, family, or neighbors about this tragic event because he may not know where they stand on it. If he does know their feelings, he doesn't want to rub salt in their still-open wound of grief, so he doesn't talk about it. He doesn't want to hurt others. Smith was affected, not necessarily directly, but it's changed his relationships with people he's known. As Police Chief Susan Rockett said earlier in this book, no one comes away from a shooting unscathed.[8] Care will be needed for a very long time.

SUMMARY

The goal is for our preventative work, outlined in previous chapters, to do the trick. We hope that through education, sharing, listening, and a whole

---

7. Clyde Smith (name changed by request), email to author, June 20, 2024.
8. Susan Rockett, interview by author, May 5, 2024.

lot of prayer, people won't turn to violence. Sometimes, though, the pull is too strong, and individuals proceed on the path of destruction anyway. Our task, then, is to recognize the warning signs and act appropriately in response to them. And when disaster still happens, our task is to be there for those left behind. It's difficult, it's heartbreaking, but it must be done. May we do so for the good of all of God's creation, moving towards a better future for each of us.

Chapter 15

It Works: Stories of Hope

When Jesus needed to make a point, he sometimes told a parable. A parable isn't necessarily a tale of events that happened but is rather a story that is told to make a larger point. Often the point of Jesus's parables sailed right over the heads of his disciples, but their truths were valuable each time. Parables still exist and are told to tell a truth in a symbolic way. With that in mind, the parable of the babies in the river is an old one and has many variations. Its origins are debated, but one of the parable's iterations that appears in multiple places tells it this way.

THE PARABLE OF THE BABIES IN THE RIVER

One day a group of villagers was working in the fields by a river. Suddenly someone noticed a baby floating downstream. A woman rushed out and rescued the baby, brought it to shore, and cared for it. During the next several days, more babies were found floating downstream, and the villagers rescued them as well. But before long there was a steady stream of babies floating downstream. Soon the whole village was involved in the many tasks of rescue work: pulling these poor children out of the stream, ensuring they were properly fed, clothed, and housed, and integrating them into the life of the village. While not all the babies, now very numerous, could be saved, the villagers felt they were doing well to save as many as they did.

Before long, however, the village became exhausted with all this rescue work. Some villagers suggested they go upstream to discover how all these babies were getting into the river in the first place. Had a mysterious illness stricken these poor children? Had the shoreline been made unsafe by an earthquake? Was some hateful person throwing them in deliberately? Was an even more exhausted village upstream abandoning them out of hopelessness?

A huge controversy erupted in the village. One group argued that every possible hand was needed to save the babies since they were barely keeping up with the current flow. The other group argued that if they found out how those babies were getting into the water further upstream, they could repair the situation up there that would save *all* the babies and eliminate the need for those costly rescue operations downstream.

"Don't you see," cried some, "if we find out how they're getting in the river, we can stop the problem and *no* babies will drown? By going upstream, we can eliminate the cause of the problem!"

"But it's too risky," said the village elders. "It might fail. It's not for us to change the system. And besides, how would we occupy ourselves if we no longer had this to do?"[1]

This story beautifully describes the situation the United States finds itself in regarding mass shootings, and it seems especially true in communities of faith. We've come up with ideas for stricter gun laws and have lobbied strongly for them. We've developed ways to tighten security and companies have been founded with expertise in how to lock our buildings more tightly. We're all trying to get it right. But who's going upstream to find out why we want to hurt one another? As discussed in earlier chapters, taking a gun away from a person or locking them out of a building will not make them reconsider their actions, decide they're calm after all, and go back to a peaceful, nonviolent life. Removing guns and hiding ourselves from perpetrators serves only to hit the pause button on the violence they've decided to commit.

We must go upstream. We must figure out why people are picking up weapons to kill and wound others. Our faith demands that we intervene before the tragedies happen. As previously noted, secular organizations have had success with mitigation efforts. We can learn from their stories and adapt them for our use. Two examples of governmental agencies stepping in to improve situations follow.

---

1. Landis Center, "Parable of the River."

Example 1: Going Upstream

The twin cities of Minneapolis/St. Paul, Minnesota, had a problem with car theft.[2] Yes, that's quite different than shootings, but much of what happened cross-applies. Car theft was on the rise in that metropolitan area, and vehicles were being stolen faster than police could react. They couldn't keep up. There simply weren't enough staff or resources to track, investigate, and retrieve all the stolen vehicles, let alone arrest, incarcerate, and charge suspects. Their success rate in finding perpetrators wasn't great: only one in ten car thefts resulted in an arrest.

Then the lightning bolt revelation came that changed things: law enforcement realized that they needed to quit chasing thieves and instead stop people from stealing. They needed to find out, metaphorically speaking, why there were babies in the river. What they discovered was that the vast majority of thefts were being done by a small percentage of people, and most of those people were young.

The city of St. Paul, exhausted from their inability to find and prosecute the thieves, decided to start a program of building relationships. Representatives from law enforcement put together a prevention program with other representatives from various agencies. Program members began having conversations with car thieves and potential car thieves. They began to talk with them, saying, "Do you understand that this act that you thought was super low-level and somewhat harmless is a felony and caused a monstrous disruption for the people in the community?" Conversations included discussions like "You were in the car. What's going on? Why was this fun?"

St. Paul has also focused on giving young people more positive outlets, offering things like free youth sports and after-school programming. Absenteeism is rampant in schools, especially after COVID-19, as some parents and students don't believe that physically going to school is necessary. St. Paul law enforcement is working with agencies to offer free Uber rides to school and mental healthcare appointments.

Melvin Carter, mayor of St. Paul, says this isn't some shocking new approach to safety. "I have children, and when it comes to keeping them safe, my first question is: How do I get to the gates up above the stairway? How do I get the plastic plugs in the outlets? When we love someone, that's how

---

2. The below is drawn from Anderson, "How One City."

It Works: Stories of Hope

we approach public safety. This is about extrapolating that same approach to a whole city." Mayor Carter understands going upstream.

The prevention program has members not just working to avoid illegal activity, but they take it to the next step and fill time by taking kids to things like plays, basketball games, and events organized by the city. They've even helped some of them find part-time jobs. "It's really about embedding yourself into their lives and becoming a pillar or teammate," says staff member Yusef Davis. "You show them like, 'Look, you don't have to do dirt to survive. There's another path for you. You just have to consciously make the decision.'"

Every Wednesday night, the group meets at a community center with parents or guardians and a therapist. It helps the parents and guardians too. One mom says a court recommended that her son attend after he got involved with a group of teenagers stealing cars. She didn't want to be named because she worried it would negatively affect her son, but she says the weekly commitment has made a big difference—even to her.

"It's helped me get resituated, like in a structure, a schedule," she told National Public Radio (NPR). "Sometimes you just gotta start somewhere. This group has helped me stabilize myself." She says you get kids on the right track by being an example of being on the right track. Yes, this was a program built from desperation and lack of resources, but it worked. The result? Car thefts fell by 40 percent.

Example 2: Going Upstream

An FBI worker talked about a case where a young man who struggled with depression was also suicidal. His parents were doing their best to focus on finances and keep a roof over the family's head, and they weren't in tune with their son's emotional struggles.

The son began to exhibit warning signs of potential violence. He started to fixate on school shooters and obsessively memorized the details of different shootings. The family became concerned and got in contact with the local sheriff, whose department did not arrest the young man. Instead, they built relationships with him. The sheriff's department contacted the FBI, and they worked together on prevention. Law enforcement workers had conversations with the young man, spent time with him, and even took him to his mental health appointments. They stepped in where his family was overextended. In the end, the young man was able to move on from his fixation with violence and go to college. He never realized that the FBI played any role in guiding him away from potential disaster.

EARLY INTERVENTION IS KEY

Mark Prieto wanted to kill Black, Jewish, and/or Muslim people in a mass shooting. His goal was to open fire at a rap concert that was to run from May 14 to 15, 2024, in downtown Atlanta, Georgia. Court records explain that Prieto, an Arizona man who was a vendor at gun shows, had been friendly with a gun show customer. They connected more than fifteen times between 2021 and 2023. In late 2023, Prieto began to talk to his acquaintance about how he supported an attack. He told the acquaintance that he thought martial law would be in place after the 2024 presidential election, so he wanted to complete his mass shooting before then. He believed Black people were not people but were monsters. Atlanta was his target because of the demographics of the city, which includes 47 percent Black or African American people. A rap concert venue was his target because he assumed there would be a high number of Black people in attendance.

The acquaintance, alarmed by Prieto's comments, turned into an informant and contacted the authorities. The FBI got involved, and an undercover agent befriended Prieto at gun shows. The agent and informant led a sting operation, leading Prieto to believe they would help him commit the mass shooting. Prieto gave the two advice on how to carry out the murders: "You want to corral them. And some people might be trying to leave out of a corner, and you want to blast those guys. Once [they] get the idea that they are trapped then there is pandemonium," Prieto said to the source and undercover agent. "Now they're in a panic. And they can't get out. Now they are going to be crawling over each other to get out." The would-be murderer also wanted to make it clear that the attack was not gang related, but that it was racially motivated. He planned to post Confederate flags at the site of the attack and to shout things such as "KKK all the way," and "Black lives don't matter, white lives matter." His top priority was a high body count.

On May 14, 2024, Prieto left Arizona for Florida with five firearms in his vehicle. Because the informant had alerted the FBI and the undercover operation had been successful in uncovering Prieto's plans, he was arrested in New Mexico as he traveled to Florida. The mass shooting attempt was successfully thwarted.[3]

3. MacDonald-Evoy, "Arizona Man."

The informant saw warning signs, knew lives were in danger, and acted appropriately. He then went to extra lengths to help prevent tragedy by working in concert with the FBI undercover agent. If the informant had simply tried to steer clear of Prieto and tried to make sure he wasn't on his hit list, innumerable lives likely would have been lost. The early intervention worked.

RELATIONSHIPS WORK

In the 1990s, Nelson Mandela and Desmond Tutu worked together on the Truth and Reconciliation Commission in South Africa. A description of a film on the commission describes the work that was done. "For over forty years, South Africa was governed by the most notorious form of racial domination since Nazi Germany. When it finally collapsed, those who had enforced Apartheid's rule wanted amnesty for their crimes. Their victims wanted justice. As a compromise, the Truth and Reconciliation Commission (TRC) was formed. Now as it investigates the crimes of Apartheid, the Commission is bringing together victims and perpetrators to reveal South Africa's brutal past."[4] By revealing the past instead of burying it, the TRC hoped to pave the way to a peaceful future.

The Restorative Justice Council describes the key points of their court-based program as follows:

- The primary aim is to repair harm.
- There should be agreement about the essential facts of the incident and an acceptance of involvement by the person who caused the harm.
- Participation is voluntary.
- The process requires acknowledgment of the harm or loss experienced, respect for the feelings of participants, and an opportunity to consider, and if possible, meet their needs.
- Where amends are made the person harmed should be the primary beneficiary, and this reparation should be acknowledged and valued.
- The person facilitating the process must act impartially.[5]

---

4. Scripps College, "Long Night's Journey," para. 1.
5. Restorative Justice Council, "Principles."

The commission received much criticism from both sides but held fast to its goal of focusing on healing rather than punishment. Justice comes in many ways, and retribution is not always part of the equation. Getting people together in a room when possible—the harmed and those doing the harming—is priceless. The victim may have a hard time forgiving the act, but they can often forgive the person. They can choose to let go of the pain.

That idea of reconciliation is important for the understanding of the theology of forgiveness. Hebrews 8 speaks of God's reaction when he found fault with people. God said, "For I will forgive their wickedness and will remember their sins no more" (Heb 8:12). Do we think God has forgotten? No. But the impact of this is that God does not remember wrongs or hold them against us. God doesn't spend time with rage burning on the back burner of God's psyche because of wrongs we've committed. Rather, he remembers it no more and lets it go. Sometimes forgiveness is setting aside the harm so we can form a relationship. God chose to set sin aside so we can have a relationship. That's a model of forgiveness that we can strive for.

EVEN AFTER TRAGEDY, HOPE CAN ALWAYS LIVE ON

The faith community of First Baptist Church in Sutherland Springs, Texas, is a strong, resilient one. Lisa Krantz, the photojournalist who spent week after week with the church and community, says her work focused not on the shooting itself, but on how the congregation held each other together afterward. She wants others to remember how they supported each other and leaned on their faith in those difficult days, weeks, and months, and continue to. The Holcombe family lost nine of its members after the shooting there. Those who remain say their faith and the support of their beloved community is how they keep going.

The church is a living example of how God's hope can triumph. They have rebuilt, not only spiritually and emotionally, but also physically. The original building that was the site of the tragedy is now a memorial. A robust new facility has been erected, where the members continue to worship, take care of each other, and serve their community. On February 5, 2018, survivor Steven Colbath said, "God had nothing to do with this. Evil came into our church and evil tried to prevail, but evil didn't win, God won."[6]

---

6. Spriester and Medina, "700 Rounds," para. 11.

SUMMARY

Hope is alive, and relationships work. If you take nothing else from this book, remember those two things. If you have an opportunity to love someone like Jesus does, you have a considerably better chance of taking action than if you stay in your house and simply pray. Prayer is important; of course it is. But we have to do more and put our faith into action. Who better is there to act than we, the church? Ministers, elders, bishops, deacons, lay people, parishioners, and all other servants of God can serve God and love others by working to stem the flow of violence.

This is how change will happen: through us, the church. I don't know how long it's going to take, but this is how we can affect lives before they're taken, before they're forever changed.

It begins by talking about it.
It begins by sharing information.
It begins with relationships.
It begins with love.
It begins by understanding that it has to come from each of us.
Let us close with a prayer.

PRAYER FOR THE POWER OF LOVE

Holy Spirit, the One who travels with us.
May we all understand how sacred life is
and see how you have created each person in your image.
We pray that your words calling us to love one another
would be enough to transform us and our communities.
And even more, may we act in ways
that show that very love to our neighbors,
trusting in the power of love to bring
hope where there is despair,
wholeness where things are torn apart,
and healing where wounds are deep. Amen.

—Rev. Dr. Pam Saturnia

Appendix A

Dylann Roof Manifesto

THE FOLLOWING DOCUMENT WAS posted by Dylann Roof on thelastrhodesian.com at 4:44 p.m. Eastern Standard Time on June 17, 2015, the day of his attack on the Emanuel African Methodist Episcopal Church in Charleston, South Carolina. His explanation helps us understand his thought processes, his goals, and where we can improve when working with potentially violent people. Spelling and grammatical issues are untouched, as this is the official court record and exactly what Roof wrote.

> I was not raised in a racist home or environment. Living in the South, almost every White person has a small amount of racial awareness, simply beause of the numbers of negroes in this part of the country. But it is a superficial awareness. Growing up, in school, the White and black kids would make racial jokes toward each other, but all they were were jokes. Me and White friends would sometimes would watch things that would make us think that "blacks were the real racists" and other elementary thoughts like this, but there was no real understanding behind it.
>
> The event that truly awakened me was the Trayvon Martin case. I kept hearing and seeing his name, and eventually I decided to look him up. I read the Wikipedia article and right away I was unable to understand what the big deal was. It was obvious that Zimmerman was in the right. But more importantly this prompted me to type in the words "black on White crime" into Google, and I have never been the same since that day. The first website I came to was the Council of Conservative Citizens. There were pages upon pages of these brutal black on White murders. I was in disbelief. At

Appendix A

this moment I realized that something was very wrong. How could the news be blowing up the Trayvon Martin case while hundreds of these black on White murders got ignored?

From this point I researched deeper and found out what was happening in Europe. I saw that the same things were happening in England and France, and in all the other Western European countries. Again I found myself in disbelief. As an American we are taught to accept living in the melting pot, and black and other minorities have just as much right to be here as we do, since we are all immigrants. But Europe is the homeland of White people, and in many ways the situation is even worse there. From here I found out about the Jewish problem and other issues facing our race, and I can say today that I am completely racially aware.

Blacks

I think it is is fitting to start off with the group I have the most real life experience with, and the group that is the biggest problem for Americans.

Niggers are stupid and violent. At the same time they have the capacity to be very slick. Black people view everything through a racial lense. Thats what racial awareness is, its viewing everything that happens through a racial lense. They are always thinking about the fact that they are black. This is part of the reason they get offended so easily, and think that some thing are intended to be racist towards them, even when a White person wouldnt be thinking about race. The other reason is the Jewish agitation of the black race.

Black people are racially aware almost from birth, but White people on average dont think about race in their daily lives. And this is our problem. We need to and have to.

Say you were to witness a dog being beat by a man. You are almost surely going to feel very sorry for that dog. But then say you were to witness a dog biting a man. You will most likely not feel the same pity you felt for the dog for the man. Why? Because dogs are lower than men.

This same analogy applies to black and White relations. Even today, blacks are subconsciously viewed by White people are lower beings. They are held to a lower standard in general. This is why they are able to get away with things like obnoxious behavior in public. Because it is expected of them.

Modern history classes instill a subconscious White superiority complex in Whites and an inferiority complex in blacks. This White superiority complex that comes from learning of how we dominated other peoples is also part of the problem I have just mentioned. But of course I dont deny that we are in fact superior.

I wish with a passion that niggers were treated terribly throughout history by Whites, that every White person had an ancestor who owned slaves, that segregation was an evil an oppressive institution, and so on. Because if it was all it true, it would make it so much easier for me to accept our current situation. But it isnt true. None of it is. We are told to accept what is happening to us because of ancestors wrong doing, but it is all based on historical lies, exaggerations and myths. I have tried endlessly to think of reasons we deserve this, and I have only came back more irritated because there are no reasons.

Only a fourth to a third of people in the South owned even one slave. Yet every White person is treated as if they had a slave owning ancestor. This applies to in the states where slavery never existed, as well as people whose families immigrated after slavery was abolished. I have read hundreds of slaves narratives from my state. And almost all of them were positive. One sticks out in my mind where an old ex-slave recounted how the day his mistress died was one of the saddest days of his life. And in many of these narratives the slaves told of how their masters didnt even allowing whipping on his plantation.

Segregation was not a bad thing. It was a defensive measure. Segregation did not exist to hold back negroes. It existed to protect us from them. And I mean that in multiple ways. Not only did it protect us from having to interact with them, and from being physically harmed by them, but it protected us from being brought down to their level. Integration has done nothing but bring Whites down to level of brute animals. The best example of this is obviously our school system.

Now White parents are forced to move to the suburbs to send their children to "good schools". But what constitutes a "good school"? The fact is that how good a school is considered directly corresponds to how White it is. I hate with a passion the whole idea of the suburbs. To me it represents nothing but scared White people running. Running because they are too weak, scared, and brainwashed to fight. Why should we have to flee the cities we created for the security of the suburbs? Why are the suburbs secure in the first place? Because they are White. The pathetic part is that these White people dont even admit to themselves why they are moving. They tell themselves it is for better schools or simply to live in a nicer neighborhood. But it is honestly just a way to escape niggers and other minorities.

But what about the White people that are left behind? What about the White children who, because of school zoning laws, are forced to go to a school that is 90 percent black? Do we really think that that White kid will be able to go one day without being picked on for being White, or called a "white boy"? And who is fighting for him? Who is fighting for these White people forced by economic circumstances to live among negroes? No one, but someone has to.

Here I would also like to touch on the idea of a Norhtwest Front. I think this idea is beyond stupid. Why should I for example, give up the beauty and history of my state to go to the Norhthwest? To me the whole idea just parralells the concept of White people running to the suburbs. The whole idea is pathetic and just another way to run from the problem without facing it.

Some people feel as though the South is beyond saving, that we have too many blacks here. To this I say look at history. The South had a higher ratio of blacks when we were holding them as slaves. Look at South Africa, and how such a small minority held the black in apartheid for years and years. Speaking of South Africa, if anyone thinks that think will eventually just change for the better, consider how in South Africa they have affirmative action for the black population that makes up 80 percent of the population.

It is far from being too late for America or Europe. I believe that even if we made up only 30 percent of the population we could take it back completely. But by no means should we wait any longer to take drastic action.

Anyone who thinks that White and black people look as different as we do on the outside, but are somehow magically the same on the inside, is delusional. How could our faces, skin, hair, and body structure all be different, but our brains be exactly the same? This is the nonsense we are led to believe.

Negroes have lower Iqs, lower impulse control, and higher testosterone levels in generals. These three things alone are a recipe for violent behavior. If a scientist publishes a paper on the differences between the races in Western Europe or Americans, he can expect to lose his job. There are personality traits within human families, and within different breeds of cats or dogs, so why not within the races?

A horse and a donkey can breed and make a mule, but they are still two completely different animals. Just because we can breed with the other races doesnt make us the same.

In a modern history class it is always emphasized that, when talking about "bad" things Whites have done in history, they were White. But when we lern about the numerous, almost countless wonderful things Whites have done, it is never pointed out that these people were White. Yet when we learn about anything important done by a black person in history, it is always pointed out repeatedly that they were black. For example when we learn about how George Washington carver was the first nigger smart enough to open a peanut.

On another subject I want to say this. Many White people feel as though they dont have a unique culture. The reason for this is that White culture is world culture. I dont mean that our culture is made up of other cultures, I mean that our culture has been adopted by everyone in the world. This makes us feel as though our culture isnt special or unique. Say for example that every business man in the world wore a kimono, that every skyscraper was in the shape of a pagoda, that every door was a sliding one, and that everyone ate every meal with chopsticks. This would probably make a Japanese man feel as though he had no unique traditional culture.

I have noticed a great disdain for race mixing White women within the White nationalists community, bordering on insanity it. These women are victims, and they can be saved. Stop.

Jew

Unlike many White naitonalists, I am of the opinion that the majority of American and European jews are White. In my opinion the issues with jews is not their blood, but their identity. I think that if we could somehow destroy the jewish identity, then they wouldnt cause much of a problem. The problem is that Jews look White, and in many cases are White, yet they see themselves as minorities. Just like niggers, most jews are always thinking about the fact that they are jewish. The other issue is that they network. If we could somehow turn every jew blue for 24 hours, I think there would be a mass awakening, because people would be able to see plainly what is going on.

I dont pretend to understand why jews do what they do. They are enigma.

Hispanics

Hispanics are obviously a huge problem for Americans. But there are good hispanics and bad hispanics. I remember while watching hispanic television stations, the shows and even the commercials were more White than our own. They have respect for White beauty, and a good portion of hispanics are White. It is a well known fact that White hispanics make up the elite of most hispanics countries. There is good White blood worht saving in Uruguay, Argentina, Chile and even Brasil.

But they are still our enemies.

East Asians

I have great respent for the East Asian races. Even if we were to go extinct they could carry something on. They are by nature very racist and could be great allies of the White race. I am not opposed at all to allies with the Northeast Asian races.

Patriotism

I hate the sight of the American flag. Modern American patriotism is an absolute joke. People pretending like they have something to be proud while White people are being murdered daily in the streets. Many veterans believe we owe them something for "protecting our way of life" or "protecting our freedom". But im not sure what way of life they are talking about. How about we protect the White race and stop fighting for the jews. I will say this though, I myself would have rather lived in 1940's American than Nazi Germany, and no this is not ignorance speaking, it is just my opinion. So I dont blame the veterans of any wars up until after Vietnam, because at least they had an American to be proud of and fight for.

An Explanation

To take a saying from a film, "I see all this stuff going on, and I dont see anyone doing anything about it. And it pisses me off.". To take a saying from my favorite film, "Even if my life is worth less than a speck of dirt, I want to use it for the good of society.".

I have no choice. I am not in the position to, alone, go into the ghetto and fight. I chose Charleston because it is most historic city in my state, and at one time had the highest ratio of blacks to Whites in the country. We have no skinheads, no real KKK, no one doing anything but talking on the internet. Well someone has to have the bravery to take it to the real world, and I guess that has to be me.

Unfortunately at the time of writing I am in a great hurry and some of my best thoughts, actually many of them have been to be left out and lost forever. But I believe enough great White minds are out there already.

Please forgive any typos, I didnt have time to check it.

Appendix B

Emanuel Samson Note

THIS NOTE WAS FOUND on the dashboard of Emanuel Samson's car after the shootings at Burnette Chapel Church of Christ. The explanation of what is written can be found in chapter 5.

Appendix C

Letter from Dylann Roof to Christian Picciolini, December 2017

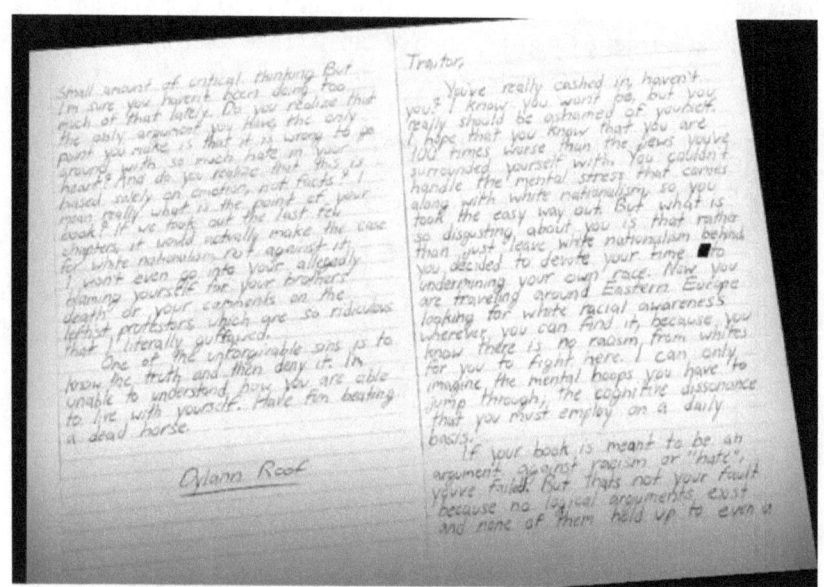

Appendix D

Letter from Emanuel Kidega Samson to Susan Presley, 2021

Hello Susan,

I hope all is well with you. Before I agree to anything, I have a few questions.

How can I be of assistance to your project exactly? What is the project about?

If you can answer these questions for me, that would be great.

Talk to you soon,

Emanuel K. Samson

Appendix E

Dylann Roof Jailhouse Drawings

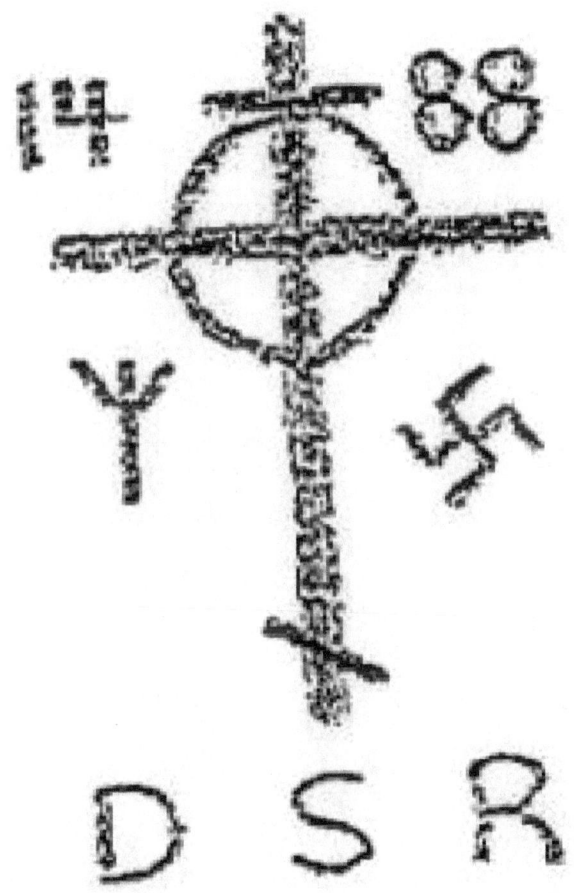

Appendix E

Dylann Roof Jailhouse Drawings

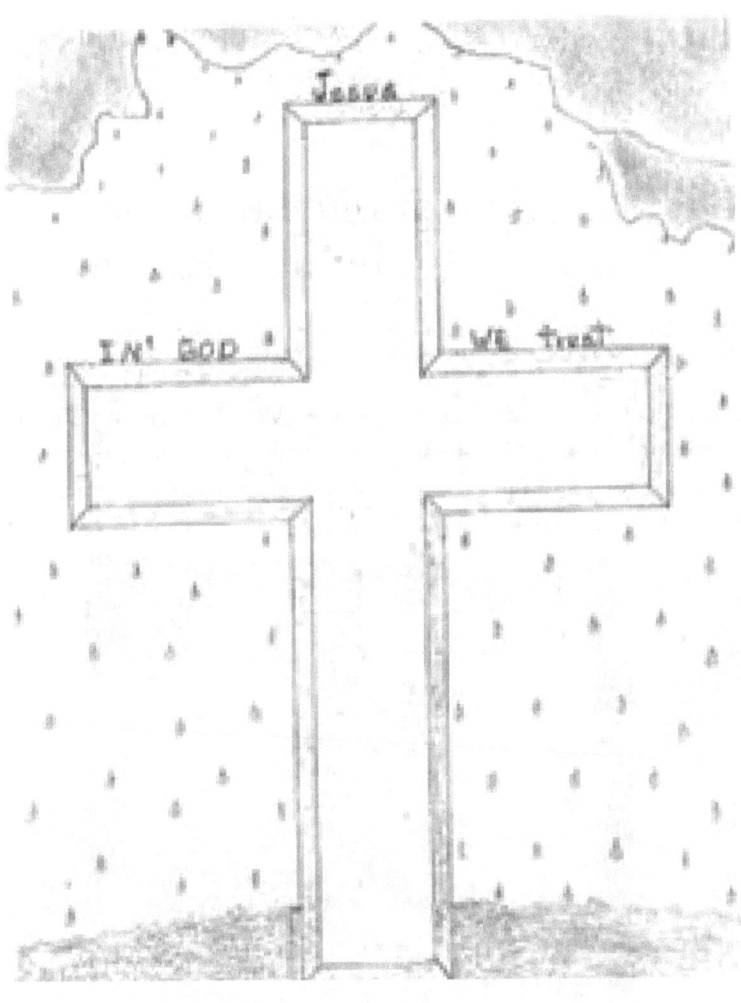

Appendix F

Letters from Dylann Roof to His Mother and Father

On the day of the shooting at Emanuel AME Church and after Roof's arrest, a journal was found in his car. Two pages had been torn out of it, and they were also left in the car. One was a letter to his mother, and the other was a more abbreviated letter to his father.

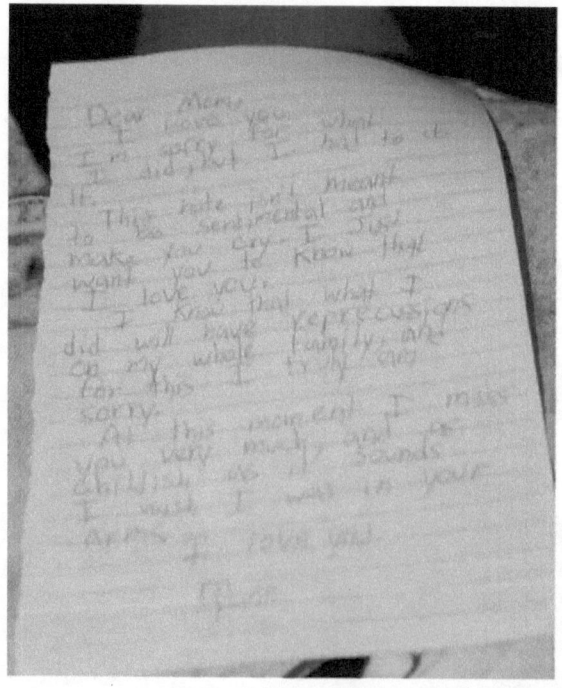

Letters from Dylann Roof to His Mother and Father

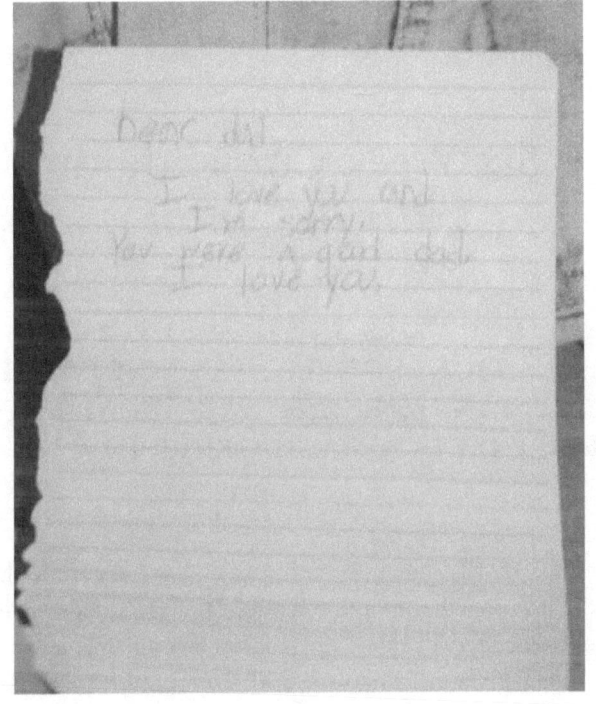

Appendix G

Six-Week Curriculum: *Unity in Conflict*

INTRODUCTION: CONFLICT AS A NET POSITIVE. CONFLICT CAN GENERATE NEW IDEAS AND HELP PEOPLE APPRECIATE EACH OTHER IN A NEW WAY.

What's at Stake?

IN THE UNITED STATES, religious, political, and social conflict has always existed and it always will, but it doesn't need to have a negative end result. No argument is needed for the importance of recognizing, addressing, and learning to deal with conflict in our world. Communities and relationships are divided, sometimes irreparably, because of a failure to address conflict in healthy, productive ways. We need look no further than our own neighborhoods and faith communities to find conflict on multiple levels: political, social, legal, and even medical as the coronavirus pandemic entered into the picture in 2020.

Avoidance of conflict can lead to deep resentments, broken relationships, and a lack of growth. Conversely, well-managed and intentionally structured conflict has the potential to help individuals, groups, and organizations grow and prosper in productive, healthy ways. Aristotle believed conflict and friendship could work well in concert. Extending the great thinker's notion, this course will show how conflict amid friendship, in a religious setting, can save the world.

Six-Week Curriculum: Unity in Conflict

Why This Study?

This curriculum is for a six-week, six-session course for Christian adults based on multiple readings. The curriculum will focus on understanding the foundational reasons conflict exists in the world and in churches in particular, and offering concrete, objective steps church leaders and laypersons can use such conflict to enact a net positive change in the church and, by extension, the world.

Though concepts and quotations will be taken from multiple authors, the main book for participants in this six-week study will be Allen R. Hilton's *A House United*. Hilton's two-pronged approach is used in this study: The first step is recognizing the church's role in endorsing and promoting conflict, and the second step is working to understand how the church can change that, modeling positive conflict resolution in ways that other entities can emulate. Participants are required to read Hilton's book prior to the start of class in order to understand the history of conflict in the US and the world, and the Christian church's complicity in the conflict. Supplemental texts are listed below. The goal of the lessons and activities is to give the students the tools to be able to recognize and repair issues within church systems and enact positive change through conflict strategies.

Who Should Be Included?

The intended audience for this curriculum is persons who might normally attend a Christian church's Bible study, as this study operates from a Christian vantage point. Optimal age groups for the study are late teenagers through older adults, and all genders can benefit from the class. Near the end of the class, practical steps for how to reach out to people outside of our churches with whom we may have had conflict will be explored.

What We'll Look At

This curriculum will focus on how conflict can be seen as a helpful growth opportunity rather than something to be avoided. Working from a Christian perspective, participants will explore multiple authors, with special emphasis on one book that participants will have read. The following works will be employed, working from a definition of conflict, through church-specific

Appendix G

conflict, and broadening the topic into society as a whole. Practical steps for engaging in conflict in positive ways are vital pieces of this curriculum.

- *A House United: How the Church Can Save the World*, by Allen Hilton. This is the key text for the class, and it is also the text that participants will read before the beginning of class. It's very reader friendly, and Hilton connects the data points of domestic unrest as they relate to violence with the church's complicity in the issue. Once the situation is explained, the author gives concrete suggestions for future action.
- *Every Congregation Needs a Little Conflict*, by George W. Bullard. This author lays the groundwork for defining conflict and the different areas in which it can occur. He shows how every church has conflict, which can be healthy if managed well, and outlines steps to make that happen.
- *The Righteous Mind: Why Good People Are Divided by Politics and Religion*, by Jonathan Haidt. The concepts used in this book cover the basics of listening. Importantly, learning to recognize similarities between speaker and listener, as well as differences, is covered effectively in this book, which lays some of the groundwork for listening skills and styles.
- "Visualising Migrant Voices: Co-Creative Documentary and the Politics of Listening," by Darcy Alexandra. For those who are visual learners, Alexandra's work brings a vital layer to understanding voices relating to the conflict surrounding the immigration debates in the United States. Through a presentation of thirteen persons of varied backgrounds, Alexandra shows the results of the immigration conflict.
- *The Dissonance of Democracy: Listening, Conflict, and Citizenship*, by Susan Bickford. Feminist theory combines with democratic theory in this book to explore conflict in political settings.
- "Terrorism in Context: The Stories We Tell Ourselves," by James Brown V, shows the three-pronged relationship between terrorism, media, and government in the US, helping the reader see media coverage of violence in a new light.
- "Blogs and the New Politics of Listening," by Stephen Coleman. The author helps explain how grassroots organizations can effect change, as well as the effectiveness of media outlets outside of major corporate media.

- *Weep Not for Your Children: Essays on Religion and Violence,* edited by Lisa Isherwood and Rosemary Radford Ruether, focuses on violence done towards women and children. This is an important facet of violence in the US, especially considering the prevalence of domestic violence targeting women, as well as school violence.
- *Reset the Heart: Unlearning Violence, Relearning Hope,* by Mai-Anh Le Tran. This author's work is referred to on multiple lessons in this curriculum, as the book defines violence and explores steps in moving forward to eradicate violence, including that which is taught within churches.

The Sessions

Session 1 lays the groundwork for conflict within our country, using authors Bickford and Tran. Political listening, an especially relevant topic in the twenty-first century, is discussed, as well as how to listen. Politics have divided our country in painful and difficult ways, but repair is possible.

In session 2, participants will explore conflict in our worship spaces through the texts by Hilton and Bullard. Definitions will be established as well as the inevitability of conflict, both healthy and unhealthy, and appropriate coping mechanisms.

Session 3 gets practical, leaning on Haidt's and Alexandra's writings to discover what tools we need to become better listeners and conflict-handlers.

In session 4, the move is made into action steps. Through Hilton's and Bullard's books, the group will define a current church conflict and create a practical conflict resolution tool.

Session 5 will focus on the skill of active listening and will take action by practicing active listening through listening to one another's stories. Coleman's and Haidt's works are used in this session.

Finally, participants in session 6 will take action through working on an area of conflict between their own worshiping body and another faith-based group. The tools learned and practiced in the first five sessions, as well as Hilton's book, will be put to work as the group creates a bridge for cooperation and understanding.

Appendix G

Next Steps

Near the end of the class, especially in session 6, opportunities will have presented themselves for further action. Optimally, the end of these sessions will not be the end of the group's action on the topic, but rather the foundation. "What's next" is a recurring theme in the study. Depending on the makeup of the class, one or more offshoot groups could be formed at the conclusion of this study, working for conflict resolutions in the area(s) the group explores in their final class.

Nuts and Bolts

What follows is the student guide, not the teacher's guide, which contains further resources and leadership ideas as well as background reading options for a fuller understanding of the topics.

All students should obtain a copy of Hilton's *A House United: How the Church Can Save the World* and read it before class begins in order to lay groundwork for the course.

Each session includes an introductory section, quote(s) of the day for centering and focusing purposes, an outline for study, and a possible activity. The optimal time for this class would be ninety minutes and include small group discussions, but the materials could be covered in sixty minutes with smaller groups.

Each chapter is presented in outline fashion. The leader may choose how they expand on the outline or add resources. Multiple readings are included in each session, but the student is not expected or required to read all resources.

What Is Success?

Each session should be considered successful if something concrete materializes out of each "What's Next?" section at the end of the meeting. Thematically, the curriculum aims toward putting our knowledge and belief into practice, so actionable steps are the goal.

Six-Week Curriculum: Unity in Conflict

SESSION 1: WHAT WE KNOW: CONFLICT HAPPENS IN OUR COUNTRY

Focus Texts for This Session

Susan Bickford, *The Dissonance of Democracy: Listening, Conflict, and Citizenship*

Mai-Anh Le Tran, *Reset the Heart: Unlearning Violence, Relearning Hope*

How do we define conflict? How does it happen? How much of it exists? Is it always a bad thing?

Introduction

There's no denying that conflict exists in our world. In our opening session of this study, the general notion of conflict, its prevalence, and its origins will be introduced. This session and the following five assume that each participant has read Allen Hilton's *A House United: How the Church Can Save the World*. If you haven't, be sure to read it this week for a fuller understanding of this course.

As we begin our study, we'll look at how listening works (or doesn't work) and how a cacophony of voices combines to sometimes overwhelm us, and we'll begin to understand how we can hear one another better. Finally, we'll look at the importance of putting beliefs and knowledge into action.

Quotes of the Day

Peace cannot be attained through violence;
it can only be attained by understanding.—Ralph Waldo Emerson

If you want to make peace with your enemy, you have to work with your enemy.
Then he becomes your partner.—Nelson Mandela

What?

Studies in communication have shown that the lack of listening in both political and social circles in our country aren't separate issues but are quite intertwined.[1] Have you noticed groups separating themselves socially in our country and in your local community based on political points of view? Some people go as far as moving to regions where more people's political ideologies match their own.

Key to managing conflict between people, both politically and socially, is listening to one another. Have you ever thought about how you listen? Do you subconsciously work on your rebuttal while the other person is speaking or tune out what strikes you as unpleasant or disagreeable? Avoidance is a tactic taken by some people to avoid naturally existing conflicts. Is this a beneficial approach?

Who?

Listening well sounds good in theory, and it sounds like it is possibly even easy to do. But with the abundance of voices demanding to be heard in our society, we can easily become overwhelmed by all the voices that demand to be heard. How often do you (or others you talk with) promote good in your conversations?

How?

We tend to focus on how to present our case, rather than on how to hear another's case.

What's Next?

Once the listening is complete, parties must move to action.

Activity

The leader should be prepared with several newspapers, whether from major cities or more local, rural areas (either is fine). Divide the papers up among the class, asking each to find an instance of lack of listening and the resulting conflict. Each participant should share their finds and discuss, depending on the time available.

---

1. Bickford, *Dissonance of Democracy*, 3.

Six-Week Curriculum: Unity in Conflict

SESSION 2: WHAT WE KNOW: CONFLICT HAPPENS IN OUR WORSHIP SPACES

Focus Texts for This Session

Allen R. Hilton, *A House United: How the Church Can Save the World*

George Bullard, *Every Congregation Needs a Little Conflict*

Introduction

What does conflict look like in churches? What types of conflict exist, and between whom? Can the existence of conflict lead to a positive result?

Quote of the Day

Five great enemies to peace inhabit us: avarice, ambition, envy, anger, and pride. If those enemies were to be banished, we should infallibly enjoy perpetual peace.—RALPH WALDO EMERSON

Definition

Defining conflict in church contexts: Two objects are trying to occupy the same space at the same time.

Types

Can be intrapersonal, interpersonal, intergroup, or subsystem

Who's Affected?

Every church has conflict, so everyone in a church, either immediately or tangentially, has the potential to be affected by conflict.

What's Next?

Ideas for healthy conflict

Activity

Take one of Bullard's twenty things to do to help avoid unhealthy conflict and expand on it.

Example

Developing a prayer culture where church members pray for each other, the church, and the leaders. The proposed activity is to come up with a system or program in a church that encourages active and ongoing participation in such a prayer group.

SESSION 3: WHAT WE NEED: OUR SKILL SETS AND TOOLS

Focus Texts for This Session

Jonathan Haidt, *The Righteous Mind: Why Good People Are Divided by Politics and Religion*

Darcy Alexandra, "Visualising Migrant Voices: Co-Creative Documentary and the Politics of Listening"

Introduction

How do we normally listen? Is there a better way to hear one another? What are our similarities and differences?

Quote of the Day

Self-understanding, rather than self-condemnation, is the way to inner peace and mature conscience.—JOSEPH L. LIEBMAN

Similarities

Find commonalities between participants in order to enable hearing of one another.

Differences

Understand the differences between how primates think and how bees think.

Together or Apart?

Groups tend to work against each other in an "us vs. them" mentality. What group are we working against?

What's Next?

Activity

Each class participant should bring a visual or audio object to the class to tell part of the story of their lives. This can be anything from a stuffed animal to wedding pictures, from a YouTube clip of their wedding to one of their pet's favorite toys. The goal is to show the power of listening through our senses other than hearing.

SESSION 4: TAKING ACTION: THE PROBLEM OF INACTION

Focus Texts for This Session

Mai-Anh Le Tran, *Reset the Heart: Unlearning Violence, Relearning Hope*

Lisa Isherwood and Rosemary Radford Ruether, *Weep Not for Your Children: Essays on Religion and Violence*

Introduction

What happens if we don't act? How can we be proactive in creating an environment of justice?

Appendix G

Quote of the Day:

We cannot merely pray to You, O God, to end war;
For we know that You have made the world in a way
That man must find his own path to peace
Within himself, and with his neighbor.

—Jack Reimer

Defining Our Terms

Tran's definition of justice is more than physical harm. It includes social injustice.

What's at Stake

A lack of examination and reevaluation of our ways of being results in inaction.

And Then What Happens?

Inaction leads to violence.

What's Next?

Activity

Have the group examine one church policy, the church bylaws, or even a denominational confession, catechism, or creed with an eye to possible ways the policy may be harmful to certain members of the community.

SESSION 5: TAKING ACTION: HEARING VOICES

Focus Texts for This Session

Stephen Coleman, "Blogs and the New Politics of Listening"

Jonathan Haidt, *The Righteous Mind: Why Good People Are Divided by Politics and Religion*

Introduction

What does "grassroots" mean? How do we know when we still need to listen, or if it's time to move to action?

Quote of the Day

We are made kind by being kind.
—Eric Hoffer

What We Do

It is instinctive to feel rather than to reason and to act based on our gut instinct rather than learning/hearing from others first.

How We Can Do It

Action must be grassroots, from the people up, not from a top-down structure.

Who Needs to Be Involved

Unless those in power are willing to hear the populace, action won't work. People at all levels of a church can and should be involved.

What's Next?

Activity

One volunteer/group member should tell a story, perhaps from their own past, and the class will practice active listening with the following tools:

- Put aside rebuttals, comments, or distracting thoughts that occur.

- Give active but silent feedback with nods, smiles, or other body language.
- Don't interrupt.
- Ask clarifying questions such as "What I'm hearing is . . ."

Upon completion, the group can comment and determine if they understood the story accurately.

SECTION 6: SAVING THE WORLD

Focus Text for This Session

Allen Hilton, *A House United: How the Church Can Save the World*

Introduction

What's our conflict project going to be? How will we get it started and move forward to bridge a divide?

In this final session, we seek to apply our knowledge about conflict, in terms of practical ways in which we can reach out to those with whom we have conflict. We will discuss the importance of putting our faith and knowledge into action. We will then discuss and create some possibilities for working towards cooperation and understanding.

Quote of the Day

The world has a way of giving what is demanded of it. If you are frightened and look for failure and poverty, you will get them, no matter how hard you may try and succeed. Lack of faith in yourself, in what life will do for you, cuts you off from the good things of the world. Expect victory and you make victory . . . bravery and faith bring both material and spiritual rewards.

—Preston Bradley

What?

Now that we've learned about conflict in society and church, the listening tools we need to address it, and the importance of taking action, it's time to practice living in unity.

Where?

Identify the largest divide between this particular church and another house of worship nearby.

Who?

Are the divisions in your church political? Social? Gender/identity based? Liberal/conservative? Racial? Economic?

What's Next?

Take steps to "include the non-includers."

Activity

1. Break into equally sized groups to create ideas for reaching out to another group of worshipers.
2. Come back together as the whole group and agree on which neighboring church, synagogue, mosque, etc. to approach.
3. Make a plan for, at the very least, the first steps in working with the other group to form bonds of unity.
4. Example: Host a joint Bible or book study between groups.

Appendix H

Pro Se Motion to Remove and Replace Appointed Counsel

DYLANN ROOF BELIEVED HIS court-appointed attorneys were inappropriate to handle his defense because they were not all white, one was Jewish, and none of them shared his racist beliefs. It was Roof's belief that there was a conflict of interest and that that caused communication difficulties. Roof filed a motion with the court to obtain new representation.

> United States of America - vs - Dylann S Roof
>
> case no. 17-3 (4th Circuit)
>
> Pro Se Motion to Remove and Replace Appointed Counsel
>
> This is a motion to dismiss and replace my currently appointed counsel due to a conflict of interest.
>
> The court is aware of my decision to represent myself at my trial, a decision based partly on differences between myself and my attorneys. As my appeals process is just beginning it is more convenient and beneficial for everyone involved to have satisfactory counsel appointed now rather than at a later date when the process has actually begun.
>
> My two currently appointed attorneys, Alexandra Yates and Sapna Mirchandani, are Jewish and Indian respectively. It is

Pro Se Motion to Remove and Replace Appointed Counsel

therefore quite literally impossible that they and I could have the same interests relating to my case.

It is also a barrier to effective communication. The lawyer appointed to represent me at my Federal trial was David Isaac Bruck, who is also Jewish. His ethnicity was a constant source of conflict even with my constant efforts to look past it.

Trust is a vital component in an attorney client relationship, and is important to the effectiveness of the defense. Because of my political views, which are arguably religious, it will be impossible for me to trust two attorneys that are my political and biological enemies. The difficulties during my trial are evidence of this.

My intentions are to have the appeals process for my case go as smoothly as possible — and to be as effective as they

Appendix H

can be, the appeals should be worked on and written by lawyers with my best interests in mind. I am confident after meeting my current attorneys that they will be unable to represent me in an efficient manner.

    For the reasons stated above I ask that the court remove and replace my current counsel.

                                  Respectfully Submitted,

                                  Dylann S Roof

Pro Se Motion to Remove and Replace Appointed Counsel

Dylann Roof 28509-171
USP PO Box 33
Terre Haute, IN
47808

Fourth Circuit Court of Appeals
Lewis F. Powell Jr United States
Courthouse Annex
1100 East Main Street, Suite 501
Richmond VA 23219-3525

Bibliography

Alexandra, Darcy. "Visualising Migrant Voices: Co-Creative Documentary and the Politics of Listening." PhD diss., Technological Institute Dublin, 2015.
Anderson, Meg. "How One City Took on Rising Car Thefts—and Brought the Numbers Down." NPR, Feb. 4, 2024. https://www.npr.org/2024/02/04/1227928003/rising-car-thefts-st-paul-minnesota-fallen-hyundai-kia.
Anti-Defamation League. "1488." ADL, n.d. https://www.adl.org/resources/hate-symbol/1488.
Associated Press. "Sheriff Didn't Pursue Sex Case Against Sutherland Springs Church Gunman." NBC News, Feb. 17, 2018. https://www.nbcnews.com/storyline/texas-church-shooting/sheriff-didn-t-pursue-sex-case-against-sutherland-springs-church-n848886.
Bailey, Phillip M., and Allison Ross. "'Whites Don't Shoot Whites': What One Man Says Kroger Shooter Told Him." *Courier Journal*, Oct. 25, 2018. https://www.courier-journal.com/story/news/crime/2018/10/25/louisville-kroger-shooting-suspect-whites-dont-shoot-whites/1759947002/.
Bales, Kevin. *New Slavery: A Reference Handbook*. Santa Barbara, CA: ABC-CLIO, 2020.
BeenVerified. "Dylann Storm Roof." BeenVerified, n.d. https://www.beenverified.com/rf/report/person?bvid=N_MTkyMDQxMTM4NzQz.
———. "Emanuel Kidega Samson." BeenVerified, n.d. https://www.beenverified.com/rf/report/person?bvid=N_MTQ2OTg4OTMwNzQ4.
Beltman, Susan, et al. "'I Really Enjoy It': Emotional Engagement of University Peer Mentors." *International Journal of Emotional Education* 11 (2019) 50–70.
Berry, John W., et al., eds. "Socialization." In *Handbook of Cross-Cultural Psychology*, 3:239–58. Boston: Allyn and Bacon, 1997.
Bickford, Susan. *The Dissonance of Democracy: Listening, Conflict, and Citizenship*. Ithaca, NY: Cornell University Press, 1996.
Bledsoe, Candice L., et al. "Silence Is Complicity: Why Every College Leader Should Know the History of Lynching." *Change: The Magazine of Higher Learning* 52 (2020) 22–25. https://doi.org/10.1080/00091383.2020.1732755.
Blomberg, Craig. *Matthew*. New American Commentary 22. Nashville: Broadman & Holman, 1992.
Breck, Arabella. "Northwestern Study: Available Gun Violence Data Doesn't Show the Full Picture." *Northwestern Now*, Aug. 1, 2019. https://news.northwestern.edu/stories/2019/08/northwestern-study-available-gun-violence-data-doesnt-show-the-full-picture/.

Bibliography

Brown, James, V. "Terrorism in Context: The Stories We Tell Ourselves." Honors thesis, University of Maine, 2019.

Bullard, George. *Every Congregation Needs a Little Conflict*. St. Louis: Chalice, 2008.

Burnette Chapel Church of Christ. "Sunday, August 16th, 2020." Facebook, Aug. 16, 2020. https://www.facebook.com/100064795865876/videos/4233343 58623873.

Camp, Lee C. "Commentary: A Response to 'White Lives Matter.'" *Christian Chronicle*, Oct. 27, 2017. https://christianchronicle.org/white-lives-matter/.

Carlin, Nathan, et al. "Preface: Special Issue in Honor of Lewis Rambo." *Pastoral Psychology* 69 (2020) 271–73.

Carlson, Britta Meiers. "Practices of Belonging: Mainline Protestant Culture and Notions of Lutheran Identity in the ELCA." *Currents in Theology and Mission* 47 (2020) 19–25.

Chaney, Matt. "22-Year-Old Releases Statement After Tennessee Church Shooting." WRIC, Sept. 26, 2017. https://www.wric.com/news/22-year-old-releases-statement-after-tennessee-church-shooting/.

Cho, Kelly Kasulis. "Many Mass Attackers Motivated by Personal and Work Grievances, Report Says." *Washington Post*, Jan. 26, 2023. https://www.washingtonpost.com/nation/2023/01/26/mass-attack-report-secret-service-workplace-violence/.

Chokshi, Niraj. "Kroger Shooting Subject Is Charged with Hate Crimes in Killings of 2 Black People." *New York Times*, Nov. 15, 2018. https://www.nytimes.com/2018/11/15/us/kroger-shooting-charges-louisville.html.

Christenson, Sig, and Zeke MacCormack. "Gunman in Church Attack Was Convicted of Fracturing Stepson's Skull." *Express News*, Aug. 11, 2018. https://www.expressnews.com/news/local/article/Gunman-in-church-attack-was-convicted-of-12336011.php.

Clark, Emily Suzanne. "Religion and Race in America." *Oxford Research Encyclopedia*, Feb. 17, 2017. https://doi.org/10.1093/acrefore/9780199329175.013.322.

Coleman, Stephen. "Blogs and the New Politics of Listening." *Political Quarterly* 76 (2005) 272–80.

Conrad, Daniel. "Wife of Texas Church Shooter Testifies in Trial Against Feds." Courthouse News Service, Apr. 7, 2021. https://www.courthousenews.com/wife-of-texas-church-shooter-testifies-in-trial-against-feds/.

Corey, Benjamin L. "Common Objections & Misunderstandings on Christian Nonviolence." Bejamin L. Corey, n.d. https://www.benjaminlcorey.com/common-objections-nonviolence/.

Corrie, Elizabeth W. *Youth Ministry as Peace Education: Overcoming Silence, Transforming Violence*. Minneapolis: Fortress, 2021.

Davis, Inez Torres. "Justice, Large and Small." Women of the ELCA, Dec. 5, 2013. https://www.womenoftheelca.org/blog/post/justice-large-small.

Department of Defense. "Report of Investigation into the United States Air Force's Failure to Submit Devin Kelley's Criminal History Information to the Federal Bureau of Investigation DODIG-2019-030." Department of Defense, Dec. 6, 2018. https://www.dodig.mil/reports.html/Article/1707300/report-of-investigation-into-the-united-states-air-forces-failure-to-submit-dev/.

Devine, Curt, and Jose Pagliery. "Sheriff Says He Got 23 Calls About Shooter's Family, but Records Show More." CNN, Feb. 27, 2018. https://www.cnn.com/2018/02/27/us/parkland-shooter-cruz-sheriff-calls-invs/index.html.

Bibliography

Dupee, David, et al. "Stanford Researchers Scoured Every Reputable Study for the Link Between Video Games and Gun Violence That Politicians Point To. Here's What the Review Found." *Fortune*, May 2, 2023. https://fortune.com/2023/05/02/stanford-researchers-scoured-every-reputable-study-link-between-video-games-gun-violence-politics-mental-health-dupee-thvar-vasan/.

ELCA. "ELCA Presiding Bishop Calls on Church to Work for Racial Justice." ELCA, Apr. 6, 2018. https://elca.org/News-and-Events/7920.

Elkins, Kathleen Gallagher. *Mary, Mother of Martyrs: How Motherhood Became Self-Sacrifice in Early Christianity*. Cambridge, MA: Feminist Studies in Religion, 2018.

Emery, Tyler. "Minutes Before Deadly Kroger Shooting, Suspect Tried to Enter Historically Black Church." KSDK, Oct. 26, 2018. https://www.ksdk.com/article/news/crime/minutes-before-deadly-kroger-shooting-suspect-tried-to-enter-historically-black-church/63-608299947.

Farberov, Snejana. "Student 'Obsessed with School Shootings' Had 'Every Intention' to Carry Out Own Massacre on Anniversary of Columbine: Cops." *New York Post*, Feb. 15, 2024. https://www.newsbreak.com/news/3335367588266-student-obsessed-with-school-shootings-had-every-intention-to-carry-out-own-massacre-on-anniversary-of-columbine-cops.

Feagin, Joe. *Systemic Racism: A Theory of Oppression*. New York: Routledge, 2006.

Federal Bureau of Investigation. "Eric Rudolph." FBI, n.d. https://www.fbi.gov/history/famous-cases/eric-rudolph.

Fomerand, Jacques. "Massacre." In *Historical Dictionary of Human Rights*, 583. 2nd ed. Historical Dictionaries of Religions, Philosophies, and Movements Series. Lanham, MD: Rowman & Littlefield, 2021.

Frazier, Herb, et al. *We Are Charleston: Tragedy and Triumph at Mother Emanuel*. Nashville: Nelson, 2016.

Glass, Michael R. "Princeton's Founding Trustees." Princeton & Slavery, n.d. https://slavery.princeton.edu/stories/founding-trustees.

Gooch, Sarah. "Recommendations to Solve the Lack of Participation in the Lunch Buddy Student Mentorship Program at Mexico High School." EdD diss., Liberty University, 2023.

Grinberg, Emanuella, and Joe Stirling. "A Picture Emerges of Church Shooting Suspect." CNN, Sept. 26, 2017. https://www.cnn.com/2017/09/26/us/tennessee-church-shooting-suspect-profile/index.html.

Guard, David. "Origins of the Ku Klux Klan and Its Significance." *Journal of Ethnophilosophical Questions and Global Ethics* 1 (2017) 13–21.

Haidt, Jonathan. *The Righteous Mind: Why Good People Are Divided by Politics and Religion*. Visalia, CA: Vintage, 2020.

Harro, Bobbie. "The Cycle of Socialization." NEA, 2010. From *Readings in Diversity and Social Justice*, edited by Maurianne Adams. https://www.nea.org/sites/default/files/2021-02/Cycle%20of%20Socialization%20HARRO.pdf.

Hawkins, Derek. "White Teen Girl Detailed Plan for Racist Attack on Black Churchgoers in Notebook, Police Say." *Washington Post*, Nov. 20, 2019. https://www.washingtonpost.com/nation/2019/11/19/white-teen-girl-detailed-plan-racist-attack-black-churchgoers-notebook-police-say/.

Hill Fletcher, Jeannine. *The Sin of White Supremacy: Christianity, Racism, and Religious Diversity in America*. Maryknoll, NY: Orbis, 2017.

Bibliography

Hilton, Allen R. *A House United: How the Church Can Save the World.* Minneapolis: Fortress, 2018.

Horsnell, Matthew. "Hypnagogic and Hypnopompic Hallucinations: Shadow People and Demon Bunnies." Narcolepsy, Aug. 21, 2020. https://narcolepsy.sleep-disorders.net/living/hallucination-types.

International Churches of Christ. "Racism Dialogue Response: Diversity: North River Church of Christ." North River Church of Christ, n.d. https://nrcoc.org/ministries/diversity/pages/icoc-racism-dialogue-response.

Isherwood, Lisa, and Rosemary Radford Ruether. *Weep Not for Your Children: Essays on Religion and Violence.* London: Routledge, 2016.

Jennings, Willie James. *The Christian Imagination: Theology and the Origins of Race.* New Haven, CT: Yale University Press, 2011.

———. "Dylann Roof Was Wrong: The Race War Isn't Coming, It's Here." Religion Dispatches, June 26, 2015. https://religiondispatches.org/dylann-roof-was-wrong-the-race-war-isnt-coming-its-here/.

Jones, Robert P. *The End of White Christian America.* New York: Simon & Schuster, 2017.

———. "The Rage of White, Christian America." *New York Times,* Nov. 10, 2016. https://www.nytimes.com/2016/11/11/opinion/campaign-stops/the-rage-of-white-christian-america.html.

———. *White Too Long.* New York: Simon & Schuster, 2020.

Khimm, Suzy. "Clementa Pinckney's Political Ministry: 'Righteous Indignation in the Face of Injustices.'" *New Republic,* June 18, 2015. https://newrepublic.com/article/122077/clementa-pinckneys-faith-fueled-his-politics.

Korkzan, Shireen. "Episcopalians to Participate in Anti-Gun Violence, Pro-Gun Safety Events in June." Episcopal News Service, May 31, 2024. https://episcopalnewsservice.org/2024/05/31/episcopalians-to-participate-in-anti-gun-violence-pro-gun-safety-events-in-june/.

Koubaridis, Andrew. "From the First Deadly Shot Until the Last—How the Texas Church Shooting Unfolded." News.com.au, Nov. 7, 2017. https://www.news.com.au/world/north-america/from-the-first-deadly-shot-until-the-last-how-the-texas-church-shooting-unfolded/news-story/aeae4f3bcf528c090099419390a5a426.

Kovaleski, Serge F., and Mary Beth Sheridan. "A Boy of Bright Promise and No Roots." *Washington Post,* Jan. 12, 2003. https://www.washingtonpost.com/archive/local/2003/01/12/a-boy-of-bright-promise-and-no-roots/aa08f90d-8528-423d-afod-ed1b0fe2d944/.

Landis Center. "The Parable of the River." Landis Center, Jan. 2015. https://landiscenter.lafayette.edu/wp-content/uploads/sites/69/2015/01/SaveBabies.pdf.

Lee, Kurtis. "Destruction of Ten Commandments Monument in Arkansas Spotlights Gray Areas of Secularism." Governing, June 29, 2017. https://www.governing.com/archive/tns-ten-commandments-oklahoma-arkansas.html.

Liptak, Adam. "Supreme Court Will Hear Case of Lee Malvo, the D.C. Sniper." *New York Times,* Mar. 18, 2019. https://www.nytimes.com/2019/03/18/us/politics/lee-malvo-supreme-court.html.

MacDonald-Evoy, Jerod. "Arizona Man Indicted for Plans to Start a 'Race War' with Mass Shooting." *Arizona Mirror,* June 13, 2024. https://sourcenm.com/2024/06/13/arizona-man-indicted-for-plans-to-start-a-race-war-with-mass-shooting/.

Bibliography

Mann, Arjan. "From Twitch to Wembley: My Evening at Critical Role LIVE." *Strand Magazine*, Nov. 21, 2023. https://www.strandmagazine.co.uk/single-post/from-twitch-to-wembley-my-evening-at-critical-role-live.

Markey, Patrick M., et al. "Video Game Play: Myths and Benefits." *American Journal of Play* 13 (2020) 87–106. https://files.eric.ed.gov/fulltext/EJ1304728.pdf.

Mentor. "Mentoring Impact. Connect with a Young Person." Mentor, n.d. https://www.mentoring.org/mentoring-impact/.

Middleton, Stephen. "Repressive Legislation: Slave Codes, Northern Black Laws, and Southern Black Codes." *Oxford Research Encyclopedia*, Feb. 28, 2020. https://oxfordre.com/americanhistory/view/10.1093/acrefore/9780199329175.001.0001/acrefore-9780199329175-e-634.

Moltmann, Jurgen. "Liberation in the Light of Hope." *Ecumenical Review* 26 (2010) 413–29.

Nebraska Emergency Management Agency et al. *Disrupting the Path to Violence: Trainer Manual*. University of Nebraska Lincoln, Jan. 1, 2019. https://ptv.unl.edu/wp-content/uploads/2019/06/Training-Manual-and-Handouts.pdf.

News 24. "WATCH: Snapchat from Charleston Victim Posted Moments Before Shooting." News 24, June 19, 2015. https://www.news24.com/news24/xarchive/archive_video/watch-snapchat-from-charleston-victim-posted-moments-before-shooting-20150619.

Office of Government Relations. "Lenten Series: Enaging the Beloved Community." Episcopal Church, Feb. 10, 2016. https://www.episcopalchurch.org/ogr/lenten-series-engaging-the-beloved-community/.

Patel, Eboo. *Acts of Faith: The Story of an American Muslim, in the Struggle for the Soul of a Generation*. Boston: Beacon, 2007.

———. *Sacred Ground: Pluralism, Prejudice, and the Promise of America*. Boston: Beacon, 2013.

Perrett, Courtney. "Lisa Krantz Wins Pulitzer Prize." Show Me Mizzou, May 14, 2024. https://showme.missouri.edu/2024/lisa-krantz-wins-pulitzer-prize/.

Peterson, Jillian, and James Densley. *The Violence Project: How to Stop a Mass Shooting Epidemic*. New York: Abrams, 2021.

Petrie, Bonnie. "A Survivor of the Sutherland Springs Shooting Recounts His Trauma and Recovery." NPR, Nov. 5, 2018. https://www.npr.org/2018/11/05/664499814/a-survivor-of-the-sutherland-springs-shooting-recounts-his-trauma-and-recovery.

Presbyterian Church (U.S.A.). "Becoming a Peace Church." Presbyterian Mission, n.d. https://www.presbyterianmission.org/ministries/peacemaking/becoming-a-peace-church. Link discontinued.

Przybylski, Andrew K., and Netta Weinstein. "Violent Video Game Engagement Is Not Associated with Adolescents' Aggressive Behaviour: Evidence from a Registered Report." *Royal Society Open Science* 6 (2019) 171474. https://doi.org/10.1098/rsos.171474.

Rao, Gautham. "The Federal Posse Comitatus Doctrine: Slavery, Compulsion, and Statecraft in Mid-Nineteenth-Century America." *Law and History Review* 26 (2008) 1–56.

Rau, Nate. "Before Antioch Church Shooting, Suspect Made Cryptic Facebook Posts." *Tennessean*, Sept. 24, 2017; updated Sept. 25, 2017. https://www.tennessean.com/story/news/2017/09/24/before-antioch-church-shooting-suspect-made-cryptic-facebook-posts/698420001/.

Bibliography

Rein, Lisa. "Mystery of Virginia's First Slaves Is Unlocked 400 Years Later." *African Diaspora Archaeology Newsletter* 9 (2006) 1–3.

Restorative Justice Council. "Principles of Restorative Practice." Restorative Justice, Nov. 15, 2012. https://restorativejustice.org.uk/sites/default/files/resources/files/Principles%20of%20restorative%20practice%20-%20FINAL%2012.11.15.pdf.

Roof, Dylann. "Crowdsourcing Appeal: Dylann Roof's Manifesto." Counter-Currents, June 20, 2015. https://counter-currents.com/2015/06/dylann-roofs-manifesto/.

Rosenberg, Eli, et al. "Who Is Devin Patrick Kelley, the Gunman Officials Say Killed Churchgoers in Sutherland Springs, Tex.?" *Washington Post*, Nov. 6, 2017. https://www.washingtonpost.com/news/morning-mix/wp/2017/11/06/who-is-devin-patrick-kelley-gunman-who-officials-say-killed-churchgoers-in-sutherland-springs/.

Rynne, Terrence. "The Pope Has Already Taught Nonviolence; Let's Put It in an Encyclical." *National Catholic Reporter*, Dec. 2, 2020. https://www.ncronline.org/opinion/guest-voices/pope-has-already-taught-nonviolence-lets-put-it-encyclical.

Sandy Hook Promise. "Gun Violence Facts About Anti-Religious Violence and Hate Crimes." Sandy Hook Promise, n.d. https://www.sandyhookpromise.org/blog/gun-violence/gun-violence-facts-about-anti-religious-violence-and-hate-crimes/.

SBC [Southern Baptist Convention]. "On Gun Violence and Mass Shootings." SBC, June 1, 2018. https://www.sbc.net/resource-library/resolutions/on-gun-violence-and-mass-shootings/.

Schmitt, Brad. "Boy Scouts to Honor 8-Year-Old Boy Who Helped Protect Relatives during Antioch Church Shootings." *Tennessean*, Feb. 28, 2018. https://www.tennessean.com/story/news/2018/02/28/boy-scouts-honor-8-year-old-boy-who-helped-protect-relatives-during-antioch-church-shootings/381240002/.

Scripps College. "Long Night's Journey into Day." Scripps College, Jan. 30, 2014. https://www.scrippscollege.edu/hi/2002-spring/film-screening-long-nights-journey-into-day.

Shaffer, Kris. *Data Versus Democracy: How Big Data Algorithms Shape Opinions and Alter the Course of History*. N.p.: Apress, 2019. Ebook.

Shelton, Caitlyn. "'He's Killed Me' Burnette Chapel Minister Calls Out to Wife During Antioch Church Shooting." Fox 17, May 20, 2019. https://fox17.com/news/local/hes-killed-me-burnette-chapel-minister-calls-out-to-wife-during-antioch-church-shooting.

Shugerman, Emily. "'He Had a Columbine Feel to Him': Former Classmates Recall Texas Shooting Suspect Devin Kelley." *Independent*, Nov. 7, 2017. https://www.independent.co.uk/news/world/americas/devin-kelley-texas-shooting-new-braunfels-high-school-columbine-a8041926.html.

South Carolina Deparment of Education. *2025 South Carolina African American History Calendar: The Lasting Legacies of the Emanuel Nine*. South African American History Calendar, 2025. https://scafricanamerican.com/wp-content/uploads/2025/01/2025-African-American-History-Calendar.pdf.

Spielberg, Steven, dir. *Minority Report*. Los Angeles: 20th Century Fox, 2002.

Spriester, Steve, and Mariah Medina. "700 Rounds in 11 Minutes: Sutherland Springs Survivor Says He's Amazed He's Alive." KSAT, Feb. 5, 2018. https://www.ksat.com/news/2018/02/06/700-rounds-in-11-minutes-sutherland-springs-survivor-says-hes-amazed-hes-alive/.

Bibliography

Stanford University. "Mass Shootings in America Online Resource." Stanford Libraries, Dec. 6, 2016. https://swap.stanford.edu/was/20161202200317/http://library.stanford.edu/projects/mass-shootings-america#.

State of Tennessee v. Emanuel Kidega Samson. "Appeal for the Criminal Court from Davidson County." Justia, Jan. 10, 2023. M2022-00148-CCA-R3-CD. https://law.justia.com/cases/tennessee/court-of-criminal-appeals/2023/m2022-00148-cca-r3-cd.html.

Stelloh, Tim, et al. "Who Is Devin Kelley, the Texas Church Shooter?" NBC News, Nov. 5, 2017. https://www.nbcnews.com/storyline/texas-church-shooting/who-devin-kelley-alleged-texas-church-shooter-n817806.

Stephens, Jenna. "Shootings: Is Dordt Prepared?" *Diamond* [student newspaper], Oct. 4, 2017.

Tallman, Brian. "You Shall Not Murder." Ligonier, May 25, 2015. https://learn.ligonier.org/articles/you-shall-not-murder.

Tamburin, Adam. "Emanuel Samson's Father Says He Begged Police to Take Son's Guns Before Church Shooting." *Tennessean*, May 22, 2019. https://www.tennessean.com/story/news/2019/05/22/emanuel-samsons-father-begged-police-take-guns-before-antioch-church-shooting/3760511002/.

———. "Jury Sentences Emanuel Samson to Life Without Parole for Antioch Church Shooting." *Tennessean*, May 28, 2019. https://www.tennessean.com/story/news/2019/05/28/emanuel-samson-sentenced-antioch-church-shooting-life-sentence/1254183001/.

———. "Lawyers Read 'Extremely Offensive' Jail Phone Calls During Emanuel Samson Murder Trial." *Tennessean*, May 23, 2019. https://www.tennessean.com/story/news/2019/05/23/emanuel-samson-antioch-church-shooting-trial-nashville-lawyers-read-offensive-jail-calls/1198111001/.

———. "Personal Turmoil Weighed on Nashville Church Shooting Suspect Emanuel K. Samson." *Tennessean*, Sept. 25, 2017. https://www.tennessean.com/story/news/2017/09/25/personal-turmoil-weighed-nashville-church-shooting-suspect-emanuel-k-samson/699960001/.

Tran, Mai-Anh Le. *Reset the Heart: Unlearning Violence, Relearning Hope*. Nashville: Abingdon, 2017.

Tryggestad, Erik. "We Do Not Go to Church Anymore." *Christian Chronicle*, July 24, 2018. https://christianchronicle.org/we-do-not-go-to-church-anymore/.

United Church of Christ. "Nonviolent Direct Action and Just Peace." United Church of Christ, n.d. https://www.ucc.org/international-policy/nonviolent_direct_action_and_just_peace/.

United States Air Force. "Proceedings of a Special Court Martial." My San Antonio, Nov. 6, 2012. https://www.mysanantonio.com/file/304/6/3046-Air%20Force%202018%20-%20Devin%20patrick%20Kelley%20trial%20transcript%2004-30-18.pdf.

United States Attorney's Office, via the Federal District Court. "Full Dylann Roof Confession." *New York Times*, Dec. 10, 2016. From video of June 18, 2015. https://www.nytimes.com/video/us/100000004815369/full-dylann-roof-confession.html.

United States Department of Justice, Office of Public Affairs. "Virginia Man Charged for Attempted Church Shooting." Office of Public Affairs, Mar. 28, 2024. https://www.justice.gov/opa/pr/virginia-man-charged-attempted-church-shooting.

United States v. Dylann Storm Roof. "Brief for the United States as Appellee." USCA4 Appeal 17-3, Doc: 132, filed Nov. 16, 2020.

Bibliography

———. "Brief of Appellant." USCA4 Appeal 17-3, Doc: 85, filed Jan. 28, 2020.

———. "Materials Subject to Judicial Notice." USCA4 Appeal 17-3, Doc: 86, filed Jan. 28, 2020.

———. "Motion for Enlargement of Appellant's Opening Brief." USCA4 Appeal 17-3, Doc: 68, filed Jan. 10, 2020.

———. "Motion to Appropriate Remedial Measures to Protect the Fairness of the Trial." Case No. 2:15-CR-472-RMG, filed Dec. 11, 2016.

———. "Pro Se Motion to Remove and Replace Appointed Counsel." USCA4 Appeal 17-3, Doc: 35, filed Sept. 18, 2017.

———. "Order." 225 F. Supp. 3d 419 (D.S.C. 2016), decided July 19, 2016.

———. "Transcript of Sealed Ex Parte Hearing Before the Honorable Richard m. Gergel, United States District Judge." 2:15-CR-472, filed Nov. 7, 2016.

White, Rozella. "The Truth Shall Set You Free." How Wise Then, June 26, 2015. https://howwisethen.com/rozella-white/.

Wilkerson, Isabel. *Caste: The Origins Of Our Discontents*. New York: Random House, 2023.

WKRN Web Staff. "Newsmaker: Joey Spann, Minister of Burnette Chapel Church of Christ." WKRN, Nov. 2, 2018. https://www.wkrn.com/news/newsmaker-joey-spann-minister-of-burnette-chapel-church-of-christ/1569418236/.

———. "Wife of Burnette Chapel Church of Christ Minister Dies After Battle with COVID-19." WKRN, Oct. 9, 2021. https://www.wkrn.com/news/wife-of-burnette-chapel-church-of-christ-minister-dies-after-battle-with-covid-19/.

Yehoshua, Tamar. "Google Search Autocomplete." Google, June 10, 2016. https://blog.google/products/search/google-search-autocomplete/.

Index

abuse
  and Devin Kelley, 92–93, 98–99
  and Dylann Roof, 62
  and Emanuel Samson, 78
  sexual, 91–93
access, to weapons, 160
action
  to avoid violence, 137–58
  vs. inaction, 203
Acts of Faith (Patel), 116
Adcock, Brittany, 91
African cultural spiritual tradition, 80–81
aggression, and gaming, 32
Alexandra, Darcy, "Visualising Migrant Voices: Co-Creative Documentary and the Politics of Listening", 196–97, 202–3
Ambrose, Jeanna, 84
AME. *see* Emanuel American Methodist Episcopal Church
American Civil War, 19
American Journal of Play, 32
ammunition, 132
anger, 2–3, 166
Ankh Ma'at Ra, 85
Anti-Defamation League, 73
Antioch, Tennessee, xvi, 11–12
anti-racism statements, 104–5
antisocial behavior
  of Devin Kelley, 54
  of Dylann Roof, 66
anti-violence
  curriculum on, 146–47
  training, 103, 158–69

Unity in Conflict course, 194–207
anxiety, 62
Apartheid, 175
apologies, 107
arming parishioners, efficacy of, 30–31
arrests, 24
Aryan Brotherhood, 62
assumptions, about mass shootings, 20–34
Atlanta, Georgia, 174–75
autism, 62, 64–65
avoidance, 137

background check, 99–100
Barth, Karl, 117
bath salts, 80, 84
Beatitudes, 103
Benedryl, 80
Bethel African Methodist Episcopal Church, 9
Bible Buddy Program, 140–44
Bickford, Susan, *The Dissonance of Democracy: Listening, Conflict, and Citizenship*, 196–97, 199
bipolar disorder, 51, 80, 83
birthright, 17–18
Bishop, Armilla, 49
Black Codes, 119
Black Lives Matter movement, 105
Black nationalism, 85
Blackburn, Cheryl, 51
"Blogs and the New Politics of Listening" (Coleman), 196–97, 204–5
Blomberg, Craig, 152
Bradley, Preston, 205

Index

Branden, Keith Allen, 58
Brennaman, Tessa, 91–92, 95–98
Bright Futures, 144
Brown, James V., "Terrorism in Context: The Stories We Tell Ourselves", 196–97
Buddhism, 17
Bullard, George W., *Every Congregation Needs A Little Conflict*, 196–97, 201–2
bullying, 79, 90, 135
Burnette Chapel Church of Christ, xvi, 11–12
  and racism, 109
  shooting at, 44–53, 185
Bush, Gregory, 8–10
Bush, Linda, 44, 48

Calvin, John, 26
Canaanites, 18
cannabis, 84, 94
car theft, 172
Carter, Danny, 49
Carter, Melvin, 172
Carter, Micah, 52
caste system, 113
Catholicism, 26
Charleston, North Carolina, xvi
Child Crime Prevention and Safety Center, 24
Child Protective Services, 91
childhood
  of Devin Kelley, 89–91
  of Dylann Roof, 62–63
  of Emanuel Samson, 77–79
children, in church, 139–40
Christian Chronicle, 52
The Christian Imagination: Theology and the Origins of Race (Jennings), 114–15
Christianity
  and Dylann Roof, 67
  martyrdom in, 16
  white foundational roots of, 114
church
  actions of, 101–11
  mass shootings at, 6
  positive change by, 117
  prayer for, 153–54
  separation from state, 19
Church of Israel, 116
Civil Rights Act, 120
civil rights movement, 102
Clinton, Bill, 62
Clinton, Hilary, 36
cognitive skills, 32–33
Colbath, David, 57, 164
Coleman, Stephen, 196–97
  "Blogs and the New Politics of Listening", 204–5
communications, with Emanuel Samson, 52, 187
community
  and Dylann Roof, 34
  and public safety, 172–73
  and relationships, 194
concealed weapons, 30–31
conflict resolution, 194–207
congregation, diverse, 44–45
connections, and relationships, 138–45
conservatives, 117
conviction
  of Dylann Roof, 42–43
  of Samson, 51–52
Corey, Benjamin L., *Undiluted: Rediscovering the Radical Message of Jesus*, 106–7
Corrie, Elizabeth W., *Youth Ministry as Peace Education: Overcoming Silence, Transforming Violence*, 110
Corrigan, Robert, 57
Corrigan, Shani, 57
Council of Conservative Citizens, 179
counselors, 135, 163–64
court records, of Dylann Roof, 69–70
Craigo-Snell, Shannon, 152
criminal history
  of Devin Kelley, 94–97
  of Dylann Roof, 66
  of Emanuel Samson, 84
criminal justice reform, 105
Crow, Wilma, 48
Crumbley, Ethan, 128
Crumbley, James, 128
Crumbley, Jennifer, 128
crusades, 16–17

Index

Cruz, Nikolas, 127–29
curriculum
  on anti-violence, 146–47
  on nonviolence, 110
  Unity in Conflict course, 194–207

darkness, vs. hope, 165
Davis, Barbara, 50
DC snipers, 10–11
death penalty, 65
Densley, James, 159
Deo vindice, 19
Department of Children's Services, 78
depression, 62, 173
destigmatization, of mental health care, 165
Deuteronomy, 18
devastation, 166
Dickerson, Catherine, 44, 48
Dierker, Sarah, 154
discipline, 135
Disrupting the Path to Violence, 129–33
The Dissonance of Democracy: Listening, Conflict, and Citizenship (Bickford), 196–97, 199
diversity, in congregation, 44–45
divine providence, 17–18
domestic terrorism, 118
domestic violence, 54, 78, 89
drawings, by Dylann Roof, 188–91
drive-by shootings, 25
drug use
  of Devin Kelley, 94
  by Dylann Roof, 65
  of Emanuel Samson, 84
Dungeons and Dragons, 32–33
"Dylann Roof Was Wrong: 'The Race War Isn't Coming, It's Here'" (Jennings), 115

Eaton, Elizabeth A., 104–5, 106
educational benchmarks, 141–44
Edwards, Jessika, 92
Edwards, Jonathan, "Sinners in the Hands of an Angry God", 101
ELCA. *see* Evangelical Lutheran Church in America

Elkins, Kathleen Gallagher, *Mary, Mother of Martyrs: How Motherhood Became Self-Sacrifice in Early Christianity*, 16
Emanuel American Methodist Episcopal Church (AME), 11–12
  and racial justice, 121
  and security systems, 29
  shooting at, xvi, xix, 35–43
EMDR (Eye Movement Desensitization and Reprocessing), 165
emergency responders, 42
Emerson, Ralph Waldo, 199
enemies, loving of, 147–48
Engle, James, 50–51
Engle, Robert Caleb, 44, 50–51, 53
Evangelical Lutheran Church in America (ELCA), 66–67
  and racism, 105, 109
Every Congregation Needs A Little Conflict (Bullard), 196–97, 201–2
exclusivity, 108

faith, 59, 147–48
faith-based community centers, 5
family dispute, 11
FBI, 130
fear, xv, 166
FEMA, 167
findhelp.org, 164
First Baptist Church, 8–9
  congregation of, 176
  shooting at, xvi, 30, 54–60
First Presbyterian Church, 140–44
forgiveness, 175–76
Francis (pope), 104
"Fruit That Works Together", 151–52
Fugitive-Slave Act, 118–19

gaming, and aggression, 32
Garza, Emily, 57
God, chosen people of, 17–19
Gooch, Sarah, 144
Great Awakening, 101
grief, 168
grievance, 2–3, 10, 129, 131, 159, 162
gun control, xvi–xvii, 127–28
gun show, 174–75

Index

guns
  access to, 4
  concealed, 30–31
  ownership, xvi–xvii

Haidt, Jonathan, *The Righteous Mind: Why Good People are Divided by Politics and Religion*, 196–97, 202–3, 205
The Handbook of Cross-Cultural Psychology, 13
hate crimes, 8–9, 112
Haymarket, Virginia, 10
Hazell, Harry "Max" II, xvii–xviii, 153, 156
healing, mindset of, 137
Health Resources and Services Administration, 163
help, prayers for, 155–56
Henry, Bonnilynn, 67
Hill, Emily, 57
Hill, Greg, 57
Hill, Maya, 45–47, 79–81, 86
Hill, Megan, 57
Hilton, A.R., *A House United: How the Church Can Save the World*, 117–20, 195–98, 201–2, 205–6
The Historical Dictionary of Human Rights, 5
Hoffer, Eric, 205
Holcombe, Bryan, 57
Holcombe, Crystal, 57
Holcombe, Danny, 57
Holcombe, Karla, 57
Holcombe, Noah, 57
Holcombe family, 57–58, 176
Holocaust, 63, 116
home support system, 144
hope
  and darkness, 165
  mindset of, 137
  stories of, 170–77
  after tragedy, 176–77
  working towards, xv
A House United: How the Church Can Save the World (Hilton), 195–98, 205–6

icons, 26
immigrants, 113
imperialism, 114
inaction, vs. action, 203
indigenous people, 17–19
indoor, vs. outdoor shootings, 25
infidelity, 62
informant, 174–75
internet, radicalization by, 63
interracial marriages, 120
intervention, 162, 174–75
interview
  of Dylann Roof, 38–39
  of Emanuel Samson, 52
  with survivors, 59
Isherwood, Lisa, *Weep Not for Your Children: Essays on Religion and Violence*, 197, 203–4
isolation, 134, 138
Israel, 18
Israel, Scott, 128
Ivey, Dave, 98

Jainism, 17
Jeffersontown, Kentucky, 8–9, 30–31
Jenkins, Marlene, 44, 47–49
Jenkins, William, 44, 47–48
Jennings, Willie James, 117
  The Christian Imagination: Theology and the Origins of Race, 114–15
  "Dylann Roof Was Wrong: 'The Race War Isn't Coming, It's Here'", 115
Jesus Christ, 147–48
  following of, 137
  light of, 1
Jiang, Rui, 10
Jim Crow laws, 115, 120
Johnson, Dennis, 57
Johnson, Sara, 57
Jones, Robert P., *White Too Long: The Legacy of White Supremacy in American Christianity*, 115–17
Jones, Vickie Lee, 8
Josephus, 16
Joshua, 18
Just Peace Pronouncement, 104
justice, 204

Index

Kelley, Danielle, 55–56, 91–92, 98
Kelley, Devin Patrick
   childhood of, 89–91
   criminal history of, 94–97
   grievance of, 129
   life of, 88–100
   and locked doors, 29
   mental health of, 94
   parents of, 90
   planning stage of, 133
   religious history of, 97–98
   religious socialization of, 13
   shooting by, xvi, 11–12, 54–60
   statements of, 99
   writings of, 99
   young adulthood of, 91–93
Kelley, Michael, 90
Kelley, Rebecca, 90
Khartoum, Sudan, 77
King, Coretta Scott, 35
King, Martin Luther, Jr., 35, 102
Koks, Florence, 82
Krantz, Lisa, xix, 100, 176
   A Tragedy Without End, 59
Krueger, Haley, 57
Ku Klux Klan, 119–22, 174, 184

lament, prayer of, 152
Langendorff, Johnnie, 58
law enforcement fatalities, 22
letters
   from Dylann Roof to parents, 192–93
   from Emanuel Samson, 185
liberals, 117
Liebman, Joseph L., 202
light, of Christ, 1
listening, 162, 200
lithium, 84
locations, of mass shootings, 24–25
locked doors, efficacy of, 25–30
love
   and enemies, 147–48
   prayer for, 177
"Loved People Love People" (McNeal), 147–48
Luker, Tammy, 49
Lunch Buddy Program, 144–46

Malvo, Lee Boyd, 10–11, 110
Mandela, Nelson, 175, 199
manifest destiny, 17–18
manifesto, of Dylann Roof, 37, 121, 179–84
Marjory Stoneman Douglas High School, 127
Marshall, Karen, 58
Marshall, Robert "Scott", 58
Martin, Trayvon, 34, 36, 73, 110, 124, 179–80
martyrdom
   in Christianity, 16
   in Islam, 16
Mary, 16
Mary, Mother of Martyrs: How Motherhood Became Self-Sacrifice in Early Christianity (Gallagher), 16
mass media, appeals to, 106–7
mass shootings
   assumptions about, 20–34
   definition of, 5
   history of, 15–19
   increase of, 2–4
   locations of, 24–25
   misconceptions about, 20–34
   news coverage of, 3–4
   in places of worship, 11–12
   and population, 21–22
   racial makeup of shooters, 23
   and racism, 112–25
   by state, 21–22
   study of, xviii
massacre, 5
Massey University, 32
Matthews, Cheryl, 128
McNeal, Micah, 147–48
McNulty, Tara, 57
medication, 165
meditation, 165
mental health
   of Devin Kelley, 94
   of Dylann Roof, 64–65
   of Emanuel Samson, 83–84
   treatment, 92
mental illness, 12, 51
mentorships, 138–45

Index

Metze, Tony, xix, 66–68, 74–76, 108–10
Mexico, Missouri, 140–44
Minneapolis, Minnesota, 172
misconceptions, about mass shootings, 20–34
misinformation, 20–21
Montgomery, Stephen, 83
Morales, David, 48
Morgan, Margaret, 118–19
mosques, 5
motivations
    of Devin Kelley, 98–99
    of Dylann Roof, 71–72
    of Emanuel Samson, 85
motives, communication of, 130
Muhammad, John Allen, 11
multiple delusions, 65
murder, 149–50
Muslims, 17

NAACP, 102
Nazis, 122, 184
Nebraska Emergency Management Agency, 129–33, 163
Neeley, Rich, 157
New Lights, 101–2
news coverage, of mass shootings, 3–4
Nicholson, J.C. (Jr.), 72
non-firearm situation, 9
nonviolence, 103–7
    curriculum on, 110
    preaching about, 147–52
    and violence, xviii
"Nonviolence: It's Not Just a Good Idea, It's a Commandment", 149–50

Obama, Barack, xvi, 43
"On Gun Violence and Mass Shootings" (Southern Baptist Convention), 105
online resources, 163–64
organized religion, 81
outdoor, vs. indoor shootings, 25
Oxford High School, 128

panic attack, 167
paper tiger, 18–19
parents
    of Devin Kelley, 90
    of Dylann Roof, 62–63
    of Emanuel Samson, 78
Park Valley Church, 10
Parker, John, xix, 69
Pastoral Psychology (Rambo), 108
Patel, Eboo
    Acts of Faith, 116
    Sacred Ground: Pluralism, Prejudice, and the Promise of America , 116
patience, 151–52
patriotism, 37, 184
peace churches, 104
Pennington, Ashley, 69
personal safety, 26
Peterson, Jillian, 159
physicians, 164
Picciolini, Christian, 72–73
    letter from Dylann Roof, 186
Pinckney, Clementa, 35–36, 39–40, 43, 75
Pitts, Mary, 49
planning stage, 55, 132–33
politics, 117
Pomeroy, Annabelle, 57, 164
Pomeroy, Frank, 57, 59, 164
Pomeroy, Sherri, xix, 60, 164–67
population, and mass shootings, 21–22
prayers, 152–57, 161, 165, 176
preaching
    about nonviolence, 147–52
    about racism, 108
preparation, of shooting, 132
Presbyterian Church, 104
Presley, Susan, letter from Emanuel Samson, 186
prevention, of violence, xvi, 127, 168–69
Prieto, Mark, 174–75
Prigg, Edward, 118–19
Prigg v. Pennsylvania, 118–19
"Pro Se Motion to Remove and Replace Appointed Counsel" (Roof), 71–72, 208–11
Prohibition, 102–3
Project Semicolon, 164, 167
Protestant Church, 26
psychiatric hospital, 94

Index

PTSD, 83, 164
Public Religion Research Institute, 115
public safety, and community, 172–73
publications, on racism, 106

race
    constructs of, 113
    radicalization by, 63
    terrorism based on, 118
race war, 71, 121, 123–24
racial justice, 36, 102
racism
    call to end, 106
    church views on, 108
    of Dylann Roof, 66–68, 74
    as form of violence, 104–5
    history of in churches, 109
    and mass shootings, 112–25
    of Roof family, 62
    within white Christianity, 114–20
Rambo, Lewis, *Pastoral Psychology*, 108
Ramos, Salvador, 167–68
RBG flag, 46
red flags, 99–100, 126–34, 159, 162
Reed, Michael Tate, 19
Reimer, Jack, 204
relationships
    building of, xviii, 129, 137, 172–73
    and community, 194
    and connections, 138–45
    purpose of, 175–76
relics, 26
religion, and violence, 15–19
religious history
    of Devin Kelley, 97–98
    of Dylann Roof, 66–67
    of Emanuel Samson, 80–81
religious justification, 17–19
religious socialization
    of Kelley, xix, 13
    of Roof, xix, 13
    of Samson, xix, 13
religious wars, 16–17
research stage, 132
Reset the Heart: Unlearning Violence, Relearning Hope (Tran), 197, 199, 203–4
Restorative Justice Council, 175–76

retaliation, 11, 112
Riches, Gloria, 82
The Righteous Mind: Why Good People are Divided by Politics and Religion (Haidt), 196–97, 202–3, 205
Risher, Sharon Washington, xix, 68, 107
Robb Elementary School, 167–68
Rockett, Susan, 30–31
Rodriguez, Richard, 57
Rodriguez, Teresa, 57
Role-Playing Games, effect of, 32–34
Roof, Dylann Storm
    at Bible Study, 36
    and community, 34
    court records of, 64–65, 69–70
    and Emanuel Samson, 44, 120–24
    grievance of, 129
    idolation of, 9
    interview of, 38–39
    jailhouse drawings of, 188–91
    letter to Christian Picciolini, 186
    letters to parents, 192–93
    life of, 61–76
    and locked doors, 28
    manifesto of, 179–84
    motivations of, 71–72
    parents of, 62–63
    pastors of, xix
    planning stage of, 132
    "Pro Se Motion to Remove and Replace Appointed Counsel", 71–72, 208–11
    racially based motives of, 10–12
    religious socialization of, 13
    shooting by, xvi
    spiritual life of, 72–73
    statements of, 73–74
    suicide plan of, 41–42
    and white supremacist groups, 37
    writings of, 73–74
Roof, Franklin Bennett, 42, 62
Roof, Joe, 62–63
Rosa, Minerva, 49
Rosa-Gonzalez, Minerva, 82
Royal Society Open Science journal, 32
RPGs. *see* Role-Playing Games
Rudolph, Eric, 116

Index

Ruether, Rosemary Radford, *Weep Not for Your Children: Essays on Religion and Violence*, 197, 203–4

Sa Neter, 85
Sacred Ground: Pluralism, Prejudice, and the Promise of America (Patel), 116
Samson, Christina, 78–80
Samson, Emanuel Kidega
  childhood of, 77–79
  communications with, 187
  comparison to Lee Boyd Malvo, 11
  court case, xix
  criminal history of, 84
  and Dylann Roof, 44, 120–24
  grievance of, 129
  interview of, 52
  life of, 77–87
  and locked doors, 28–29
  mental health of, 83–84
  motivations of, 85
  parents of, 78
  planning by, 45, 132
  racially based motives of, 10–11
  religious history of, 80–81
  shooting by, xvi
  statements of, 85–86
  suicidal ideation of, 79
  writings of, 85–86
Samson, Vanansio, 85
sanctuary, 3
Sanders, Felicia, 40
Sanders, Tywanza, 41
Sandy Hook Project, 98
Saturnia, Pam, 177
schizoaffective disorder, 83
schizophrenia spectrum disorder, 62, 64–65, 80
school zoning laws, 182
Second Amendment, xvi–xvii
security
  false sense of, 28
  team, 30–31
segregation, 102, 120, 123–24, 181
self-defense, xviii
sentencing
  of Dylann Roof, 42–43
  of Samson, 51–52
separation, of church and state, 19
sermons
  change from, 104
  outlines of, 147–52
Seventh Day Adventist Church, 10
sexual assault, 89, 98–99
shadow people, 80–81
Sheppard, Polly, testimony of, 40–41
Shields, Michelle, 55, 93, 98
shooter drills, 133
shooter preparation
  by Devin Kelley, 55–56
  by Dylann Roof, 36–39
  by Emanuel Samson, 46–47
shooting, stopping of, 40–41, 50–51, 58
Sikh temple, 6
Simmons, Daniel L., 40
"Sinners in the Hands of an Angry God" (Edwards), 101
slave revolt, 35
slavery, 115, 118–19, 181
sleep problems, 80
Smith, Clyde, 167
Smith, Melanie Crow, 44, 47–48, 52, 87
social equality, 36
social media, 2
social skills, 32–33
socialization, 13, 114
South Africa, 175
Southern Baptist Convention, "On Gun Violence and Mass Shootings", 105
Southern Baptists, 115
Southern Christian Leadership Conference (SCLC), 102
Southern Poverty Law Center, 85
Spann, Joey, 47–48, 81–82
  injury of, 44
  life now, 53
  plea for unity by, xx
  "Time Sure is Precious", 87
  "We Do Not Go to Church Anymore", 52
Spann, Peggy, 44, 47–49, 53, 87
speaking up, 160–61
spiritual advisor, 69
spiritual life, of Dylann Roof, 72–73
Sri Lankan Civil War, 17

Index

St. Paul, Minnesota, 172
Stafford, Linda, 49
Stallard, Maurice E., 8
Stanford Brainstorm Lab, 32
Stanford University, 5
statements
   of Devin Kelley, 99
   of Dylann Roof, 73–74
   of Emanuel Samson, 85–86
   on nonviolence, 104–5
Stephenson, David, 119–20
stranger danger, 24
Styrt, Katie, 155
Suboxone, 65
Sudan, 77–78
suicidal ideation, 45, 79, 83
Suicide & Crisis Lifeline, 163
suicide plan, of Dylann Roof, 41–42
Sunday School, 104
support, 176
supremacy issues, 147
survivors, care for, 164–68
Sutherland Springs Baptist Church, 164, 167
Sutherland Springs shooting, xix
Sutherland Springs, Texas, 54
synagogues, 5–6

tactical gear, 132
telephone resources, 163–64
temples, 5
"Terrorism in Context: The Stories We Tell Ourselves" (Brown), 196–97
testimony, of Polly Sheppard, 40–41
theft, 26
therapy, 165
Thompson, Myra, 36
threats, 129
"Time Sure is Precious" (Spann), 87
tragedy, hope after, 176–77
training classes, 161–63
Tran, Mai-Anh Le, *Reset the Heart: Unlearning Violence, Relearning Hope*, 197, 199, 203–4
troubled people, building relationships with, 137
Truth and Reconciliation Commission, 175–76

Tutu, Desmond, 175

unarmed security license, 45
Undiluted: Rediscovering the Radical Message of Jesus (Corey), 106–7
United Church of Christ (UCC), 104
United States Air Force (USAF), 55, 88, 92, 100, 167
Unity in Conflict course
   curriculum of, 194–207
   goal of, 147
Universal Negro Improvement Association, 46
Uvalde school shooting, xix, 167–68

vandalism, 26
vengeance, 121
Vesey, Denmark, 35
veterans, 163
video games, effect of, 32–34
violence
   frequency in places of worship, 4–11
   and gun access, 4
   justification of, 132
   and nonviolence, xviii
   path to, 130–32, 161–62
   prayer against, 154–57
   prevention of, 117, 127, 137–58, 157
   and religion, 15–19
   warning signs of, 173
The Violence Project: How to Stop a Mass Shooting Epidemic (Densley and Peterson), 159
"Visualising Migrant Voices: Co-Creative Documentary and the Politics of Listening" (Alexandra), 196–97, 202–3
Voting Rights Act, 120

Ward, Brooke, 57
Ward, Joann, 57
Warden, Peggy Lynn, 58
warning signs, xv, 89, 127–34, 173, 175
Warren, Linda, xix
Warren, Peter, xix
Washington, Booker T., 35
"We Do Not Go to Church Anymore" (Spann), 52–53

Index

weapons
  access to, 160
  history, 99
  obtention of, 132
Weep Not for Your Children: Essays on Religion and Violence (Isherwood and Ruether), 196, 203–4
Wesley, John, 101
White, Lula, 57, 98
White, Rozella Haydee, 74
white Christianity, racism within, 114–20
white men, as perpetrators, 23
white supremacism, 122–23
  groups, 36–37
  symbols of, 73–74
White Too Long: The Legacy of White Supremacy in American Christianity (Jones), 115–16
Whorton, Zane, 154, 156
Wilkerson, Isabel, 113

Willeford, Stephen, 58
Williams, Billy, 9
Willoughby, Jack, 98
Workman, Kris, 166
workplace violence, 54
writings
  of Devin Kelley, 99
  of Dylann Roof, 73–74
  of Emanuel Samson, 85–86

young adulthood
  of Devin Kelley, 91–93
  of Dylann Roof, 63–64
  of Emanuel Samson, 79
youth, in church, 139–40
youth groups, 104
Youth Ministry as Peace Education: Overcoming Silence, Transforming Violence (Corrie), 110

Zimmerman, George, 179

www.ingramcontent.com/pod-product-compliance
Lightning Source LLC
Chambersburg PA
CBHW031355230426
43670CB00006B/545